200 ALL-AMERICAN HOME PLANS

BLUE RIBBON DESIGNER SERIES™

Popular Home Styles From Across America

D1275286

HOME PLANNERS, INC.
TUCSON, ARIZONA

Published by Home Planners, Inc.
Editorial and Corporate Offices:
3275 West Ina Road, Suite 110
Tucson, Arizona 85741

Distribution Center:
29333 Lorie Lane
Wixom, Michigan 48393

Rickard D. Bailey, President and Publisher
Cindy J. Coatsworth, Publications Manager
Paulette Mulvin, Senior Editor
Jan Prideaux, Project Editor
Kellie Gibson, Book Designer

Photo Credits
Front Cover: (top image:) Susan DuPlessis
           (center image:) © Andrew D. Lautman
           (bottom image:) © Andrew D. Lautman
Back Cover: © Andrew D. Lautman

First Printing, September 1994
10 9 8 7 6 5 4 3 2 1

Printed in the United States of America

Library of Congress Catalog Card Number: 94-076447

ISBN softcover: 1-881955-17-6

On the front cover: Design DD9645 (top), see page 49; Design DD2615
(center), see page 16; Design DD2283 (bottom), see page 27.

On the back cover: Design DD3309, see page 131.

TABLE of CONTENTS

EDITOR'S NOTE As each chapter in America's architectural history closes, a new one opens—shaped not only by its past, but enriched by the forecast of events and experiences. Each exciting new episode develops its own story like a well-written novel, containing a beginning (the past), a middle (the present) and an ending (the future). It is this evolution of design that becomes a part of our heritage. This fine collection of home plans offers an historic journey of styles, filled with the spirit of our stouthearted ancestors, that allows us to do more than simply savor their memories. These favored All-American styles combine the architectural integrity of the past with amenity-filled interiors and the luxurious details of today—making them truly modern-day classics. This book and its richly rewarding home designs will provide a legacy to be built upon, not only for today, but for many generations to come.

About The Designers

The Blue Ribbon Designer Series™ is a collection of books featuring the home plans of a diverse group of outstanding home designers and architects known as the Blue Ribbon Network of Designers. This group of companies is dedicated to creating and marketing the finest possible plans for home construction on a regional and national basis. Each of the companies exhibits superior work and integrity in all phases of the stock-plan business including modern, trendsetting floor planning, a professionally executed blueprint package and a strong sense of service and commitment to the consumer.

Design Basics, Inc.

For nearly a decade, Design Basics, a nationally recognized home design service located in Omaha, has been developing plans for custom home builders. Since 1987, the firm has consistently appeared in *Builder* magazine, the official magazine of the National Association of Home Builders, as the top-selling designer. The company's plans also regularly appear in numerous other shelter magazines such as *Better Homes and Gardens, House Beautiful* and *Home Planner*.

Design Traditions

Design Traditions was established by Stephen S. Fuller with the tenets of innovation, quality, originality and uncompromising architectural techniques in traditional and European homes. Especially popular throughout the Southeast, Design Traditions' plans are known for their extensive detail and thoughtful design. They are widely published in such shelter magazines as *Southern Living* magazine and *Better Homes and Gardens*.

Alan Mascord Design Associates, Inc.

Founded in 1983 as a local supplier to the building community, Mascord Design Associates of Portland, Oregon, began to successfully publish plans nationally in 1985. With plans now drawn exclusively on computer, Mascord Design Associates quickly received a reputation for homes that are easy to build yet meet the rigorous demands of the buyers' market, winning local and national awards. The company's trademark is creating floor plans that work well and exhibit excellent traffic patterns. Their motto is: "Drawn to build, designed to sell."

Larry E. Belk Designs

Through the years, Larry E. Belk has worked with individuals and builders alike to provide a quality product. After listening to over 4,000 dreams and watching them become reality all across America, Larry's design philosophy today combines traditional exteriors with upscale interiors designed for contemporary lifestyles. Flowing, open spaces and interesting angles define his interiors. Great emphasis is placed on providing views that showcase the natural environment. Dynamic exteriors reflect Larry's extensive home construction experience, painstaking research and talent as a fine artist.

Larry W. Garnett & Associates, Inc.

Starting as a designer of homes for Houston-area residents, Garnett & Associates has been marketing designs nationally for the past ten years. A well-respected design firm, the company's plans are regularly featured in *House Beautiful, Country Living, Home* and *Professional Builder*. Numerous accolades, including several from the Texas Institute of Building Design and the American Institute of Building Design, have been awarded to the company for excellence in architecture.

Home Planners, Inc.

Headquartered in Tucson, Arizona, with additional offices in Detroit, Home Planners is one of the longest-running and most successful home design firms in the United States. With over 2,500 designs in its portfolio, the company provides a wide range of styles, sizes and types of homes for the residential builder. All of Home Planners' designs are created with the care and professional expertise that fifty years of experience in the home-planning business affords. Their homes are designed to be built, lived in and enjoyed for years to come.

Donald A. Gardner, Architects, Inc.

The South Carolina firm of Donald A. Gardner was established in response to a growing demand for residential designs that reflect constantly changing lifestyles. The company's specialty is providing homes with refined, custom-style details and unique features such as passive-solar designs and open floor plans. Computer-aided design and drafting technology resulting in trouble-free construction documents places the firm at the leading edge of the home plan industry.

The Sater Group, Inc.

The Sater Group, Inc. has a long established tradition of providing South Florida's most diverse and extraordinary custom designed homes. Their goal is to fulfill each client's particular need for an exciting approach to design by merging creative vision with elements that satisfy a desire for a distinctive lifestyle. This philosophy is proven, as exemplified by over 50 national design awards, numerous magazine features and, most important, satisfied clients. The result is an elegant statement of lasting beauty and value.

New England and Cape Cod Designs

AMERICA WAS A BRAVE, new world offering new freedoms to the early colonial settlers. From this newly developed country emerged a diversity of settlements, farming practices, and ethnic and religious backgrounds that would impact building styles for centuries to come. The local experiences of the colonists tempered the building traditions brought to America not only by the English, but the Dutch, German, French and Spanish cultures as well.

Simplicity of design was the common thread throughout much of the early period of New England architecture. Built by the first generations of Americans, these homes displayed an austerity that reflected the lifestyles their builders had left behind. A simple beauty presented itself in these homes, and the quality of construction proved to be exceptional, verified by the number of original homes still standing today. Common materials of the early New England homes included clapboard, shingles, cut stone, and brick or stucco, depending upon the region. Design DD8042 offers a wonderful example of a Colonial cottage that characterizes the successful blending of some of these building materials.

The Cape Cod is one of the earliest types of dwellings built by the early settlers and remains one of today's most desired home styles. The environment played a key role in the selection of building materials, and form followed function when building these homes. Cape Cod homes were small, symmetrical 1½-story houses constructed with clapboard exteriors. They often included massive central or end chimneys that warmed the rooms around them and steeply-pitched roofs that shed the heavy snow loads of the severely cold winters. Expansion of these homes was simple, and if a need for additional space arose, the house could be added to from either side. Design DD2622 features a delightful Cape Cod that allows for future expansion, while Designs DD2520 and DD2563 portray the appeal of an already expanded plan.

From the early Cape Cod, a series of new styles emerged. First was the Cape Ann Colonial which originated in Cape Ann, Massachusetts, distinguished by its gambrel roof. Next appeared the Garrison Colonial, a two-story house with a second-story overhang at the front portion of the exterior. Traditional ornamentation consisted of four carved pineapple or acorn-shaped drops below the overhang. On the heels of the Garrison style came the Dutch Colonial—an indigenous American style built in the 1600s by Dutch settlers in Pennsylvania—recognized by its stone walls and gambrel roof with outwardly flaring eaves.

Completing this early New England circle of architecture was the Salt Box, referred to in the South as a "Catslide." The harsher the climate, the more protection needed to be built into the house itself. The Salt Box offered a prime example of this consideration with its steeply gabled roof extending down to the first floor at the rear of the design, always oriented to the north to aid in warding off the frigid winter winds.

The rich collection of designs found in this section shares the exterior flavor of their earlier New England counterparts, but possesses the functional livability required for the energetic lifestyles of today.

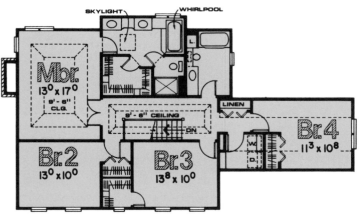

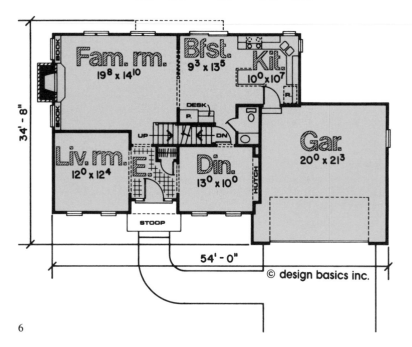

© design basics inc.

Design DD7207

First Floor: 998 square feet
Second Floor: 1,206 square feet
Total: 2,204 square feet

● A touch of New England abides in this comfortable family home. A bright entry opens to a formal living room to the left and, to the right, a formal dining room with space for a hutch. A warming fireplace with built-in bookcases provides the focal point for the generous family room, perfect for informal gatherings. The U-shaped kitchen is a cook's delight, combining with the sunlit breakfast room to provide an airy, spacious feeling. The second floor houses the sleeping zone. Sure to please is the master suite, where the bedroom is highlighted by a vaulted ceiling. The master bath features a skylit dressing area, a whirlpool tub and a walk-in closet. Three secondary bedrooms, a full bath and a convenient laundry room complete the upstairs.

Design by
Design
Basics,
Inc.

Design DD9343

First Floor: 1,000 square feet
Second Floor: 993 square feet
Total: 1,993 square feet

● At less than 2,000 square feet, this plan captures the heritage and romance of an authentic Colonial home with many modern amenities. Stylish, yet economical to build, here's a classic design for move-up buyers. A central hall leads to the formal rooms at the front where showpiece furnishings can be displayed. For daily living, the informal rooms can't be beat. A bookcase and large linen cabinet are thoughtful touches upstairs. Further evidence of tasteful design is shown in the master suite. A volume ceiling, large walk-in closet and whirlpool tub await the fortunate homeowner. Each secondary bedroom has bright windows to add natural lighting and comfort.

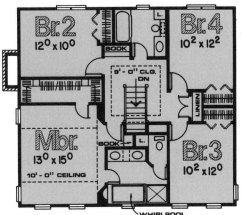

Design by
Design
Basics,
Inc.

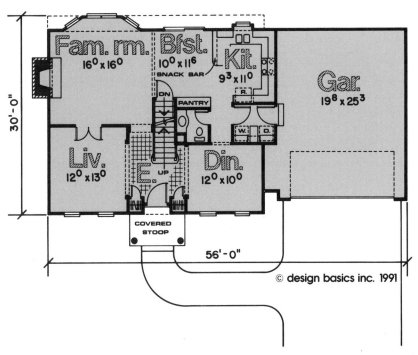

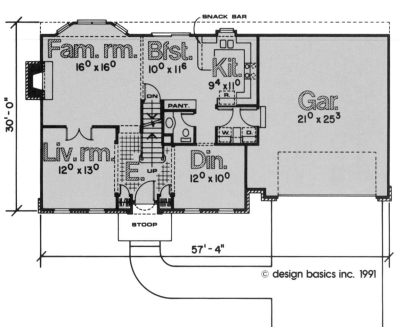

Design by
Design
Basics,
Inc.

Design DD9344

First Floor: 1,000 square feet
Second Floor: 1,345 square feet
Total: 2,345 square feet

● Repeating window detailing, an arched entry and a brick facade highlight the exterior of this modern, two-story Colonial home. Formal rooms at the front provide entertaining ease. The dining room is served by a convenient passageway for quick kitchen service while bright windows and French doors add appeal to the living room. A relaxing family room has a bayed conversation area plus a clear view through the sunny dinette into the gourmet kitchen. Features include wrapping counters, a snack bar, two Lazy Susans and a generous pantry. Upstairs, a U-shaped hall with a view to below offers separation to all four bedrooms. Bedroom 2 has its own bath. Homeowners will love the expansive master retreat. This oasis features a private sitting room, two walk-in closets, compartmented bath, separate vanities and a window-brightened whirlpool tub.

ATTIC STORAGE/EXPANDABLE AREA

BATH 3

BEDRM 3
13-8 X 11-8

SEAT

Design by
Larry E. Belk
Designs

WIDTH 78-10

SCREENED PORCH

SINK ICE REFG

GREENHOUSE WINDOW

COPYRIGHT 1993 LARRY E. BELK

GARAGE

FP

KEEPING RM
13-4 X 16-0

KITCHEN
11-4 X 16-0

PAN

FP

LIVING ROOM
16-0 X 16-0

MASTER BATH

BAR

MASTER BEDRM
12-6 X 16-0

DEPTH 57-9

UTIL

BUILT IN

DINING ROOM
12-6 X 15-0

FOYER

LIN CAB

BATH 2

PORCH

BEDRM 2
12-10 X 15-6

10 FT CEILINGS DOWNSTAIRS

Design DD8042

First Floor: 2,173 square feet
Second Floor: 304 square feet
Total: 2,477 square feet

● A pleasing blend of textures
and interesting window treatments
is the key to the charisma of this
enchanting cottage; it will capture
your heart. The spacious interior is
a delight—from the comfortable
living room and columned dining
room—perfect for formal entertaining—to the lavish master suite
which offers a relaxing and private
retreat. The welcoming space of the
cheery kitchen, combined with the
keeping room and its cozy fireplace, will become a favored place
for informal gatherings. Access to a
screened porch further enhances its
appeal. Bedroom 2 has its own
bath and walk-in closet and completes the first floor. The upstairs
contains Bedroom 3 and a full bath.

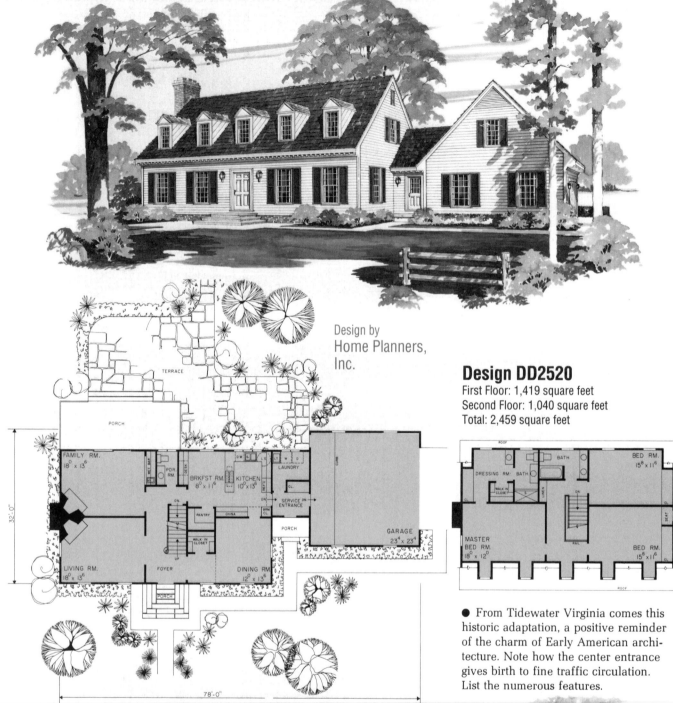

Design by
Home Planners,
Inc.

TERRACE

PORCH

Design DD2520

First Floor: 1,419 square feet
Second Floor: 1,040 square feet
Total: 2,459 square feet

FAMILY RM.
18⁰ x 13⁶

BRKFST RM.
8⁰ x 11⁶

KITCHEN
10⁰ x 13⁶

LAUNDRY

SERVICE
ENTRANCE

PORCH

GARAGE
23⁴ x 23⁴

PDR.
RM.

DESK

PANTRY

CHINA

WALK-IN
CLOSET

UP

LIVING RM.
18⁰ x 13⁶

FOYER

DINING RM.
12⁰ x 13⁶

PORCH

32'-0"

78'-0"

DRESSING RM.

BATH

BATH

BED RM.
15⁸ x 11⁶

WALK IN
CLOSET

LINEN

DN

MASTER
BED RM.
18⁰ x 12⁰

RAIL

BED RM.
15⁸ x 11⁶

ROOF

ROOF

SEAT

● From Tidewater Virginia comes this
historic adaptation, a positive reminder
of the charm of Early American architecture. Note how the center entrance
gives birth to fine traffic circulation.
List the numerous features.

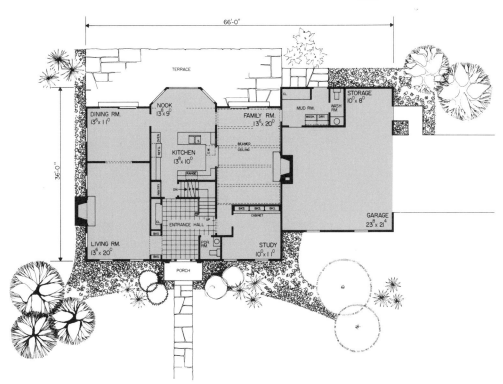

BED RM.
13⁴ x 14⁴

BATH

DRESSING RM.

WALK-IN CLOSET

BATH

WALK-IN CLOSET

ROOF

ROOF

DN

BED RM.
13⁶ x 14⁴

BED RM.
13⁸ x 10²

MASTER BED RM.
13⁶ x 19⁶

Design by
Home Planners, Inc.

66'-0"

36'-0"

TERRACE

DINING RM.
13⁶ x 11⁰

NOOK
13⁶ x 9⁰

FAMILY RM.
13⁶ x 20⁰

MUD RM.

STORAGE
10' x 8⁰

WASH RM.

WASH DRY

BEAMED CEILING

KITCHEN
13⁰ x 10⁰

OVEN

REF'G

S

C.W.

RANGE

PANTRY

DN

BKS BKS BKS

CABINET

GARAGE
23⁸ x 21⁴

LIVING RM.
13⁶ x 20⁰

BKS

ENTRANCE HALL

PDR RM

STUDY
10' x 11⁰

PORCH

Design DD2610

First Floor: 1,505 square feet
Second Floor: 1,344 square feet
Total: 2,849 square feet

● This full two-story traditional will be noteworthy wherever built. It strongly recalls images of a New England of yesteryear. And well it might, for the window treatment is delightful. The front entrance detail is inviting. The narrow horizontal siding and the corner boards are appealing as are the two massive chimneys. The center entrance hall is large with a handy powder room nearby. The study has built-in bookshelves and offers a full measure of privacy. The interior kitchen has a pass-through to the family room and enjoys all that natural light from the bay window of the nook. A beamed ceiling, fireplace and sliding glass doors are features of the family room. The mud room highlights a closet, laundry equipment and an extra wash room. Study the upstairs with four bedrooms, two baths and plenty of closets. An excellent arrangement for all.

11

Design DD2622

First Floor: 624 square feet
Second Floor: 624 square feet
Total: 1,248 square feet

● This Colonial adaptation provides a functional design that allows for expansion in the future. A cozy fireplace in the living room adds warmth to this space as well as the adjacent dining area. The roomy L-shaped kitchen features a breakfast nook and an over-the-sink window. Upstairs, two secondary bedrooms share a full bath with double vanity. The master bedroom is on this floor as well. Its private bath contains access to attic storage. An additional storage area over the garage can become a bedroom, office, or study in the future. For information on customizing this design, call 1-800-521-6797, ext. 800.

Design by
Home Planners,
Inc.

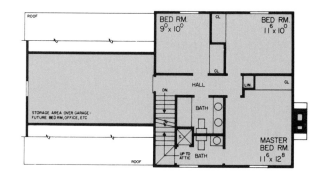

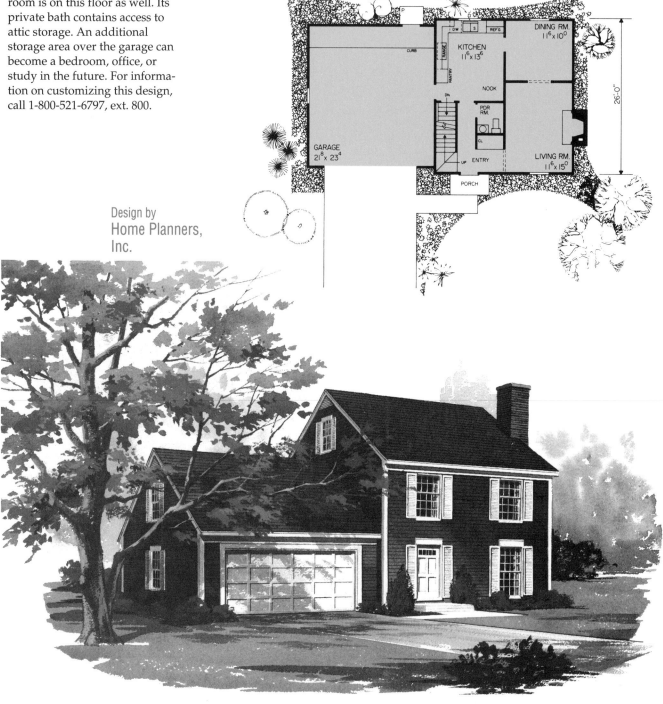

Design DD2540

First Floor: 1,306 square feet
Second Floor: 1,360 square feet
Total: 2,666 square feet

● This comfortable Colonial home puts a good foot forward in family living. The entry hall is wide and gracious to receive guests (and comes complete with a powder room for convenience). Flanking it are the family room with fireplace and the formal living room. A dining room has sliding glass doors to a rear terrace and leads directly to the L-shaped kitchen with island range. A handy utility area features washer/dryer space and storage and has an exterior door to the two-car garage. Upstairs are four bedrooms with two full baths. The master bedroom has a sitting room, dressing area, walk-in closet and bath with dual vanities.

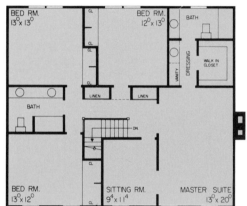

Design by
Home Planners, Inc.

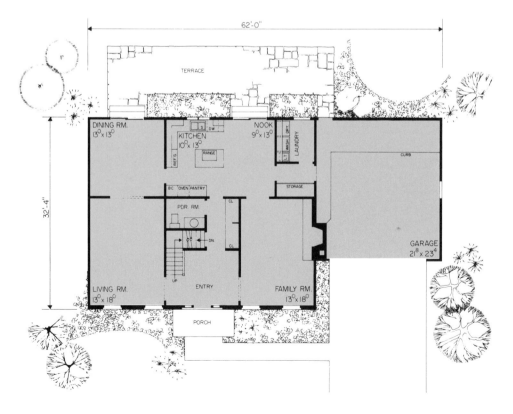

Design DD9821

First Floor: 2,070 square feet
Second Floor: 790 square feet
Total: 2,860 square feet

Design by
Design Traditions

● The striking combination of wood frame, shingles and glass creates the exterior of this classic cottage. The foyer opens to the main level layout. To the left of the foyer is a study with a warming hearth and a vaulted ceiling. To the right is the formal dining room. A great room with an attached breakfast area is to the rear near the kitchen. A guest room is nestled in the rear of the plan for privacy. The master suite provides an expansive tray ceiling, a glass sitting area and easy passage to the outside deck. Upstairs, two bedrooms are accompanied by a loft for a quiet getaway. This home is designed with a basement foundation.

Width 58'-4"
Depth 54'-10"

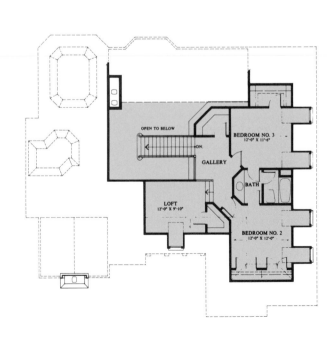

Design DD9822

First Floor: 1,944 square feet
Second Floor: 954 square feet
Total: 2,898 square feet

● This story-and-a-half home combines warm informal materials with a modern livable floor plan to create a true New England classic. The dining room, study and great room work together to create one large, exciting space. Just beyond the open rail, the breakfast room is lined with windows. Plenty of counter space and storage make the kitchen truly usable. The master suite, with its tray ceiling and decorative wall niche, is a gracious and private owners' retreat. Upstairs, two additional bedrooms each have their own vanity within a shared bath while the third bedroom or guest room has its own bath and walk-in closet. This home is designed with a basement foundation.

Design by
Design Traditions

WIDTH 51'-6"
DEPTH 73'

● Here are two more examples of the rambling Cape Cod house that illustrate just how delightful the appearance of those added dependents can be. The appealing result is houses with varying roof planes, projecting and recessed exterior walls and interesting, irregular configurations. In addition to charm, these two houses deliver exceptional country-estate livability for the growing, active family. Each one has a central entrance leading to a foyer, but from there the many features are distinct.

Design DD2615

First Floor: 2,563 square feet
Second Floor: 552 square feet
Total: 3,115 square feet

Design by
Home Planners,
Inc.

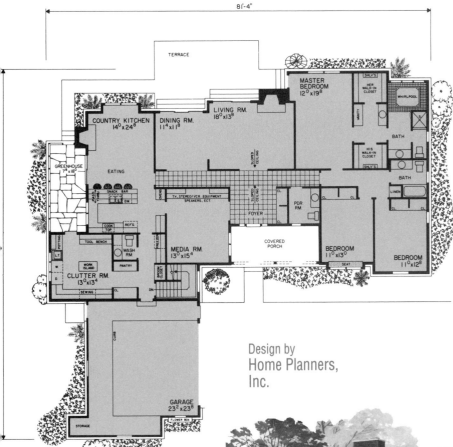

81'-4"

TERRACE

MASTER BEDROOM 12⁰x19⁸

COUNTRY KITCHEN 14⁰x24⁸

DINING RM. 11⁴x11⁸

LIVING RM. 18⁰x13⁸

HER WALK-IN CLOSET

SHLV'S

WHIRLPOOL

VANITY

BATH

GREENHOUSE 7⁸x18⁰

EATING

SNACK BAR

HIS WALK-IN CLOSET

SHLV'S

BATH

LINEN

SLOPED CEILING

SLOPED CEILING

T.V.,STEREO/VCR EQUIPMENT SPEAKERS, ECT.

FOYER

PDR RM

CL

CL

CL

COOK TOP

REFG.

COVERED PORCH

BEDROOM 11⁰x13⁰

SEAT

BEDROOM 11⁰x12⁸

POTTING

TOOL BENCH

WORK ISLAND

WASH RM.

PANTRY

MEDIA RM. 13⁰x15⁴

CLUTTER RM. 13⁰x13⁴

SEWING

BROOM CLOSET

DN.

CURB

GARAGE 23²x23⁸

STORAGE

FLOWER BOX

Design by
Home Planners,
Inc.

Design DD2880
Square Footage: 2,907

● This comfortable traditional home offers plenty of modern livability. A clutter room off the two-car garage is an ideal space for a workbench, sewing or hobbies. Across the hall is a media room and the perfect place for a stereo, VCR and more. A spacious gathering area and a country kitchen with a snack bar to the right of the greenhouse (great for fresh herbs) is an ideal place for informal gatherings with family and friends. The formal living room with a fireplace and the dining room provide access to the rear grounds. An amenity-filled spacious master suite features His and Her walk-in closets, a relaxing whirlpool tub and access to the rear terrace. Two large secondary bedrooms share a full bath. For information on customizing this design, call 1-800-521-6797, ext. 800.

QUOTE ONE™

Cost to build? See page 216
to order complete cost estimate
to build this house in your area!

17

Design DD2921

First Floor: 3,215 square feet
Second Floor: 711 square feet
Total: 3,926 square feet

● Organized zoning by room functions makes this traditional design a comfortable home for living. A central foyer facilitates flexible traffic patterns. Quiet areas of the house include a media room and luxurious master bedroom suite with a fitness area, spacious closet space and a bath, as well as a lounge or writing area. Informal living areas of the house include a sun room and a large country kitchen. The second floor holds two bedrooms and a lounge. For information on customizing this design, call 1-800-521-6797, ext. 800.

Cost to build? See page 216 to order complete cost estimate to build this house in your area!

Design by
Home Planners,
Inc.

Design by
Home Planners,
Inc.

QUOTE ONE™

Cost to build? See page 216
to order complete cost estimate
to build this house in your area!

COVERED PORCH

SKYLIGHT   SKYLIGHT   SKYLIGHT

TERRACE

BRKFST RM
13² x 11⁸

LIVING RM
13⁰ x 17²

DINING
8⁸ x 9¹⁰

SLOPED CEILING   SLOPED CEILING

RAILING

P'TRY

DESK

SNACK BAR

DW   S

KITCHEN
13² x 9⁶

COOK TOP

OVEN   REFG

LAUNDRY
8⁴ x 7⁸

CL

LT   W   D

STORAGE
11⁰ x 8⁴

DN

SLOPED CEILING

FOYER

CL

BATH

WALK-IN CLOSET

BATH

LINEN

STUDY/
BEDROOM
10⁰ x 10⁴

CL

CL

PORCH

GARAGE
19⁸ x 20⁴

SLOPED CEILING   SLOPED CEILING

MASTER
BEDROOM
13⁴ x 13⁰

BEDROOM
13⁴ x 10⁸

SEAT

52'-6"

58'-0"

Design DD3340
Square Footage: 1,611

● You may not decide to
build this design simply because of its delightful covered porch. But it certainly
will provide its share of
enjoyment if this plan is
your choice. Notice also how
effectively the bedrooms are
arranged out of the traffic
flow of the house. One bedroom could double nicely as
a TV room or study. The living room/dining area is
highlighted by a fireplace,
sliding glass doors to the
porch, and an open staircase
with built-in planter to the
basement.

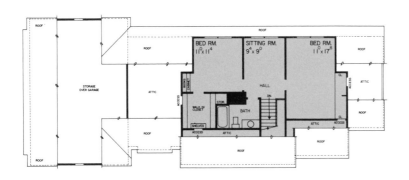

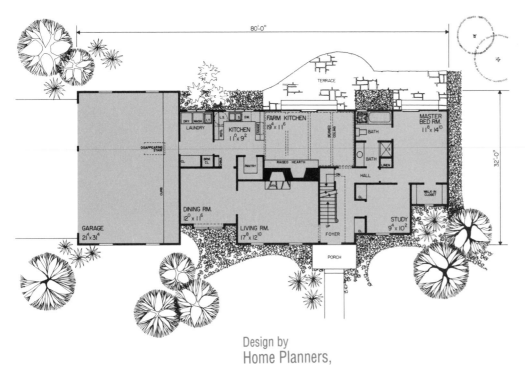

Design by
Home Planners,
Inc.

Design DD2563

First Floor: 1,500 square feet
Second Floor: 690 square feet
Total: 2,190 square feet

● This charming Cape Cod
will definitely capture your
heart with its warm appeal. This
home offers you and your family a wealth of livability. Inside,
to the left of the foyer, is a formal living room with a cozy
fireplace and an adjacent dining
room. To the right is a study. An
efficient kitchen and a large,
farm kitchen eating area will be
enjoyed by all. Access to the terrace is provided by sliding glass
doors from both the farm
kitchen and the master bedroom. The master suite enjoys a
pampering bath and a large
walk-in closet. The second floor
contains a sitting room, two
secondary bedrooms and a full
bath. For information on customizing this design, call
1-800-521-6797, ext. 800.

Cost to build? See page 216
to order complete cost estimate
to build this house in your area!

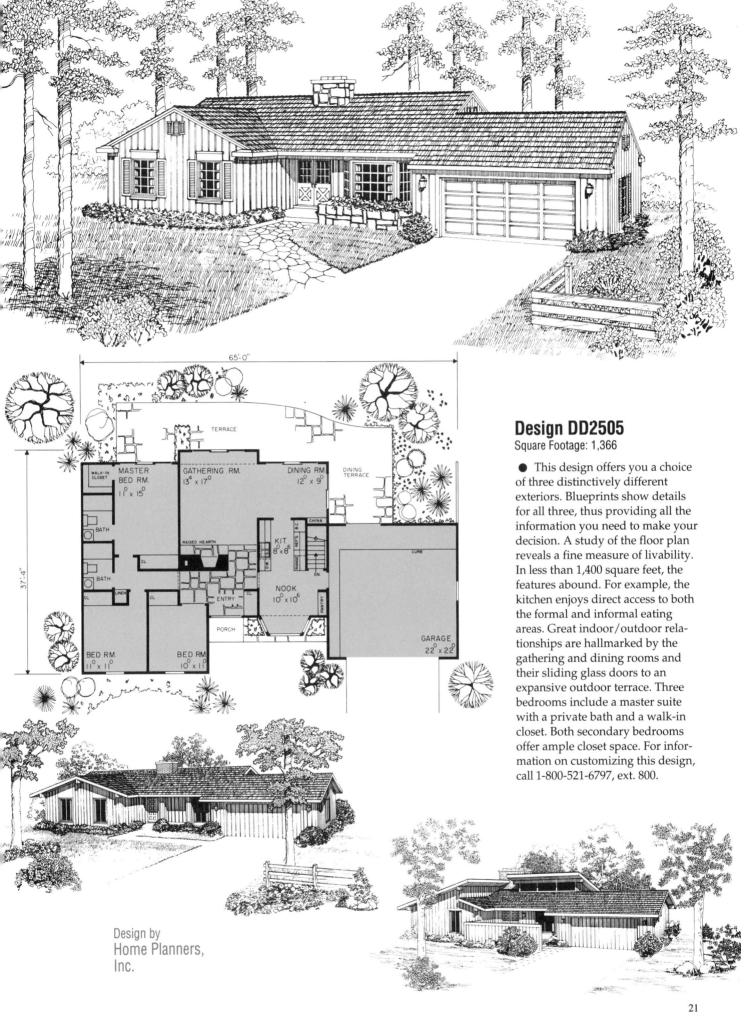

Design DD2505
Square Footage: 1,366

● This design offers you a choice of three distinctively different exteriors. Blueprints show details for all three, thus providing all the information you need to make your decision. A study of the floor plan reveals a fine measure of livability. In less than 1,400 square feet, the features abound. For example, the kitchen enjoys direct access to both the formal and informal eating areas. Great indoor/outdoor relationships are hallmarked by the gathering and dining rooms and their sliding glass doors to an expansive outdoor terrace. Three bedrooms include a master suite with a private bath and a walk-in closet. Both secondary bedrooms offer ample closet space. For information on customizing this design, call 1-800-521-6797, ext. 800.

Design by
Home Planners,
Inc.

21

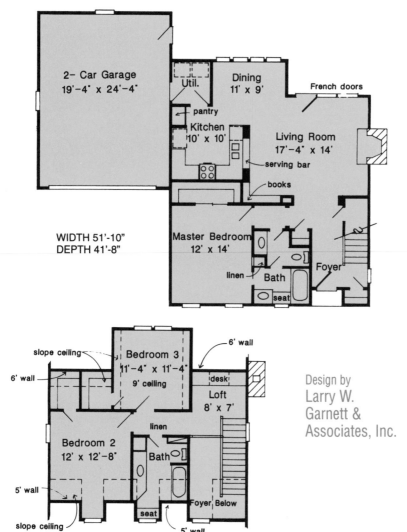

Design DD8958

First Floor: 980 square feet
Second Floor: 546 square feet
Total: 1,526 square feet

● You'll feel right at home in this traditional-style house. A living room defined by a fireplace, French doors and built-in-bookshelves sets the tone for first-floor livability. A U-shaped kitchen benefits from such features as a pantry and a conveniently accessed dining area. A utility room supplies passage from the garage to the main house. The master bedroom enjoys first-floor frontal views and a compartmented bath. Two more bedrooms, set up-stairs, share a delightful full bath with a linen closet and a window seat. Each bedroom yields a walk-in closet. Also particularly mentionable: the loft with a built-in desk that sits atop the stairs.

Design by
Larry W.
Garnett &
Associates, Inc.

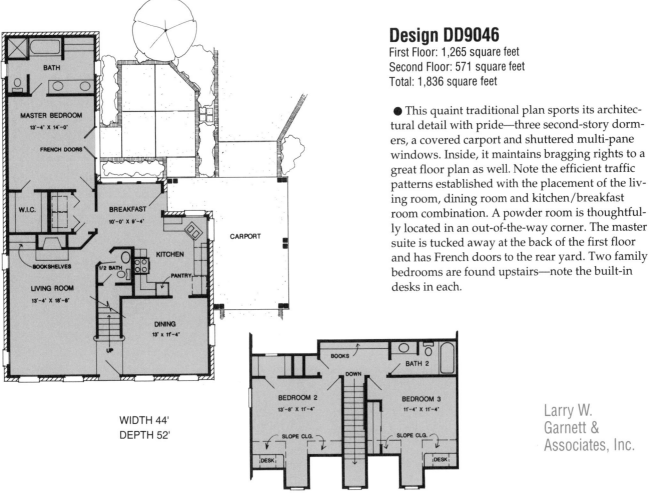

BATH

MASTER BEDROOM
13'-4" X 14'-0"

FRENCH DOORS

W.I.C.

BREAKFAST
10'-0" X 9'-4"

CARPORT

KITCHEN

BOOKSHELVES

1/2 BATH

PANTRY

LIVING ROOM
13'-4" X 18'-8"

DINING
13' x 1f'-4"

UP

WIDTH 44'
DEPTH 52'

BOOKS

DOWN

BATH 2

BEDROOM 2
13'-8" X 11'-4"

BEDROOM 3
11'-4" X 11'-4"

SLOPE CLG.

SLOPE CLG.

DESK

DESK

Design DD9046

First Floor: 1,265 square feet
Second Floor: 571 square feet
Total: 1,836 square feet

● This quaint traditional plan sports its architectural detail with pride—three second-story dormers, a covered carport and shuttered multi-pane windows. Inside, it maintains bragging rights to a great floor plan as well. Note the efficient traffic patterns established with the placement of the living room, dining room and kitchen/breakfast room combination. A powder room is thoughtfully located in an out-of-the-way corner. The master suite is tucked away at the back of the first floor and has French doors to the rear yard. Two family bedrooms are found upstairs—note the built-in desks in each.

Larry W.
Garnett &
Associates, Inc.

23

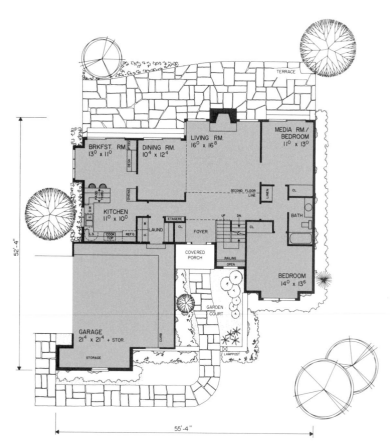

Design DD2927 First Floor: 1,425 square feet; Second Floor: 704 square feet; Total: 2,129 square feet

● This charming Early American adaptation with stone-and-board exterior is just as charming on the inside. Features include a complete second-floor master bedroom suite with a balcony overlooking the living room. There is also a studio and a master bathroom. The first floor features a convenient kitchen with a pass-through to a breakfast room. There's also a formal dining room just steps away at the rear of the house. An adjacent rear living room enjoys its own fireplace. Other features include a rear media room or optional third bedroom. A downstairs bedroom enjoys an excellent front view while the garden court will be enjoyed by all. For information on customizing this design, call 1-800-521-6797, ext. 800.

GEORGIAN, FEDERAL *and* GREEK REVIVAL STYLES

DURING THE 18TH CENTURY, a flourishing young America—having found ways to achieve the basic necessities—now turned her attention to the art of living. The new homes constructed during this period were exceptionally grand and elegant, well proportioned, composed for formal effect and richly embellished with ornamentation. These new trends in design were in favor from the sophisticated city dwellers in Boston to the country gentlefolk in Maryland.

The Georgian-style home was first introduced as a basic two- or three-story, large, rectangular-shaped home. A brick exterior was customary, laid in a Flemish- or English-bond pattern, and the roof featured slate or copper shingles. Classic lines and ornamentation such as quoins, cornices with tooth-like dentils, Palladian-style windows and pediment gables are well represented by Designs DD2683 and DD9126. Windows were multi-paned and aligned both horizontally and vertically in symmetrical rows.

The wealthy and social elite of these times were daring in their actions but conservative in their attitudes. Identifying primarily with the Federalist party, these "new patricians" looked to England once again for cultural leadership. However, the sense of American identity had developed, and the majority demanded an American style of architecture for the average working man as well as the privileged. The purpose of American architecture was apparent: to bring comfort, dignity and quality to all classes of the population.

Federal-style homes served this purpose and were designed as multi-story, box-shaped houses with either a hip or flat roof. The features of this style were more flexible and delicate than early Georgian designs. This is evident in the more fragile hardware and door ornamentation of Designs DD2662 and DD9299. Exteriors were most often clapboard or Flemish-bond patterned brick, and windows contained small glass panes. The tops of many of these homes often featured an ornate portico or a belvedere and balustrades, known as a "widow's walk," as part of their ornamentation.

By the early 1800s, America's admiration for Greece had reached a burning intensity, due in part to that country's own fight for independence, and it was in the spirit of Greek architecture that America found its artistic ideal. Greek Revival spoke to a nation that welcomed innovation and aspired to greatness. During this period the nation's population grew dramatically and her western boundary now met the Pacific. As the popularity of this classic style spread to the West Coast, these homes were often sold disassembled and shipped by way of Cape Horn to their waiting builders.

The Greek Revival style was a two-, sometimes three-story symmetrical home, elaborately detailed, that featured the characteristics of Greek temples. Designs DD2668 and DD2984 offer accurate interpretations of this elegant style. Porches are supported by square or round columns and cornice lines are emphasized with a wide, divided band of trim, frieze above and architrave below. Front doors are sometimes surrounded by narrow sidelights with transom lights above.

The following pages of this section offer wonderful examples of the splendor of these styles, presented with updated, contemporary floor plans suited to meet the needs of today's most active lifestyles.

Design DD2668

First Floor: 1,206 square feet; Second Floor: 1,254 square feet
Total: 2,460 square feet

● This elegant exterior houses a very livable plan. Every bit of space has been put to good use. The front country kitchen is a good place to begin. It is efficiently planned with its island cook top, built-ins and pass-thru to the dining room. The large great room will be the center of all family activities. Quiet times can be enjoyed in the front library. Study the second floor sleeping areas.

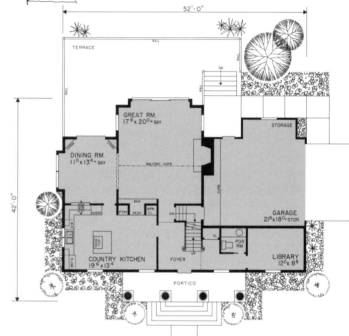

Design by
Home Planners,
Inc.

Cost to build? See page 216
to order complete cost estimate
to build this house in your area!

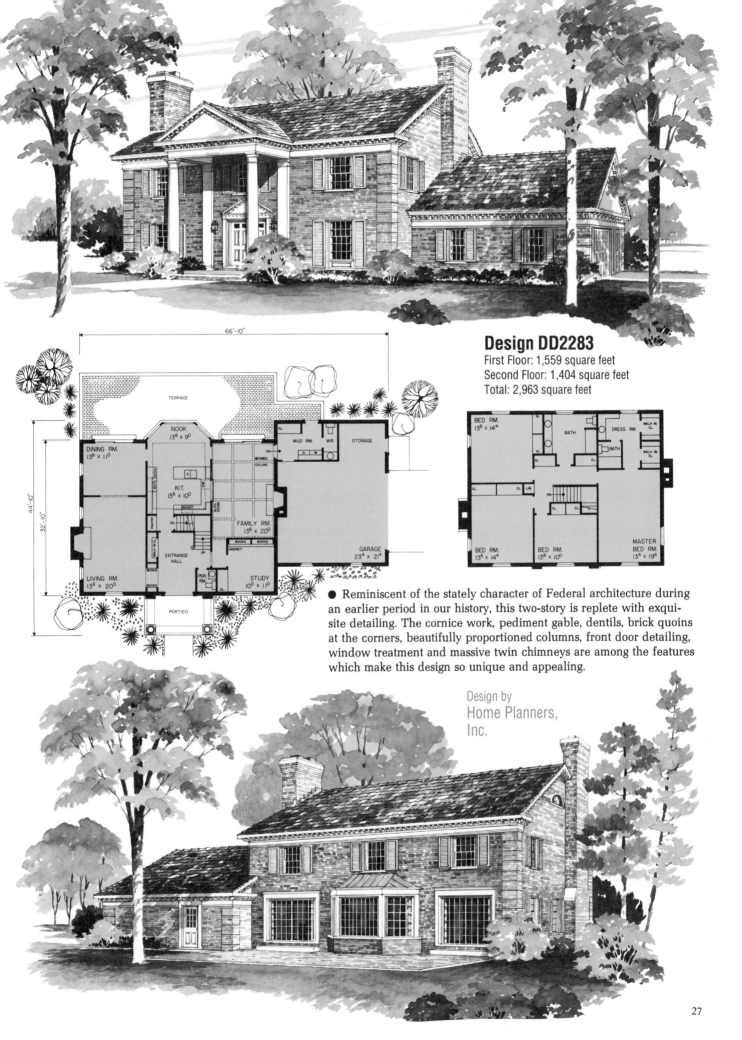

Design DD2283

First Floor: 1,559 square feet
Second Floor: 1,404 square feet
Total: 2,963 square feet

66'-10"

TERRACE

NOOK
13⁶ x 9⁰

MUD RM.   W.R.   STORAGE

DINING RM.
13⁶ x 11⁰

BEAMED CEILING

KIT.
13⁶ x 10⁰

FAMILY RM.
13⁶ x 20⁰

GARAGE
23⁴ x 21⁴

44'-10"   32'-10"

ENTRANCE HALL

BOOKS   BOOKS

CABINET

LIVING RM.
13⁶ x 20⁰

PDR. RM.

STUDY
10⁰ x 11⁰

PORTICO

BED RM.
13⁶ x 14⁴   BATH   DRESS. RM.   WALK-IN CL.

BATH   WALK-IN CL.

DN.

BED RM.
13⁶ x 14⁴   BED RM.
13⁶ x 10⁰   MASTER BED RM.
13⁶ x 19⁶

● Reminiscent of the stately character of Federal architecture during an earlier period in our history, this two-story is replete with exquisite detailing. The cornice work, pediment gable, dentils, brick quoins at the corners, beautifully proportioned columns, front door detailing, window treatment and massive twin chimneys are among the features which make this design so unique and appealing.

Design by
Home Planners,
Inc.

Design DD2984

First Floor: 3,116 square feet
Second Floor: 1,997 square feet
Total: 5,113 square feet

● An echo of Whitehall, built in 1765 in Anne Arundel County, Maryland, resounds in this home. Its classic symmetry and columned facade herald a grand interior. There's no lack of space whether entertaining formally or just enjoying a family get-together, and all are kept cozy with fireplaces in the gathering room, study, and family room. An island kitchen with attached breakfast room handily serves the nearby dining room. Four second floor bedrooms include a large master suite with another fireplace, a whirlpool, and His and Hers closets in the bath. Three more full baths are found on this floor.

Design by
Home Planners, Inc.

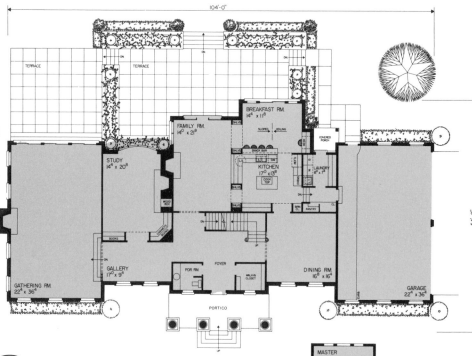

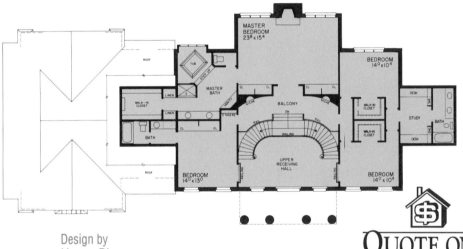

Design by
Home Planners,
Inc.

QUOTE ONE™

Cost to build? See page 216
to order complete cost estimate
to build this house in your area!

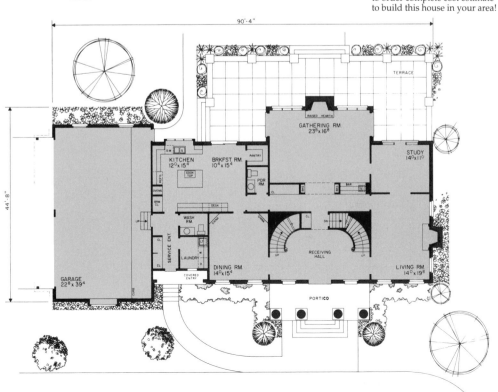

Design DD2889

First Floor: 2,349 square feet
Second Floor: 1,918 square feet
Total: 4,267 square feet

● This is truly a classic design. Some of the exterior highlights of this two-story include the pediment gable with cornice work and dentils, the beautifully proportioned columns, the front door detailing and the window treatment. Behind the facade of this design is an equally elegant interior. Imagine greeting your guests in the large receiving hall. It is graced by two curving staircases and opens to the formal living and dining rooms. Beyond the living room is the study. It has access to the rear terrace. Those large, informal occasions for family get-togethers or entertaining will be enjoyed in the spacious gathering room. It has a centered fireplace flanked by windows on each side, access to the terrace and a wet bar. The work center is efficient: a kitchen with island cooktop, breakfast room, washroom, laundry and service entrance. The second floor also is outstanding. Three family bedrooms and two full baths are joined by the feature-filled master bedroom suite.

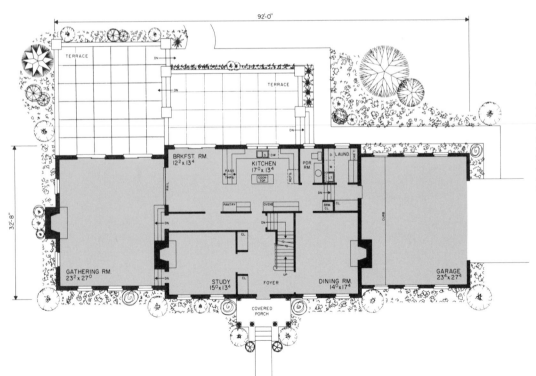

Design DD2683

First Floor: 2,126 square feet
Second Floor: 1,882 square feet
Total: 4,008 square feet

● This stately two-story home
combines the grace of the past
with modern amenities. The
luxurious master suite provides
a quiet retreat featuring a fireplace, a pampering master bath,
a dressing room with a huge
walk-in closet and a spacious
lounge.

Design by
Home Planners,
Inc.

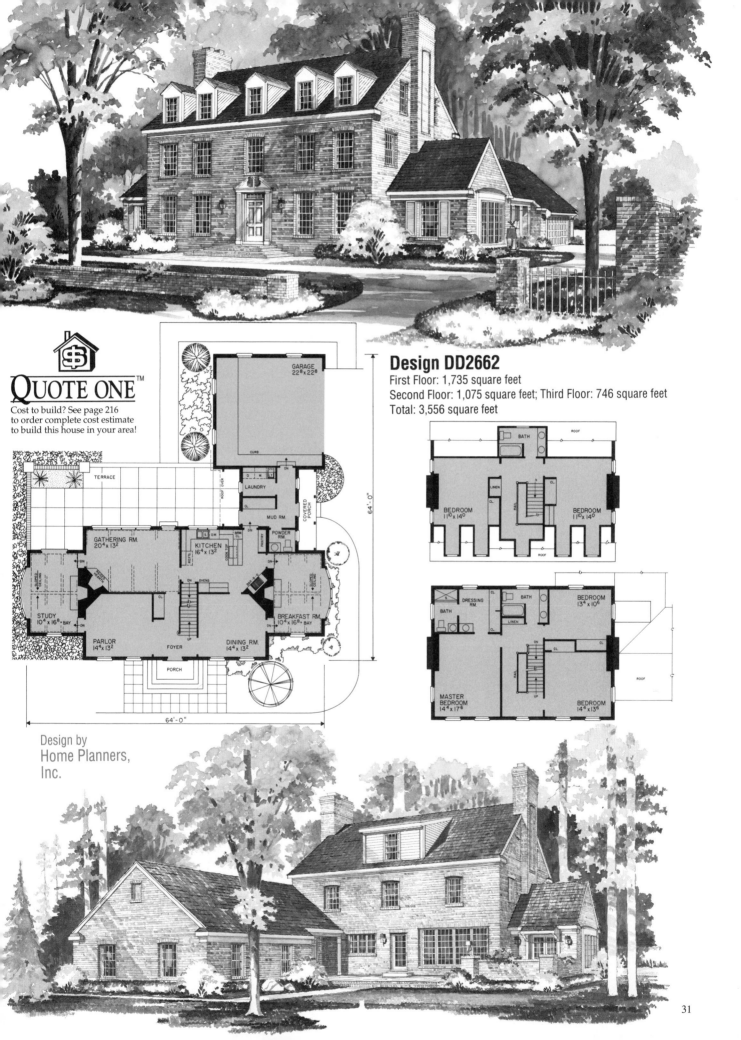

QUOTE ONE™

Cost to build? See page 216
to order complete cost estimate
to build this house in your area!

Design by
Home Planners,
Inc.

Design DD2662

First Floor: 1,735 square feet
Second Floor: 1,075 square feet; Third Floor: 746 square feet
Total: 3,556 square feet

First Floor labels:

GARAGE 22⁸ x 22⁸
TERRACE
LAUNDRY
MUD RM.
COVERED PORCH
POWDER RM.
GATHERING RM. 20⁴ x 13²
KITCHEN 16⁴ x 13²
PANTRY
BREAKFAST RM. 10⁴ x 16⁸ BAY
STUDY 10⁴ x 16⁸ BAY
PARLOR 14⁴ x 13²
FOYER
DINING RM. 14⁴ x 13²
PORCH

64'-0"

Third Floor labels:

BATH
ROOF
LINEN
BEDROOM 11¹⁰ x 14⁰
BEDROOM 11¹⁰ x 14⁰

Second Floor labels:

DRESSING RM.
BATH
BATH
LINEN
BEDROOM 13⁴ x 10⁶
MASTER BEDROOM 14⁴ x 17⁶
BEDROOM 14⁴ x 13⁶
ROOF

Design DD9126

First Floor: 2,157 square feet
Second Floor: 1,346 square feet
Total: 3,503 square feet

● Traditional styling at its best—this plan is a true work of art. The entry foyer contains a curved staircase to the second floor and is open to the formal dining room. The living room has a fireplace as does the family room. A quiet study features built-in shelves and is tucked away to the rear of the plan. Note the master bedroom on the first floor. It boasts a double walk-in closet, corner shower and large tub. Four bedrooms upstairs revolve around a game room with vaulted ceiling. Bedroom 5 has a window seat and double closets.

Design by
Larry W.
Garnett &
Associates, Inc.

Width 70'-6"
Depth 73'-4"

2-Car Garage

Util.

1/2 Bath

Porch

Study
12' x 12'-8"

Books

Breakfast
11'-8" x 10'

Kitchen
12' x 14'

Living Room
17' x 17'

Bath

Plant Shelf

Family Room
16'-8" x 14'-8"
14' Clg.

Gallery

Master Bedroom
14'-2" x 17'-4"

Dining
14'-2" x 11'-8"

Foyer

9' Clg. Throughout First Floor
Unless Otherwise Noted

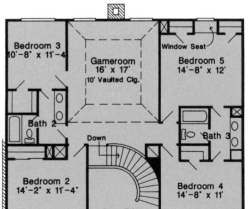

Bedroom 3
10'-8" x 11'-4"

Gameroom
16' x 17'
10' Vaulted Clg.

Window Seat

Bedroom 5
14'-8" x 12'

Bath 2

Down

Bath 3

Bedroom 2
14'-2" x 11'-4"

Foyer Below

Bedroom 4
14'-8" x 11'

8' Clg. Throughout Second Floor
Unless Otherwise Noted

Design DD9095

First Floor: 2,824 square feet
Second Floor: 1,334 square feet
Total: 4,158 square feet

● If you're looking for a plan that delivers a wealth of fine features, this one
should appeal to you. Fireplaces in the
dining room, living room and study keep
all warm and snug. A window-surround-
ed breakfast nook starts the day with
sunshine. Built-ins abound: bookcases in
the library loft, study and gallery; wine
rack in the family room; niche in the hall;
and bookcases and cabinets in two
upstairs bedrooms. The family room has
a vaulted ceiling and is overlooked by
the balcony from above. A three-car
garage serves automotive needs.

Design by
Larry W.
Garnett &
Associates, Inc.

Bedroom 3
14' x 14'-4"

Family Room Below

Bath 4

Books

Bath 3   Linen

Balcony

Library Loft

Books

42" High Wall

Bedroom 2
14' x 15'

Bedroom 4
11'-4" x 15'

Desk   Books/
Cabinets

Books/
Cabinets

Foyer Below

Width 77'-8"
Depth 86'-10"

3-Car Garage

Util.

French Door   Raised   Foyer
            Gallery
Porch

French Doors   Fixed   French Door
        French Doors

Family Room
15'-8" x 18'
Volume Clg.

Books/Cabinets

Master Bedroom
17'-4" x 15'-4"

Living Room
21'-8" x 14'-4"

Niche

Bath

Linen

Bath
2

Gallery

Buffet   Wine Rack

Pantry

Closet
16'-8" x 8'-8"

Books/Cabinets

Breakfast
10'-8" x 14'

French Doors

Books

Kitchen
12' x 10'

Study
13'-4" x 14'

Dining
13' x 16'

Foyer

French Doors

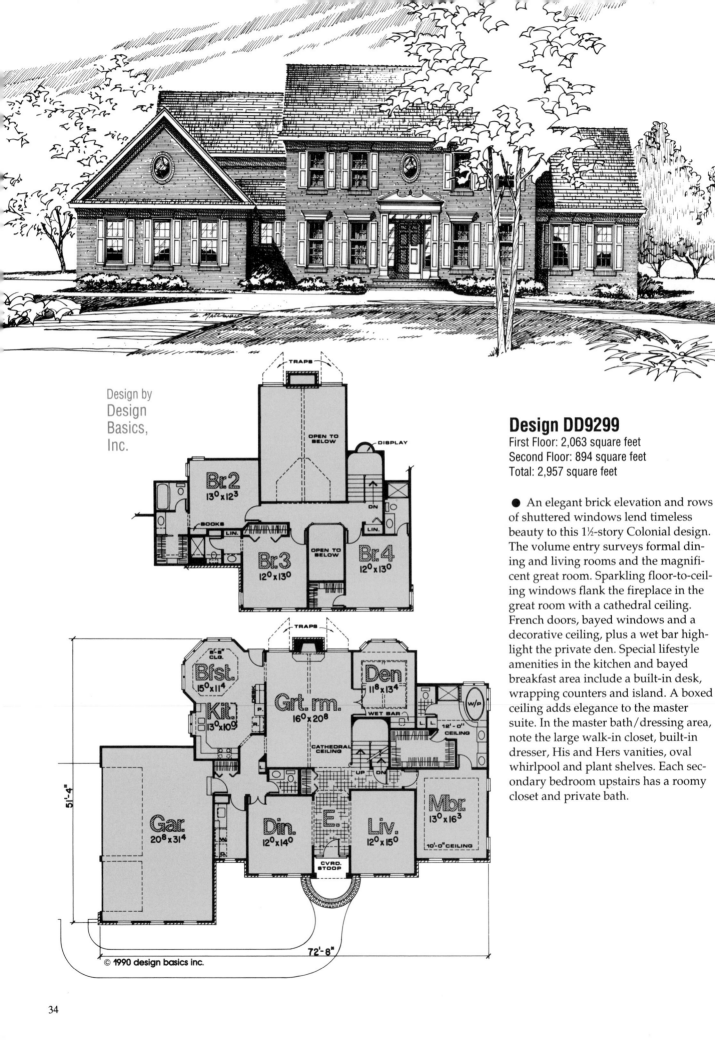

Design by
**Design
Basics,
Inc.**

TRAPS

**OPEN TO
BELOW**

DISPLAY

Br.2
13⁰ x 12³

BOOKS LIN.

LIN.

Br.3
12⁰ x 13⁰

**OPEN TO
BELOW**

Br.4
12⁰ x 13⁰

DN

Design DD9299

First Floor: 2,063 square feet
Second Floor: 894 square feet
Total: 2,957 square feet

● An elegant brick elevation and rows
of shuttered windows lend timeless
beauty to this 1½-story Colonial design.
The volume entry surveys formal dining and living rooms and the magnificent great room. Sparkling floor-to-ceil-
ing windows flank the fireplace in the
great room with a cathedral ceiling.
French doors, bayed windows and a
decorative ceiling, plus a wet bar highlight the private den. Special lifestyle
amenities in the kitchen and bayed
breakfast area include a built-in desk,
wrapping counters and island. A boxed
ceiling adds elegance to the master
suite. In the master bath/dressing area,
note the large walk-in closet, built-in
dresser, His and Hers vanities, oval
whirlpool and plant shelves. Each secondary bedroom upstairs has a roomy
closet and private bath.

TRAPS

Bfst.
15⁰ x 11⁴

Grt. rm.
16⁰ x 20⁸

Den
11⁸ x 13⁴

Kit.
13⁰ x 10⁹

WET BAR

**CATHEDRAL
CEILING**

12'-0"
CEILING

W/P

Gar.
20⁸ x 31⁴

Din.
12⁰ x 14⁰

E.

Liv.
12⁰ x 15⁰

UP **DN**

Mbr.
13⁰ x 16³

10'-0" CEILING

**CVRD.
STOOP**

51'-4"

72'-8"

© 1990 design basics inc.

Design DD9390

First Floor: 1,865 square feet
Second Floor: 774 square feet
Total: 2,639 square feet

● A magnificent brick facade with a 3-car, side-load garage conceals a well-organized floor plan. A tiled foyer leads to the formal dining room, with wet bar and hutch space, on the left and a parlor on the right. Straight ahead is a spacious great room with arched windows flanking a fireplace. The kitchen offers a snack bar peninsula and adjoins a bayed breakfast area. The first-floor master bedroom includes a large walk-in closet and French doors leading to a master bath with angled whirlpool and shower with glass block. The second floor provides three bedrooms and two full baths. A reading seat flanked by two cabinets overlooks the volume entry.

Design by
Design Basics, Inc.

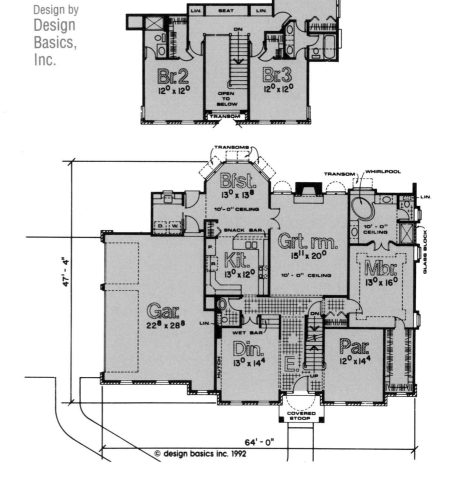

Design DD7208 First Floor: 1,675 square feet
Second Floor: 1,605 square feet; Total: 3,280 square feet

● A grand and glorious split staircase makes a lasting first impression in this stately two-story home. The striking family room is lit by a beveled wall of windows while a wet bar, built-in book cases and an entertainment center provide the finishing touches. The spacious kitchen is sure to please, featuring an island cooktop with a snack bar, a planning desk and a sunny bayed breakfast area. Quiet and private, the second floor accommodates the sleeping areas. Each secondary bedroom enjoys a walk-in closet; two bedrooms share a Hollywood bath and a third enjoys a private bath. The master suite offers uncommon elegance with French doors opening into the master bedroom with its tray ceiling, a gazebo sitting area and a separate off-season closet. Enter the master bath through French doors and enjoy its relaxing whirlpool tub, an open shower and built-in dressers in the large walk-in closet.

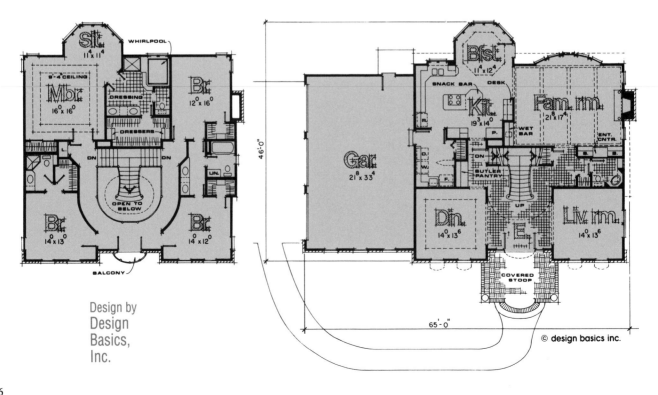

Design by
Design
Basics,
Inc.

Design DD9367 First Floor: 2,500 square feet
Second Floor: 973 square feet; Total: 3,473 square feet

● Step between the columns and into the entry of this grandiose design. The first floor offers maximum livability with 2,500 square feet. Large living and dining rooms flank a formal staircase. One of the most dramatic rooms in the house is the great room with a fourteen-foot-high beamed ceiling, a fireplace and wonderful views. Fancy the octagon-shaped break-fast nook or the kitchen with abundant counter space. This house incorporates four bedrooms with the master bedroom on the first floor. A tiered ceiling, two walk-in closets and a luxurious bath with His and Hers vanities, shower and a spa tub all characterize this room. On the second floor you'll find three bedrooms: two share a full bath, one has a private bath.

Design by
Design
Basics,
Inc.

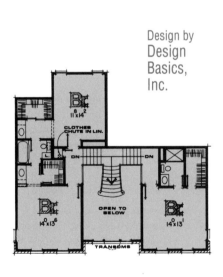

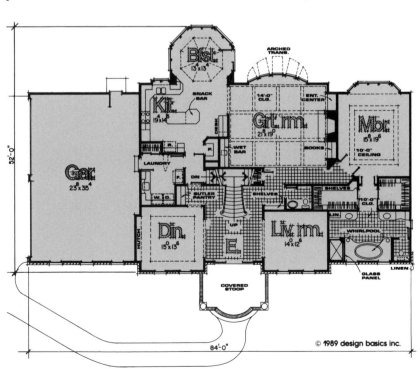

© 1989 design basics inc.

Design DD9837

First Floor: 1,847 square feet
Second Floor: 1,453 square feet
Total: 3,300 square feet

● To suit those who favor classic styling, this elegant manor home features a dramatic brick exterior which is further emphasized by the varied roofline and the finial atop the uppermost gable. The main level opens with a two-story foyer and formal rooms on the right. The living room contains a fireplace set in a bay window. The dining room is separated from the living room by a symmetrical column arrangement. The more casual family room is to the rear. For guests, a bedroom and bath are located on the main level. The second floor provides additional bedrooms and baths for family as well as a magnificent master suite. This home is designed with a basement foundation.

Width: 63'-3"
Depth: 47'

Design by
Design Traditions

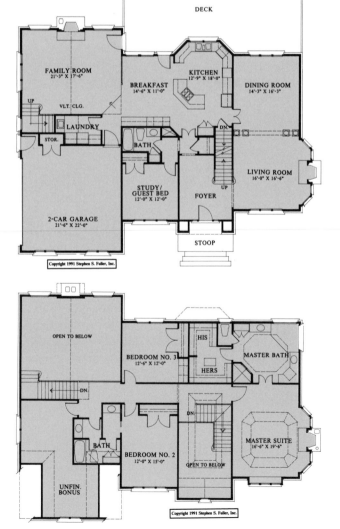

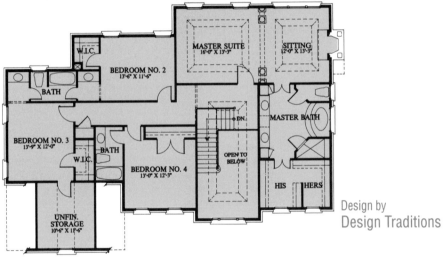

W.I.C.

BATH

BEDROOM NO. 2
13'-6" X 11'-6"

MASTER SUITE
16'-0" X 13'-3"

SITTING
12'-0" X 13'-3"

BEDROOM NO. 3
13'-9" X 12'-0"

BATH

W.I.C.

BEDROOM NO. 4
13'-0" X 12'-3"

DN.

OPEN TO BELOW

MASTER BATH

HIS   HERS

UNFIN. STORAGE
10'-6" X 11'-6"

Design by
Design Traditions

Design DD9899

First Floor: 1,554 square feet
Second Floor: 1,648 square feet
Total: 3,202 square feet

● The classic styling of this brick traditional will be respected for years to come. The formidable double-door entry with transom and Palladian window reveals the shining foyer within. It is flanked by the spacious dining room and formal study or parlor. A large family room with a full wall of glass conveniently opens to the breakfast room and kitchen. The master suite features a spacious sitting area with its own fireplace and tray ceiling. Two additional bedrooms share a bath, while a fourth bedroom has its own private bath. This home is designed with a basement foundation.

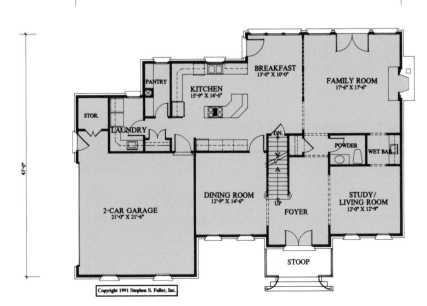

60'-0"

43'-0"

PANTRY

KITCHEN
15'-9" X 14'-6"

BREAKFAST
13'-0" X 10'-0"

FAMILY ROOM
17'-6" X 17'-6"

STOR.

LAUNDRY

2-CAR GARAGE
21'-0" X 21'-6"

DINING ROOM
12'-9" X 14'-6"

DN.

UP

FOYER

POWDER

WET BAR

STUDY/ LIVING ROOM
12'-0" X 12'-9"

STOOP

Design DD9844 Square Footage: 2,090 (without basement)

● Grace and elegance in one-story living abound in this traditional country home. It contains all the necessary elements of a convenient floor plan as well: an inviting great room with a fireplace, an elegant formal dining room, an efficient kitchen with an attached breakfast nook, a guest room/office and three bedrooms including a relaxing master suite. This winning combination is sure to please even the most discriminating homeowner. A large, unfinished basement area allows for future expansion.

Width 61'
Depth 72'-6"

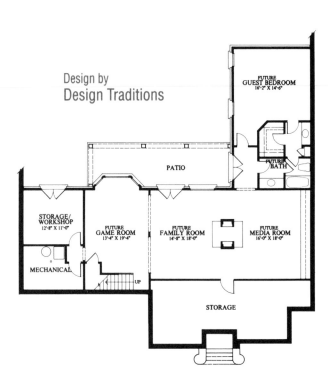

Design by
Design Traditions

Design DD9884
Square Footage: 2,120

● Arched-top windows act as graceful accents for this wonderful design. Inside, the floor plan is compact but commodious. A central family room serves as the center of activity. It has a fireplace and connects to a lovely sun room with rear porch access. The formal dining room is to the front of the plan and is open to the entry foyer. A private den also opens off the foyer with double doors. It has its own private, cozy fireplace. The kitchen area opens to the sun room and it contains an island work counter. Bedrooms are split, with the master suite to the right side of the design and family bedrooms to the left. There are also three full baths in this plan. This home is designed with a basement foundation.

Design by
Design Traditions

BEDROOM NO. 3
11'-6" X 11'-0"

BATH

MASTER BATH

W.I.C.

BEDROOM NO. 2
11'-4" X 11'-0"

SUN ROOM
12'-0" X 13'-9"

PORCH

MASTER BEDROOM
13'-4" X 15'-8"

BREAKFAST
10'-0" X 9'-0"

FAMILY ROOM
18'-0" X 14'-0"

LAUNDRY

KITCHEN
12'-0" X 13'-9"

BATH

DN.

TWO CAR GARAGE
20'-4" X 20'-8"

DINING ROOM
10'-6" X 13'-6"

FOYER

DEN
11'-4" X 12'-6"

STOOP

Width 62'
Depth 62'-6"

Design DD9714

First Floor: 1,468 square feet
Second Floor: 483 square feet
Total: 1,951 square feet

● Grand roof heights and multi-pane windows on the outside of this stately traditional lead the way to a convenient three-bedroom floor plan. The 51-foot width allows the plan to be built on a narrow lot. The two-level entrance foyer allows natural light to penetrate from the windows above. The foyer opens directly to the formal dining room and also to the rear great room where a cathedral ceiling, fireplace and arched window above the exterior door are enhancements to enjoy. The master bedroom has His and Hers walk-in closets and a master bath with double-bowl vanity, separate shower and whirlpool tub. The second level offers two additional bedrooms, a full bath and plenty of storage.

WIDTH 51'-3"
DEPTH 67'-2"

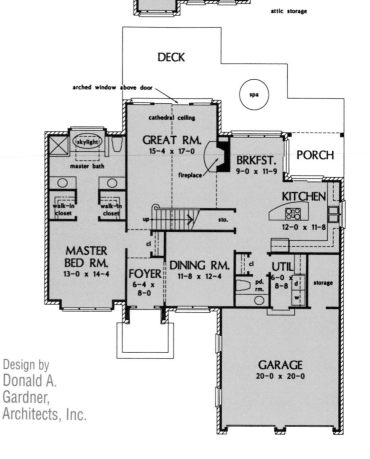

Design by
Donald A.
Gardner,
Architects, Inc.

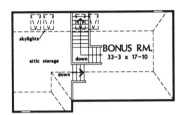

skylights

attic storage

BONUS RM.
33-3 x 17-10

down

down

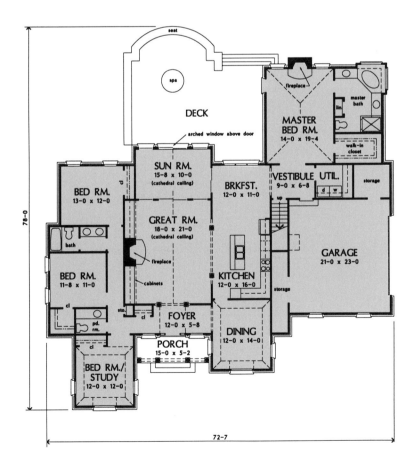

seat

spa

DECK

arched window above door

SUN RM.
15-8 x 10-0
(cathedral ceiling)

BRKFST.
12-0 x 11-0

fireplace

**MASTER
BED RM.**
14-0 x 19-4

master
bath

lin

walk-in
closet

VESTIBULE

UTIL.
9-0 x 6-8

storage

BED RM.
13-0 x 12-0

GREAT RM.
18-0 x 21-0
(cathedral ceiling)

up

GARAGE
21-0 x 23-0

bath

fireplace

BED RM.
11-8 x 11-0

cabinets

KITCHEN
12-0 x 16-0

storage

cl

sto.

cl

cl

pd.
rm.

FOYER
12-0 x 5-8

DINING
12-0 x 14-0

cl

PORCH
15-0 x 5-2

**BED RM./
STUDY**
12-0 x 12-0

78-0

72-7

Design DD9709

Square Footage: 2,663
Bonus Room: 653 square feet

● This stately one-story home displays large arched windows, round columns, a covered porch, and brick veneer siding. The arched window in the clerestory above the entrance provides natural light to the interior. The great room boasts a cathedral ceiling, a fireplace, built-in cabinets, and book-shelves. Sliding glass doors lead to the sun room. The L-shaped kitchen services the dining room, the breakfast area and the great room. The master bedroom suite, with a fireplace, uses private passage to the deck and its spa. Three additional bedrooms—one could serve as a study—are at the other end of the house for privacy. This plan is available with a crawl-space foundation.

Design by
Donald A.
Gardner,
Architects, Inc.

Design DD3503

First Level: 1,748 square feet
Second Level: 1,748 square feet
Third Level: 1,100 square feet
Total: 4,596 square feet

● A brick exterior serves as a nice introduction to this charming home. Enter the eleven-foot-high foyer and take a seat in the warm living room with its welcoming, warming fireplace. Built-in shelves grace the hallway as well as the living and dining rooms. The handy kitchen, with its island and snack bar, opens up into a conversation room with a sun-filled bay and a fireplace. The service entrance leads to both the laundry and the garage. This house features four bedrooms: the spacious master suite with a fireplace, a bay-windowed sitting area, a walk-in closet and a whirlpool; two family bedrooms that share a full bath with a double-bowl vanity; and a guest bedroom that shares the third floor with the library. This design would work well on a narrow lot.

Design by
Home Planners,
Inc.

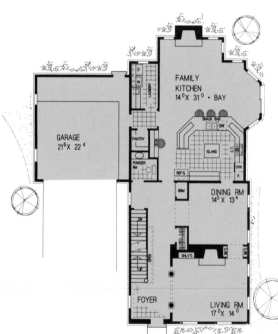

Width 50'
Depth 63'

44

SOUTHERN FARMHOUSES, COASTAL *and* ATLANTIC STYLES

AMONG AMERICA'S MOST CHERISHED DWELLINGS are the farmhouses of the Southern, Coastal and Atlantic regions. Typified by their simplicity and honest appeal, these homes cast a spell that is all their own. More than a home, frequently a family's heritage, these houses were often passed down from one generation to the next. At the turn of the 19th Century, ninety-five percent of the population in these regions was involved with some aspect of farming. The distinctive contrast in farmhouse styles was strongly influenced by geography and varied greatly due to the local availability of building materials, the building traditions of the settlers, and whether farmhouses were constructed during the pre-railroad or post-railroad eras.

The most common features of the early Southern farmhouses were the use of wood siding and a large, front or wraparound porch. Designed for practical purposes, porches encouraged comfortable outdoor livability due to the shorter and less confining Southern winters than those of their Midwestern counterparts. For a look at some contemporary versions of the classic Southern farmhouse, see Designs DD9606 and DD9632. By the late 18th Century, the now-familiar full, shed-roofed porch was universal, and if expansion was required, it was achieved by adding a rearward addition or enlarging the front porch. The principal variation to these additions involved porch size and shape, the placement of chimneys and different patterns of the rearward extensions. For a brief time in the 1930s, many Southern farmhouses employed either much smaller entry porches or none at all, believed most likely to be an attempt at imitating the Cape Cod shape which had become so popular.

The early farmhouses of the Coastal South were primarily linear, hall-and-parlor homes—meaning they were two rooms wide and one room deep. One-story homes were far more common than those built in the North due to the milder climate, therefore requiring a lesser need for more interior space. Prior to the railroads, the only means of efficiently transporting materials such as lumber, brick and quarried stone was by water. This meant that coastal towns and villages had access to a much larger variety of building materials, making it easier for this region to follow the most current architectural fashions, often building more elaborate and sophisticated homes. Designs DD9742 and DD9804 offer marvelous contemporary adaptations of the refined farmhouses commonly found in the coastal area.

The Atlantic region's early farmhouses were initially built by German immigrants who introduced building techniques using horizontally placed square-hewn logs interlocked at the corners. This linear plan was most commonly built with one or two end chimneys. The major drawback with this form of building was the difficulty encountered when there was a need for expansion. Changes took place as the availability of building materials grew; many of these farmhouses increased from one to two stories, featured wood siding, and were often decorated with dormered windows, yet the large porch that had proven so functional was always retained.

This section presents wonderful examples of the heritage that has remained so much a part of the American farmhouse, while providing amenity-filled interiors for today's modern homeowner.

Design DD9621

First Floor: 1,325 square feet
Second Floor: 453 square feet
Total: 1,778 square feet

● For the economy-minded family desiring a house with lots of distinction, this compact design has all the amenities available in larger plans. A wraparound covered porch, a front Palladian window and dormer and rear arched windows all provide exciting visual elements to the exterior. The spacious great room has a fireplace, a cathedral ceiling and arched clerestory windows. A second-level balcony overlooks this gathering area. The kitchen is centrally located for maximum flexibility in layout and features a pass-through to the great room. Besides the generous master suite with a full bath, there are two family bedrooms located on the second level sharing a full bath with a double vanity. Note the ample attic storage space. Please specify basement or crawlspace foundation when ordering.

FRONT

REAR

Design by
Donald A.
Gardner,
Architects, Inc.

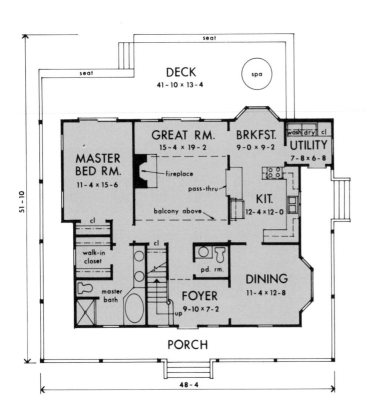

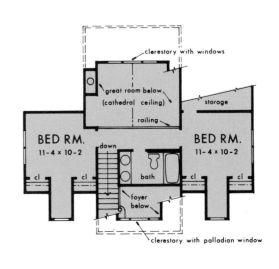

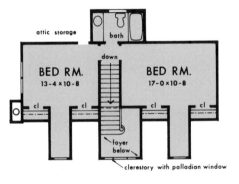

attic storage

bath

BED RM.
13-4 × 10-8

down

BED RM.
17-0 × 10-8

cl   cl   cl   cl

foyer
below

clerestory with palladian window

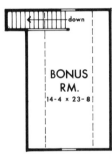

down

BONUS
RM.
14-4 × 23-8

Design by
Donald A.
Gardner,
Architects, Inc.

Design DD9606

First Floor: 1,289 square feet
Second Floor: 542 square feet
Total: 1,831 square feet

● This cozy country cottage is perfect for the growing family—offering both an unfinished basement option and a bonus room. Enter through the two-story foyer with a Palladian window in a clerestory dormer above. The master suite is on the first floor for privacy and accessibility. Its accompanying bath boasts a whirlpool tub with a skylight above and a double-bowl vanity. The second floor contains two bedrooms, a full bath and plenty of storage. Note that all first-floor rooms except the kitchen and utility room boast nine-foot ceilings. This plan is available with either a basement or crawlspace foundation. Please specify when ordering.

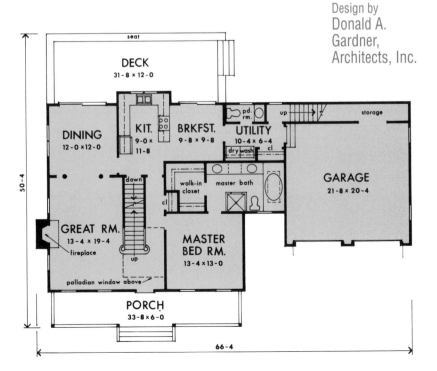

seat

DECK
31-8 × 12-0

DINING
12-0 × 12-0

KIT.
9-0 ×
11-8

BRKFST.
9-8 × 9-8

pd.
rm.

UTILITY
10-4 × 6-4

dry wash   cl

up

storage

GARAGE
21-8 × 20-4

50-4

down

walk-in
closet

master bath

GREAT RM.
13-4 × 19-4

fireplace

up

MASTER
BED RM.
13-4 × 13-0

palladian window above

PORCH
33-8 × 6-0

66-4

Design DD9632

First Floor: 1,756 square feet
Second Floor: 565 square feet
Total: 2,321 square feet

Design by
Donald A.
Gardner,
Architects, Inc.

● A wraparound covered porch at the front and sides of this house and an open deck at the back provide plenty of outside living area. The spacious great room features a fireplace, cathedral ceiling, and clerestory with an arched window. The first-floor master bedroom contains a generous closet and a master bath with garden tub, double-bowl vanity, and shower. The second floor sports two bedrooms and a full bath with double-bowl vanity. This plan includes a crawl-space foundation.

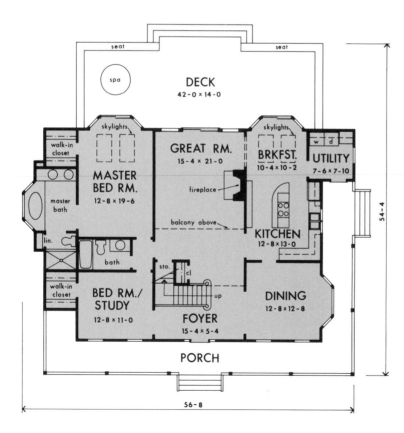

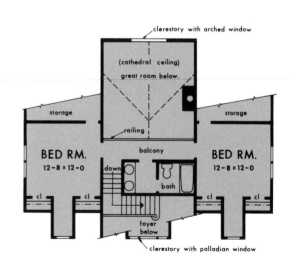

B. NATHAN.

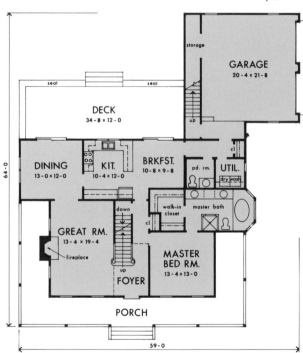

storage

GARAGE
20-4 x 21-8

DECK
34-8 x 12-0

seat   seat

DINING
13-0 x 12-0

KIT.
10-4 x 12-0

BRKFST.
10-8 x 9-8

pd. rm.

UTIL.
dry wash

cl

64-0

walk-in
closet

master bath

cl

GREAT RM.
13-4 x 19-4

fireplace

down

up
FOYER

MASTER
BED RM.
13-4 x 13-0

PORCH

59-0

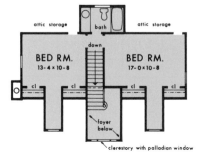

attic storage   attic storage

bath

down

BED RM.
13-4 x 10-8

BED RM.
17-0 x 10-8

cl   cl   cl   cl

foyer
below

clerestory with palladian window

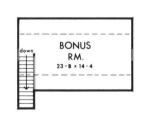

down

BONUS
RM.
23-8 x 14-4

Design DD9645

First Floor: 1,356 square feet
Second Floor: 542 square feet
Total: 1,898 square feet

● This cozy country cottage is perfect for the growing family—offering both an unfinished basement option and a bonus room. Enter through the two-story foyer with a Palladian window in a clerestory dormer above. The master suite is on the first floor for privacy and accessibility. Its accompanying bath boasts a whirlpool tub with a skylight above and a double-bowl vanity. The second floor contains two bedrooms, a full bath and plenty of storage. Note that all first-floor rooms except the kitchen and utility room boast nine-foot ceilings. This plan is available with either a basement or crawlspace foundation. Please specify when ordering.

Design by
Donald A.
Gardner,
Architects, Inc.

49

Design DD9742

Square Footage: 1,954
Bonus Room: 436 square feet

● This beautiful brick country home has all the amenities needed for today's active family. Covered front and back porches along with a rear deck provide plenty of room for outdoor enjoyment. Inside, the focus is on the large great room with its cathedral ceiling and welcoming fireplace. To the right, columns separate the kitchen and breakfast area while keeping this area open. Chefs of all ages will appreciate the convenience of the kitchen with its center island and additional eating space. The master bedroom provides a splendid private retreat, featuring a cathedral ceiling and a large walk-in closet. The luxurious master bath shares a double-bowl vanity, a separate shower and a relaxing skylit whirlpool tub. At the opposite end of the plan, two additional bedrooms share a full bath. A skylit bonus room above the garage allows for additional living space.

Design by
Donald A.
Gardner,
Architects, Inc.

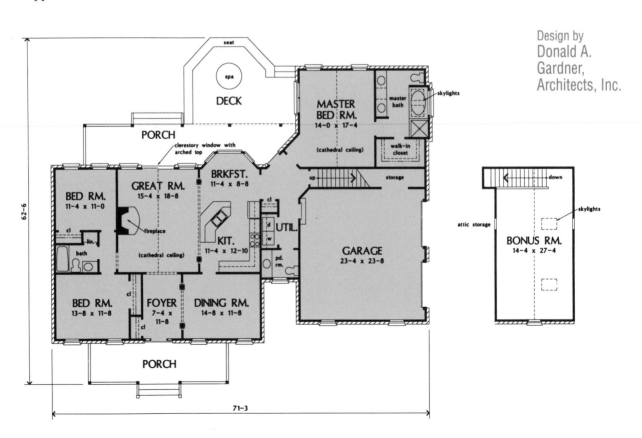

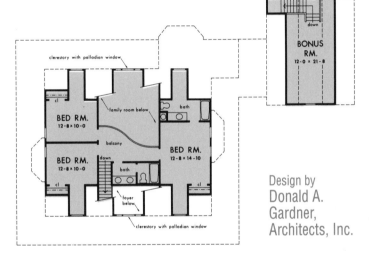

Design DD9669

First Floor: 1,759 square feet
Second Floor: 888 square feet
Total: 2,647 square feet

● This complete four-bedroom country farmhouse ignites a passion for both indoor and outdoor living with the well-organized open layout and the continuous flowing porch and deck encircling the house. Front and rear Palladian window dormers allow natural light to penetrate the foyer and family room below as well as adding exciting visual elements to the exterior. The dramatic family room with sloped ceiling envelopes a curved balcony. The master suite includes a large walk-in closet, a special sitting area, and a master bath with whirlpool tub, shower and double bowl vanity. A bonus room over the garage adds to the completeness of this house.

Design by
Donald A.
Gardner,
Architects, Inc.

Design DD9001

First Floor: 1,308 square feet
Second Floor: 751 square feet
Total: 2,059 square feet

● A wraparound veranda and simple, uncluttered lines give this home an unassuming elegance that is characteristic of its farmhouse heritage. The kitchen overlooks an octagon-shaped breakfast room with full-length windows. The master bedroom features plenty of closet space and an elegant bath. Located within an oversized bay window is a garden tub with adjacent planter and glass-enclosed shower. Upstairs, two bedrooms share a bath with separate dressing and bathing areas. The balcony sitting area is perfect as a playroom or study. Plans for a detached two-car garage are included.

Design by
Larry W. Garnett & Associates, Inc.

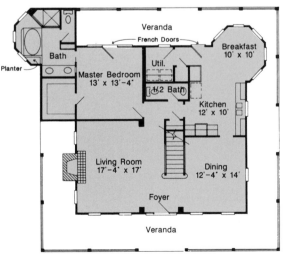

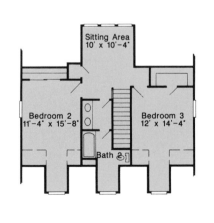

Width 53'
Depth 45' - 4"

Design DD9002

First Floor: 1,504 square feet
Second Floor: 690 square feet
Total: 2,194 square feet

● The symmetry and grace of the turn-of-the-century farmhouse is captured in this design. The veranda provides plenty of shade for outdoor activities. Inside, the kitchen with center-island work counter opens to the breakfast area with a full-length bay window. The master bedroom features a walk-in closet and abundant linen storage. A corner tub and glass-enclosed shower highlight the bath. An optional French door allows access to a swimming pool, or possibly a private spa. Upstairs, the balcony overlooks the living room below. Two bedrooms each have walk-in closets and private dressing areas. Plans for a detached two-car garage are included.

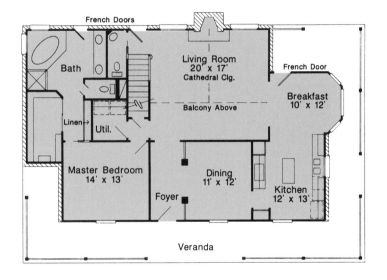

Design by
Larry W.
Garnett &
Associates, Inc.

Width 57' - 4"
Depth 37' - 8"

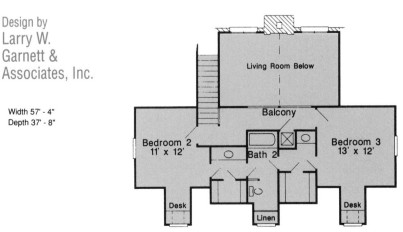

53

Design DD9087

First Floor: 2,263 square feet
Second Floor: 787 square feet
Total: 3,050 square feet

Design by
Larry W.
Garnett &
Associates, Inc.

● Excellent outdoor living is yours with this 1½-story home. The wrapping covered front porch gives way to a center hall entry with flanking living and dining rooms. The living room features a media center, two-way fireplace and columned entry. The attached garden room has French doors to the front porch and French doors to a smaller covered porch that is also accessed through the master bedroom suite. The family room is complemented by a fireplace, built-in bookshelves and another covered porch. An angled island counter separates it from the kitchen. Upstairs are three bedrooms and two full baths. Bedroom 4 has a beautiful bumped out window while Bedrooms 2 and 3 have dormer windows.

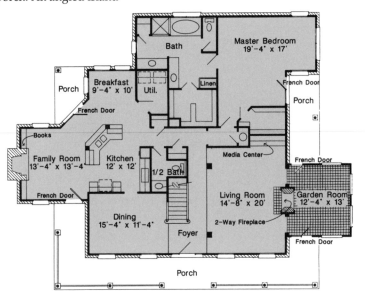

Width 68'-10"
Depth 52'-4"

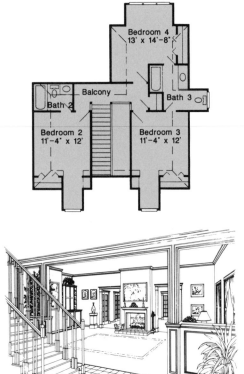

Living Room

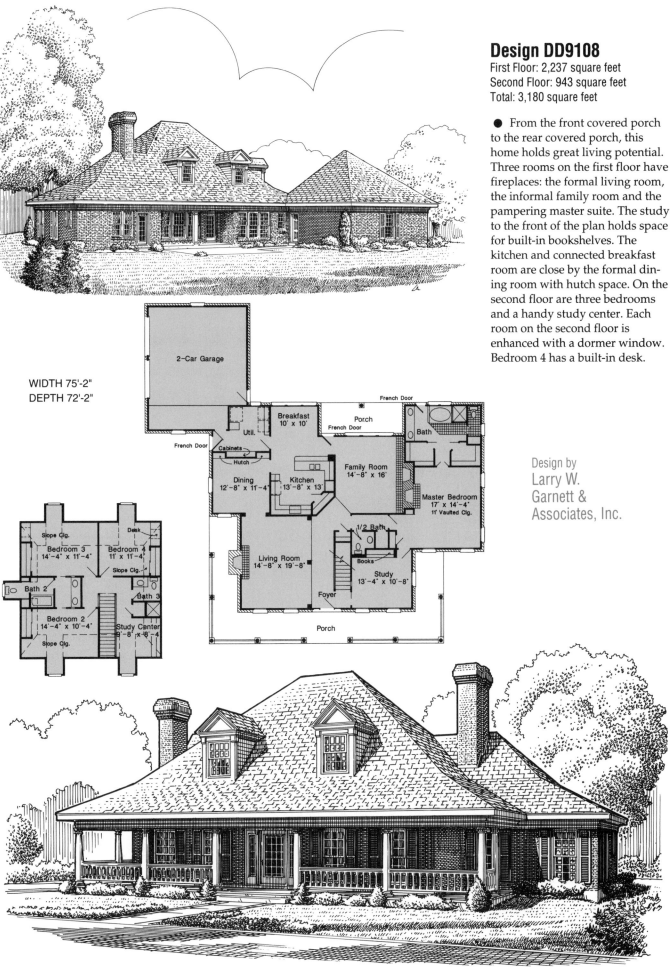

Design DD9108

First Floor: 2,237 square feet
Second Floor: 943 square feet
Total: 3,180 square feet

● From the front covered porch to the rear covered porch, this home holds great living potential. Three rooms on the first floor have fireplaces: the formal living room, the informal family room and the pampering master suite. The study to the front of the plan holds space for built-in bookshelves. The kitchen and connected breakfast room are close by the formal dining room with hutch space. On the second floor are three bedrooms and a handy study center. Each room on the second floor is enhanced with a dormer window. Bedroom 4 has a built-in desk.

WIDTH 75'-2"
DEPTH 72'-2"

2-Car Garage

French Door

Breakfast
10' x 10'

Porch

French Door

French Door

Bath

Util.

Cabinets

Hutch

Family Room
14'-8" x 16'

Dining
12'-8" x 11'-4"

Kitchen
13'-8" x 13'

Master Bedroom
17' x 14'-4"
11' Vaulted Clg.

Living Room
14'-8" x 19'-8"

1/2 Bath

Books

Study
13'-4" x 10'-8"

Foyer

Porch

Slope Clg.

Desk

Bedroom 3
14'-4" x 11'-4"

Bedroom 4
11' x 11'-4"

Slope Clg.

Bath 2

Bath 3

Bedroom 2
14'-4" x 10'-4"

Study Center
9'-8" x 8'-4"

Slope Clg.

Design by
Larry W.
Garnett &
Associates, Inc.

55

Design DD8000

Square Footage: 2,540

● A gabled stucco entry with over-sized columns emphasizes the arched glass entry of this winsome one-story brick home. Arched windows on either side of the front door add symmetry and style to this pleasing exterior. An arched passage flanked by twin bookcases and plant ledges—perfect for plants and collectibles—provides interest to the living room. Pass through the arch and find three of the bedrooms in this split-bedroom plan. Bedroom 4 may also be a study and can be entered from double French doors off the living room. A large, efficient kitchen shares space with an octagonal-shaped breakfast area and a family room with a fireplace. The master bedroom is entered through angled double doors and features a cathedral ceiling. Attention centers immediately on the columned and arched entry to the relaxing master bath with its central whirlpool tub. This plan is available with either a crawlspace or slab foundation. Please specify when ordering.

Design by
Larry E. Belk
Designs

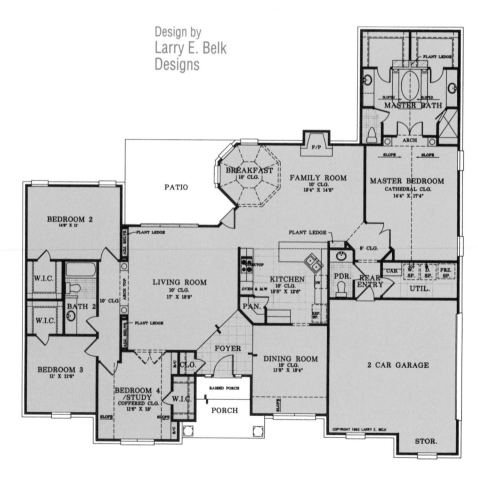

Width 70'
Depth 65'

Design DD8009

Square Footage: 2,326

● A brick exterior with an accent of stucco will definitely draw attention to this one-story home. Side-by-side windows with a half-round transom located in the dining room and a gable porch provide the finishing touches to the appealing elevation. Special note should be taken of the angled, foyer with its high ceiling that presents definition of the dining and great room with three columns and graceful connecting arches. High ceilings throughout the home make it appear much larger than it actually is. The efficient kitchen contains a snack bar and a large work island while the connecting utility room offers freezer space and a walk-in pantry. The sleeping wing is located on the opposite side of the house. The master suite is complete with a luxury master bath and a huge walk-in closet. The study is enhanced with double French doors for entry. A slight modification to this room reverses the closet and door location, offering a fourth bedroom in its place. This plan is available with either a crawlspace or slab foundation. Please specify when ordering.

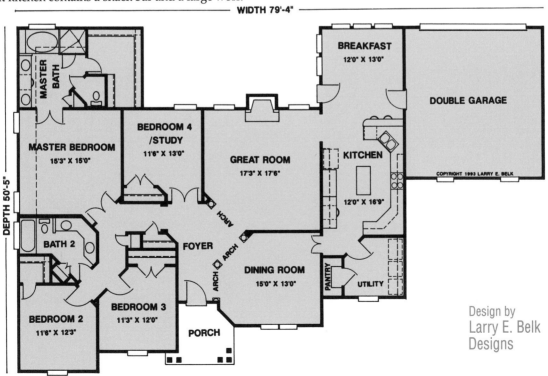

Design by
Larry E. Belk
Designs

57

Design DD8015
Square Footage: 2,598

● An elegant combination of brick and stucco gives this home enormous curb-appeal. An arch-top window in the dining room is duplicated in the dormer and adds interest to this lovely elevation. Inside, elegant columns with connecting arches lead the way to the great room and the dining room, as well as to the adjacent kitchen, breakfast and family rooms, all served by a see-through fireplace. The master bedroom and bath are located at the rear of the home with two additional bedrooms located nearby. A study is situated off the foyer and finds entrance through double French doors. This room may also serve as a bedroom by simply reversing the location of the closet and door to provide private access. This plan is available with either a crawlspace or slab foundation. Please specify when ordering.

Width 65'-10"
Depth 73'

Design by
Larry E. Belk
Designs

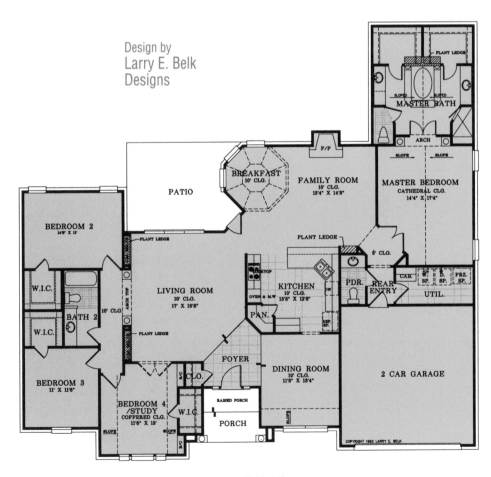

Design by
Larry E. Belk
Designs

Width 69'
Depth 63'-6"

Design DD8071
Square Footage: 2,517

● A graceful stucco arch supported by columns gives this home instant curb appeal. Stucco quoins are used to further accent its traditional brick finish. Inside, the angled foyer steps down into the living room and draws the eye to a duplicate of the exterior arch with columns. Built-in display shelves on either side provide plenty of room for books or treasures. Step down again to enter the formal dining room. The kitchen features a coffered ceiling and is conveniently grouped with a sunny bayed breakfast room and the family room, the perfect place for informal gatherings. Upon entering the master suite, the master bath becomes the focal point. Columns flank the entry to this luxurious bath with a whirlpool tub as its centerpiece. His and Hers walk-in closets, a separate shower and a double-bowl vanity complete the design. This plan is available with either a crawlspace or slab foundation. Please specify when ordering.

◄ 72' ►

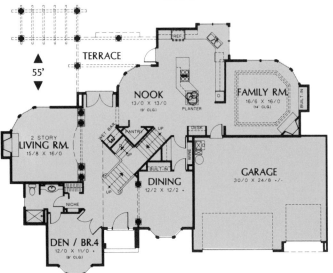

Design DD9517

First Floor: 1,920 square feet
Second Floor: 1,552 square feet
Total: 3,472 square feet
Bonus Room: 252 square feet

● Details certainly do make the difference! Bay windows flanking the high-arched entry produce dramatic effects for this delightful two-story stucco home. Living areas radiate around the foyer which also contains the stairway to the second floor. To the right is the dining room, to the left, a two-story living room with a welcoming fireplace—a great area for formal entertaining. To the rear of the plan lies the informal living area. An expansive family room, complete with a corner fireplace and a built-in entertainment center, shares space with the large, efficient kitchen and breakfast nook. Access to the rear terrace is provided for outdoor enjoyment. The second floor contains a grand master suite featuring a relaxing master bath highlighted by a corner spa tub, a separate shower and a huge walk-in closet. Two secondary bedrooms, each with a full bath and a bonus room, complete the upstairs.

Design by
**Alan Mascord
Design Associates, Inc.**

Design DD8073

First Floor: 2,110 square feet
Second Floor: 1,168 square feet
Total: 3,278 square feet

● A stucco exterior serves as a super introduction to this open, spacious home. From the foyer, enter the formal living room and dining room, defined by a series of columns connected by graceful arches. The kitchen, bayed breakfast room and sunlit family room are conveniently arranged to provide a spacious area for family gatherings. A well-placed corner fireplace in the family room serves all three areas and adds a warm, cozy feel to this space. The master suite is located on the opposite side of the home and features a luxurious master bath with a corner whirlpool tub, a separate shower, His and Hers vanities and a grand walk-in closet. Three secondary bedrooms and a full bath share the second floor with a bay-windowed recreation room, providing a great play area for children and adults alike. This plan is available with either a crawlspace or slab foundation. Please specify when ordering.

Design by
Larry E. Belk
Designs

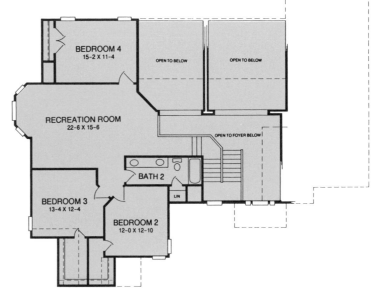

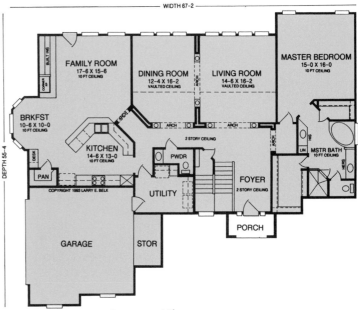

61

Design DD9918 First Floor: 1,710 square feet
Second Floor: 1,470 square feet; Total: 3,180 square feet

● Many generously sized, shuttered windows flood this stunning home with the clear, warming light of outdoors. The two-story foyer with its tray ceiling makes a dramatic entrance. To the right, a banquet-sized dining room offers space for a buffet, while the large kitchen allows easy access to the bay-windowed breakfast room. To the left is a versatile room which can serve as a living room, a study or a guest room. Beyond the foyer is the great room which sports a cheering fireplace flanked by bookcases. An open-railed stairway leads to three bedrooms on the second floor. The exquisite master suite is truly a room to live in, with its stylish tray ceiling and warming fireplace. Its elegance is intensified right down to the bay window and huge walk-in closet with a built-in dressing table. This home is designed with a basement foundation.

Design by
Design Traditions

Width 61'-6"
Depth 50'-6"

Design DD9804

First Floor: 2,199 square feet
Second Floor: 1,235 square feet
Total: 3,434 square feet

● The covered front porch of this home warmly welcomes family and visitors. To the right of the foyer is a versatile option room. On the other side is the formal dining room, located just across from the open great room with its skylights, French doors and fireplace—which also opens into the breakfast room. The kitchen ,with its bay window, includes a cooking island/ breakfast bar. Adjacent to the breakfast room is the sun room. At the rear of the main level is the master suite, which features a decorative tray ceiling and a lavish bath loaded with features. Just off the bedroom is a private deck. On the second level, three additional bedrooms and two baths are found. This home is designed with a basement foundation.

WIDTH 62'-6"
DEPTH 54'-3"

Design by
Design Traditions

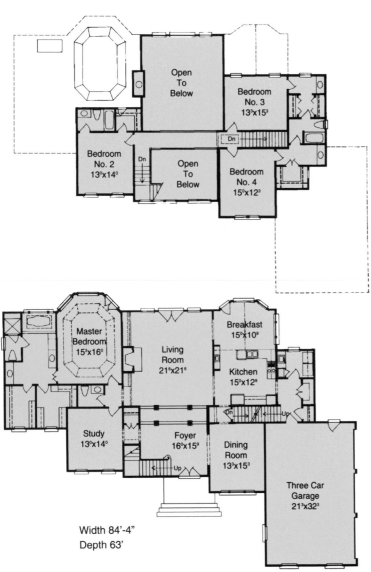

Width 84'-4"
Depth 63'

Design DD9919

First Floor: 2,461 square feet
Second Floor: 1,114 square feet
Total: 3,575 square feet

● A myriad of glass and ornamental stucco detailing complement the asymmetrical facade of this two-story home. This unique stair-stepped facade provides each room at the front of the home with a corner view. Inside, the striking, two-story foyer provides a dramatic entrance, accented by the sweeping balustered stair and bathed in sunlight from the large triple-arched windows. To the left is the formal dining room. An efficient L-shaped kitchen and a bayed breakfast nook are conveniently located off the dining area. The living room, with its welcoming fireplace, opens through double doors to the rear terrace. The private master suite provides access to the rear terrace and an adjacent study. The master bath is sure to please with its relaxing garden tub, a separate shower, grand His and Hers walk-in closets and a compartmented toilet. The second floor contains three large bedrooms—one with a private bath—while the others share a bath. This home is designed with a basement foundation.

Design by
Design Traditions

Design DD9920

First Floor: 2,951 square feet
Second Floor: 1,805 square feet
Total: 4,756 square feet

● Simple stucco details and shuttered windows create a subtle and tasteful country character for this charming home. Inside, the second-floor gallery, the adjacent library, the banquet-size dining room and the huge two-story living room are accentuated with interesting windows. French doors offer easy access to the patio area from the master bedroom, while providing a warm, naturally lit environment. The master bath pampers with its soothing garden bath and oversized walk-in closet. A well-designed kitchen, vaulted breakfast area and welcoming family room continue the provincial spirit of the home. Upstairs, private baths and walk-in closets provide plenty of space for each of the four bedrooms. The open-rail gallery and balcony over the family room connect the upstairs bedrooms with the living area below. This home is designed with a basement foundation.

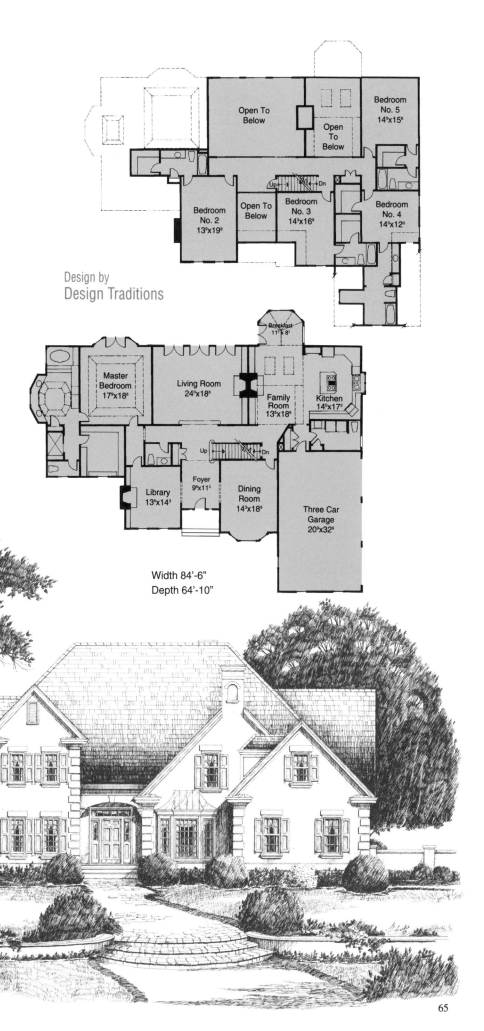

Design by
Design Traditions

Width 84'-6"
Depth 64'-10"

Design DD9921

First Floor: 2,832 square feet
Second Floor: 1,394 square feet
Total: 4,226 square feet
Bonus Room/Bedroom: 425 square feet

● Arched windows and a sculpted bay window provide personality and charm to this lovely two-story stucco home. Inside, the arrangement of rooms is well-suited for a variety of lifestyles. The large dining room and study off the foyer provide the opportunity for formal receiving and entertaining. Access from the dining room to the kitchen is provided through a service alcove. For informal gatherings, look to the spacious kitchen, the multi-windowed breakfast room or the cozy keeping room with its welcoming fireplace. The centrally located great room provides opportunities for either formal or informal gatherings. Conveniently, yet privately located, the master suite is designed to take full advantage of the adjacent study and family area. A vaulted master bath and His and Hers walk-in closets highlight this impressive and functional suite. The second floor contains three bedrooms, three full baths and a bonus room that can also function as a bed-room. This home is designed with a basement foundation.

Design by
Design Traditions

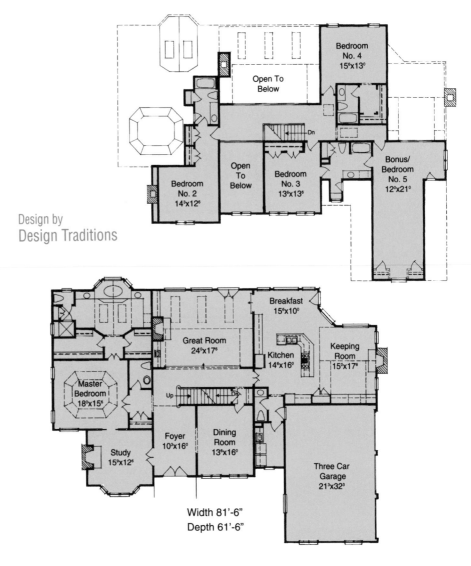

Width 81'-6"
Depth 61'-6"

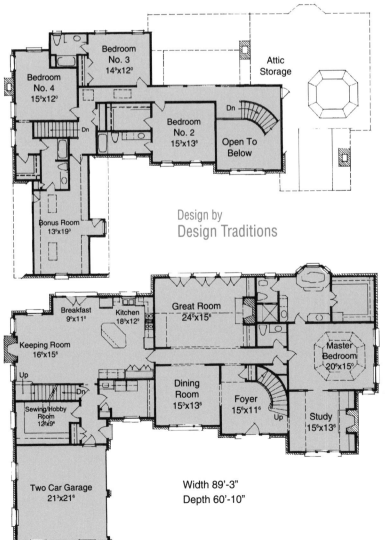

Bedroom
No. 3
14⁶x12⁰

Attic
Storage

Bedroom
No. 4
15⁰x12⁰

Bedroom
No. 2
15³x13⁶

Dn

Open To
Below

Dn

Bonus Room
13⁰x19³

Design by
Design Traditions

Breakfast
9⁰x11⁰

Kitchen
18⁶x12⁹

Great Room
24⁰x15⁶

Keeping Room
16⁰x15⁶

Master
Bedroom
20⁶x15⁰

Up

Dining
Room
15³x13⁶

Foyer
15⁶x11⁶

Dn

Sewing/Hobby
Room
12⁶x9⁰

Up

Study
15⁶x13⁰

Two Car Garage
21³x21⁶

Width 89'-3"
Depth 60'-10"

Design DD9922

First Floor: 3,030 square feet
Second Floor: 1,510 square feet
Total: 4,540 square feet
Bonus Room: 324 square feet

● Brick details, casement windows and large expanses of glass
add an Old World touch of glam-
our to this gracious two-story
home. Inside, asymmetrical shapes
create an interesting twist to this
functional floor plan. Sunlight
floods the two-story foyer which is
highlighted by the sweeping
curves of the balustrade. For formal occasions, look to the spacious
dining room, the inviting study
and the vaulted great room. The
master suite provides a quiet
retreat with access to the study
through paneled pocket doors.
Luxury abounds in the spacious
master bedroom and sumptuous
master bath complete with a relaxing garden tub, dual vanities and a
huge walk-in closet. The kitchen,
breakfast room and keeping room
provide a well-designed family living area. Three private secondary
bedrooms with full baths are contained on the second floor. A bonus
room is also featured on the second
floor, perfect for a childrens den.
This home is designed with a basement foundation.

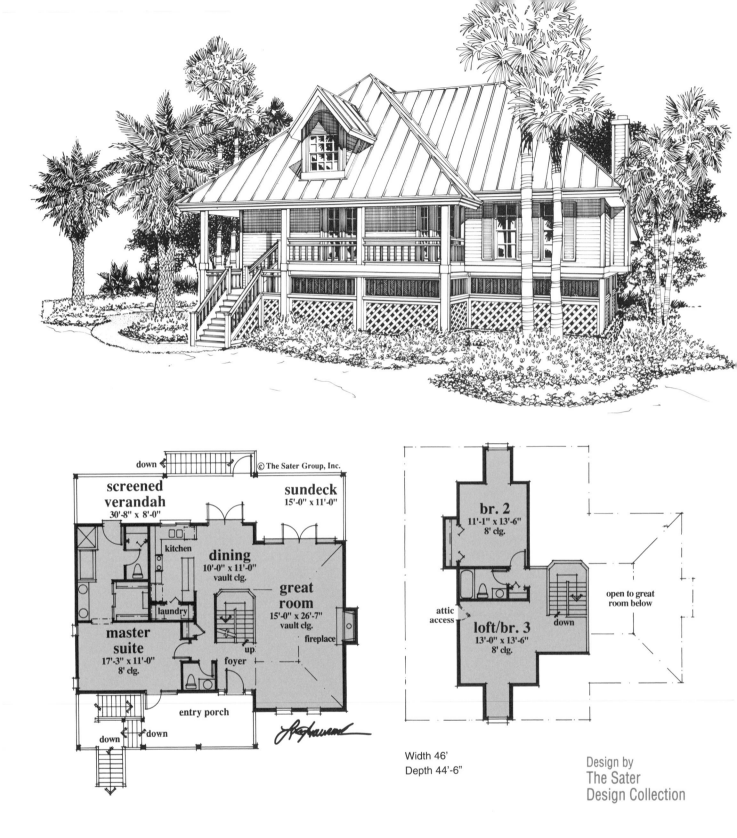

© The Sater Group, Inc.

screened verandah
30'-8" x 8'-0"

sundeck
15'-0" x 11'-0"

down

kitchen

dining
10'-0" x 11'-0"
vault clg.

great room
15'-0" x 26'-7"
vault clg.

fireplace

laundry

master suite
17'-3" x 11'-0"
8' clg.

up

foyer

entry porch

down   down

down

br. 2
11'-1" x 13'-6"
8' clg.

attic access

loft/br. 3
13'-0" x 13'-6"
8' clg.

down

open to great room below

Width 46'
Depth 44'-6"

Design by
**The Sater
Design Collection**

Design DD6617 First Floor: 1,189 square feet; Second Floor: 575 square feet; Total: 1,764 square feet

● An abundance of porches and a deck encourage year-round indoor-outdoor relationships in this classic two-story home. The spacious living room with its cozy fireplace and the adjacent dining room, both with access to the screened porch/deck area, are perfect for formal or informal entertaining. An efficient kitchen and a nearby laundry room make chores easy. The private master suite offers access to the screened porch and leads into a relaxing master bath complete with a walk-in closet, a tub and separate shower, double-bowl lavs and a compartmented toilet. Bedroom 2 shares the second floor with a full bath and a loft which may be used as a third bedroom.

Design DD6616 First Floor: 1,136 square feet; Second Floor: 636 square feet; Total: 1,772 square feet

● This two-story coastal design is sure to please with its warm character and decorative widow's walk. The covered entry—with its dramatic transom window—leads to a spacious living room highlighted by a warming fireplace. To the right, the dining room and kitchen combine to provide a delightful place for mealtimes inside or out, with access to

a side deck through double doors. Bedroom 2, a study and a full bath complete the first floor. The luxurious master suite is located on the second floor for privacy and features an oversized walk-in closet and a separate dressing area. The pampering master bath enjoys a relaxing whirlpool tub, a double-bowl vanity and a compartmented toilet.

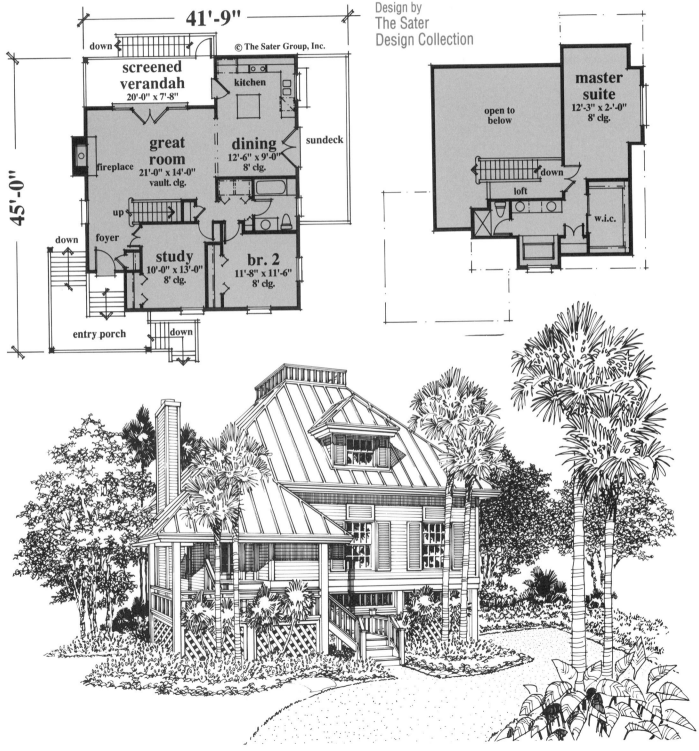

Design by
The Sater
Design Collection

© The Sater Group, Inc.

41'-9"

45'-0"

down

screened
verandah
20'-0" x 7'-8"

kitchen

great
room
21'-0" x 14'-0"
vault. clg.

dining
12'-6" x 9'-0"
8' clg.

sundeck

fireplace

up

down

foyer

study
10'-0" x 13'-0"
8' clg.

br. 2
11'-8" x 11'-6"
8' clg.

entry porch

down

open to
below

master
suite
12'-3" x 2'-0"
8' clg.

down

loft

w.i.c.

© The Sater Group, Inc.

Design DD6615

First Floor: 1,736 square feet; Second Floor: 640 square feet
Lower Level: 840 square feet; Total: 3,216 square feet

● Lattice panels, shutters, a balustrade and a metal roof add character to this delightful coastal home. Double doors flanking a fireplace open to the sun deck from the spacious great room sporting a vaulted ceiling. Access to the veranda is provided from this room also. An adjacent dining room provides views of the rear grounds and space for formal and informal entertaining. The glassed-in nook shares space with the L-shaped kitchen and a center work island. Bedrooms 2 and 3, a full bath and a utility room complete this floor. Upstairs, a sumptuous master suite awaits. Double doors extend to a private deck from the master bedroom. His and Hers walk-in closets lead the way to a grand master bath featuring an arched whirlpool tub, a double-bowl vanity and a separate shower.

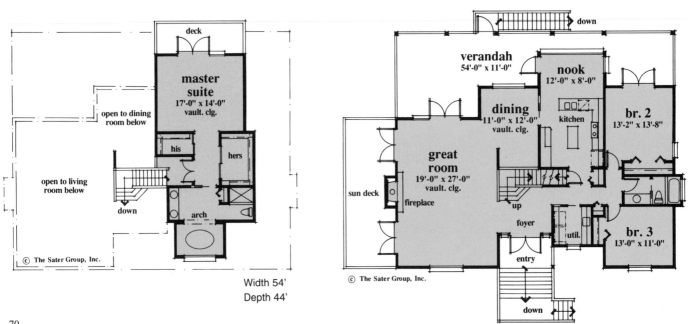

Width 54'
Depth 44'

MIDWEST and PLAINS FARMHOUSES

MANY ADVENTUROUS AMERICAN SETTLERS moved westward into the Midwestern and Plains regions, and a different style of farmhouse was born. As the woodlands gave way to the Midwestern plains, the timber gave way to the grasslands. New building techniques and alternatives were essential due to the lack of lumber, dictating that many of the first Midwestern farmhouses be built from available stone.

Early construction took place prior to the arrival of the railroad and the original one-story Plains farmhouses were constructed from a primitive—yet innovative—style of masonry made from sod blocks. In sod construction, the top few inches of soil, along with the roots of the hardy plains grasses, were cut with a special plow into brick-shaped sections. Laid in the same manner as brick, these sod blocks were highly successful, providing excellent insulation from both the summer heat and the severely cold winters. Over much of the plains, streams supplied a meager border of small trees which produced short timbers for roof supports. Initially, the sod block used to construct the farmhouses was also utilized as roofing, laid over these timber supports. However, this method did not meet with much success. Due to the severe weather conditions, finding materials for watertight roofing was of the highest priorities, and in many cases, the roof was eventually replaced by fully framed roofs with shingles, making these homes not only comfortable, but energy efficient as well.

As the railroad expanded across America, so did the availability of lumber for construction. The early homes built of sod were now abandoned for farmhouses constructed of wood, and those changes brought about a transformation in style. The one-story farmhouse maintained its popularity because it offered resistance to the sweeping winds of the Plains, but the introduction of the expanded two-story farmhouse proposed a welcome alternative to the relatively long and confining winters, making the larger homes much more desirable. Many of the new two-story homes were then designed with a gable front and wing that became common to the two stories.

During the evolution of these farmhouses, one well-established aspect of these homes never changed—namely, the large, sheltering wraparound porches. Throughout history the porch has remained an essential part of the farmhouse design; not only because of its aesthetically pleasing qualities, but because of its utmost value in dealing with the elements. These practical solutions that our spirited ancestors presented have matured into a heritage of style that is still appreciated today. Designs DD9851, DD9861, DD2946, DD9298 and DD9711 offer a look at the best of this style as interpreted by modern designers.

Our adaptations of the Midwestern farmhouse styles in this section retain the rugged charm and the feeling of sturdiness present in the time-honored originals, yet feature the practical convenience essential for today's style of living.

Design DD9300

First Floor: 1,137 square feet
Second Floor: 917 square feet
Total: 2,054 square feet

● Colonial detailing and gracious amenities makes this home ideal for a variety of lifestyles. A bright dining room opens to a hard-surfaced entry. Access the private den with bookcase via French doors. Family gatherings are comfortable in the great room with fireplace, built-in bookcase and large bayed windows at the rear. An island kitchen benefits from a pantry, desk and sunny breakfast area with outdoor access. The upstairs landing is brightened by a skylight. In the master bedroom there is a vaulted ceiling, plus a dressing area featuring a walk-in closet with mirrored bi-pass doors and window seat. Secondary bedrooms share a hall bath with window seat while the front bedroom has its own window seat. Truly, this is a delightful home inside and out!

Design by
Design
Basics,
Inc.

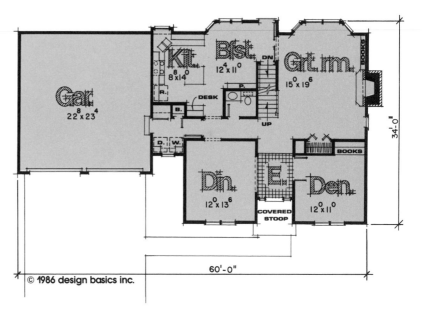

© 1986 design basics inc.

Design DD9214

First Floor: 1,188 square feet
Second Floor: 1,172 square feet
Total: 2,360 square feet

● Beginning with the interest of a wraparound porch, there's a feeling of country charm in this two-story plan. Formal dining and living rooms, visible from the entry, offer ample space for gracious entertaining. The large family room is truly a place of warmth and welcome with its gorgeous bay window, fireplace and French doors to the living room. The kitchen, with island counter, pantry and desk, makes cooking a delight. Upstairs, the secondary bedrooms share an efficient compartmented bath. The expansive master suite has its own luxury bath with double vanity, whirlpool, walk-in closet and dressing area.

Design by
Design
Basics,
Inc.

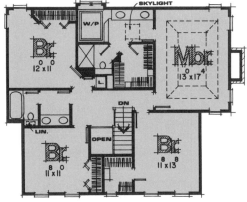

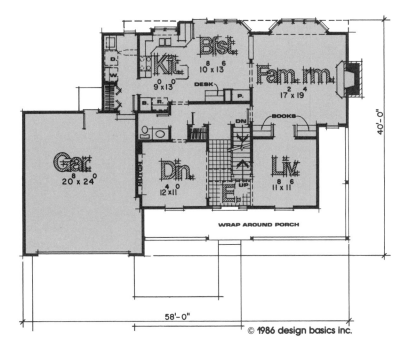

Design DD9312

First Floor: 1,150 square feet
Second Floor: 1,120 square feet
Total: 2,270 square feet

● Lap siding, special windows and a covered porch enhance the elevation of this popular style. The spacious two-story entry surveys the formal dining room with hutch space. An entertainment center, through-fireplace and bayed windows add appeal to the great room. Families will love the spacious kitchen, breakfast and hearth room. Enhancements to this casual living area include a through-fireplace, gazebo dinette, wrapping counters, an island kitchen and planning desk. An efficient U-shaped staircase routes traffic throughout. Comfortable secondary bedrooms and a sumptuous master suite feature privacy by design. Bedroom 3 is highlighted by a half round window, volume ceiling and double closets while Bedroom 4 features a built-in desk. The master suite has a vaulted ceiling, large walk-in closet, His and Hers vanities, compartmented stool/shower area and an oval whirlpool tub.

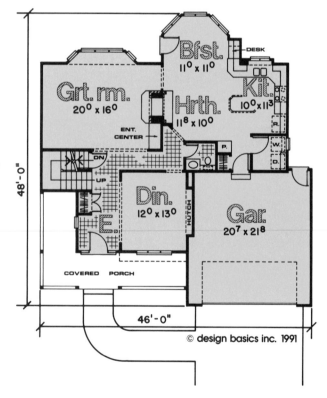

© design basics inc. 1991

Design by
Design
Basics,
Inc.

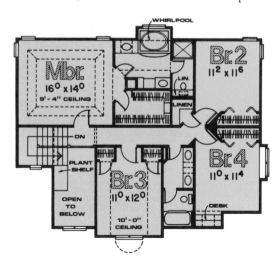

74

Design DD9235

First Floor: 919 square feet
Second Floor: 927 square feet
Total: 1,846 square feet

● Wonderful country design begins with the wraparound porch of this plan. Explore further and find a two-story entry with a coat closet and plant shelf above and a strategically placed staircase alongside. The island kitchen with a boxed window over the sink is adjacent to a large bay-windowed dinette. The great room includes many windows and a fireplace. A powder bath and laundry room are both conveniently placed on the first floor. Upstairs, the large master suite contains His and Hers walk-in closets, corner windows and a bath area featuring a double vanity and whirlpool tub. Two pleasant secondary bedrooms have interesting angles and a third bedroom in the front features a volume ceiling and arched window.

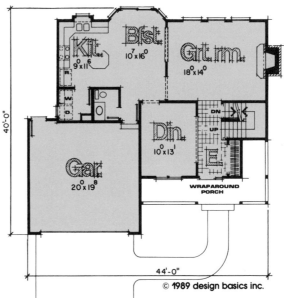

© 1989 design basics inc.

Design by
Design
Basics,
Inc.

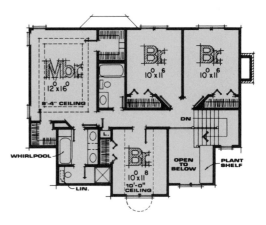

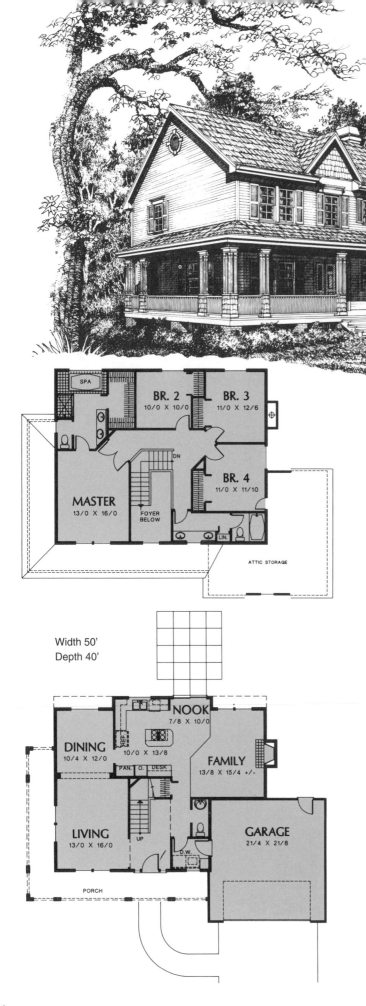

Design by
Alan Mascord
Design Associates, Inc.

Design DD9497

First Floor: 1,037 square feet
Second Floor: 1,090 square feet
Total: 2,127 square feet

● Cedar siding makes a beautiful difference in this two-story country plan. Its symmetrical floor plan serves the needs of family living. Main living areas radiate from the entry hall: the formal living room is to the left and connects directly to the dining room; the family room is to the right and behind the garage. An L-shaped kitchen includes an island cooktop and a casual eating area that contains sliding glass doors to a rear terrace. The bedrooms are on the second floor and center around the open-railed staircase. The master bedroom contains a gigantic walk-in closet and a whirlpool tub and separate shower. Family bedrooms share a full bath with double-sink vanity.

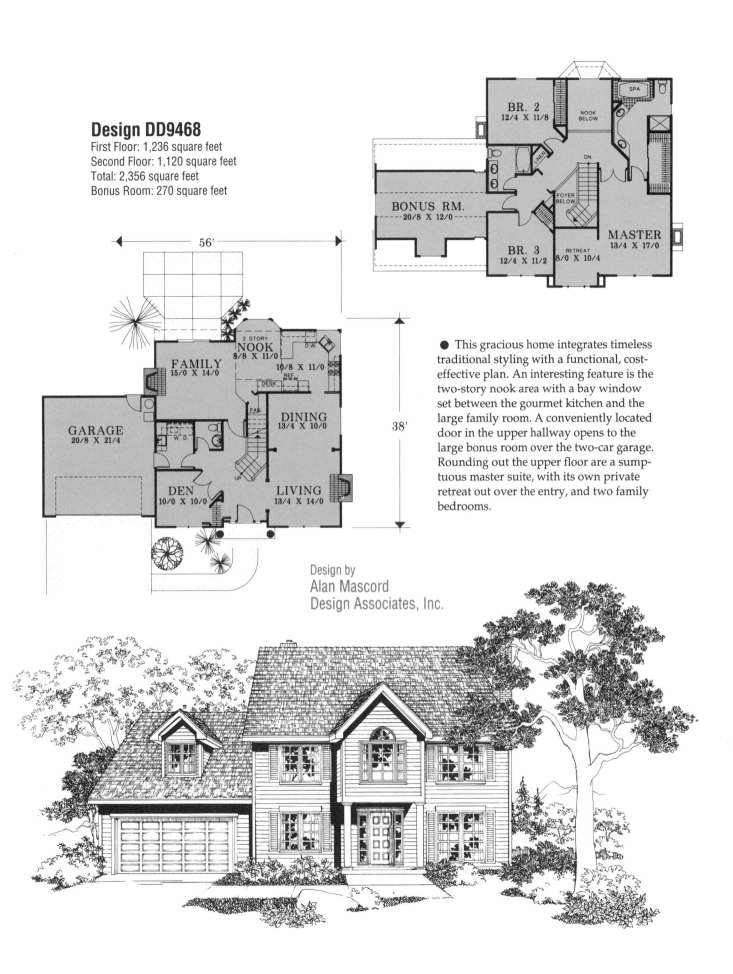

Design DD9468

First Floor: 1,236 square feet
Second Floor: 1,120 square feet
Total: 2,356 square feet
Bonus Room: 270 square feet

BR. 2
12/4 X 11/8

NOOK
BELOW

SPA

LINEN

DN.

BONUS RM.
20/8 X 12/0

FOYER
BELOW

MASTER
13/4 X 17/0

BR. 3
12/4 X 11/2

RETREAT
8/0 X 10/4

56'

2 STORY
NOOK
8/8 X 11/0

D.W.

10/8 X 11/0

FAMILY
15/0 X 14/0

DESK

REF.

PAN.

38'

GARAGE
20/8 X 21/4

W. D.

DINING
13/4 X 10/0

UP

DEN
10/0 X 10/0

LIVING
13/4 X 14/0

● This gracious home integrates timeless traditional styling with a functional, cost-effective plan. An interesting feature is the two-story nook area with a bay window set between the gourmet kitchen and the large family room. A conveniently located door in the upper hallway opens to the large bonus room over the two-car garage. Rounding out the upper floor are a sumptuous master suite, with its own private retreat out over the entry, and two family bedrooms.

Design by
Alan Mascord
Design Associates, Inc.

Copyright 1992 Stephen S. Fuller, Inc.

Design DD9851

First Floor: 2,210 square feet
Second Floor: 1,070 square feet
Total: 3,280 square feet

● A generous front porch enhances the living area of this home with its sheltering welcome and Americana detailing. This classic style is also echoed in the use of wood siding, shuttered windows and stone finish work on two chimneys. The main level begins with a two-story foyer with a tray ceil-ing. Double doors open into the study with an exposed beamed ceiling and a fireplace. Left of the foyer lies the dining room drenched in natural sunlight. Across the hall, the great room with a fireplace, a wet bar and two sets of French doors provides a great gathering place. The master suite is located at the end of the main hallway. It features a tray ceiling and a complete master bath with a separate shower, a water closet and dual vanities. The large walk-in closet completes the suite. Staircases from the great room and foyer lead to the upper level. Two additional bedrooms—each with a walk-in closet and a vanity—share the tub area. A third bedroom has a gen-erous walk-in closet and a private bath. This home is designed with a basement foundation.

Width 60'-6"
Depth 58'-6"

Design by
Design Traditions

Copyright 1992 Stephen S. Fuller, Inc.

Design by
Design Traditions

PORCH

BREAKFAST
13'-4" X 9'-0"

BEDROOM/
OFFICE
10'-4" X 11'-0"

GREAT ROOM
17'-0" X 17'-8"

KITCHEN
13'-4" X 10'-6"

DN.

BATH

LAUNDRY

TWO CAR GARAGE
20'-6" X 19'-6"

DINING ROOM
11'-4" X 12'-10"

FOYER
5'-4" X
12'-10"

PORCH

MASTER
BATH

MASTER BEDRDOOM
16'-4" X 13'-6"

BEDROOM NO. 2
10'-4" X 12'-0"

BATH

BEDROOM/
STUDY
11'-2" X 12'-0"

Width 61'
Depth 70'-6"

Design DD9853
Square Footage: 2,090

● This traditional home features board-and-batten and cedar shingles in an attractively proportioned exterior. Finishing touches include a covered entrance and a porch with column detailing and an arched transom, flower boxes and shuttered windows. The foyer opens to both the dining room and great room beyond with French doors opening onto the porch. Through the double doors to the right of the foyer is the combination bedroom/study. A short hallway leads to a full bath and a secondary bedroom with ample closet space. The master bedroom is spacious, with walk-in closets on both sides of the entrance to the master bath. With separate vanities, shower and toilet, the master bath forms a private retreat at the rear of the home. Convenient to both the great room and dining room, the kitchen opens to an attractive breakfast area featuring a bay window. An additional room is remotely located off the kitchen, providing a retreat for today's at-home office or guest. This home is designed with a basement foundation.

Design DD9908 First Floor: 1,944 square feet; Second Floor: 1,055 square feet; Total: 2,999 square feet

● Interesting rooflines, multi-level eaves and a two-story double-bay window create a unique cottage farmhouse appearance for this charming home. A combination of columns and stone create a cozy and inviting porch. The grand foyer leads to the formal dining room and large great room, both graced with columns. The great room features a cozy fireplace and opens to the deck through French doors. The breakfast room, divided from the great room by an open stair-case, shares space with an efficient L-shaped kitchen and nearby laundry room, making domestic endeavors easy to accomplish. The right wing is devoted to a sumptuous, amenity-filled master suite with convenient access to the study for after-hours research or quiet reading. The second floor contains three secondary bedrooms and two baths for family and guests. This home is designed with a basement foundation.

Width 51'-6"
Depth 72'

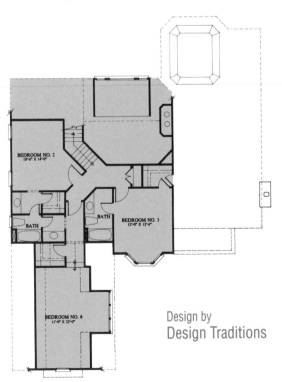

Design by
Design Traditions

Copyright 1992 Stephen S. Fuller

Design DD9861

First Floor: 1,960 square feet
Second Floor: 965 square feet
Total: 2,925 square feet

● The facade of this charming home is Americana at its best, with a rocking-chair porch, a bay window and dormers above, finished in stone and wood siding and faithfully detailed.

The main level features an easy flow, beginning with the dining room to the right of the foyer. The great room features a large hearth and French doors to the patio, and leads directly to the breakfast area and kitchen. Storage closets and a counter-top desk area highlight the kitchen which, along with the laundry room, is conveniently located to the rear of the home. Left of the foyer is an attractive study with a large bay window. The master suite, featuring a bay-windowed sitting area, large master bath with double vanities, a shower and ample closet space, completes the main level. On the upper level, Bedroom 2 features a full bath and has three dormer windows overlooking the front lawn. The third and fourth bedrooms share another full bath. This home is designed with a basement foundation.

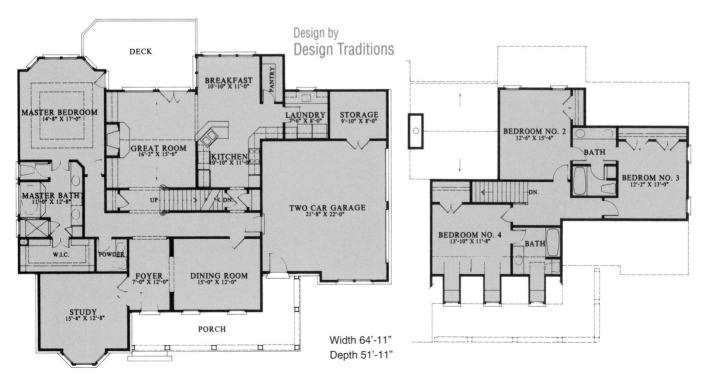

Design by
Design Traditions

Width 64'-11"
Depth 51'-11"

Quote One™
Cost to build? See page 216
to order complete cost estimate
to build this house in your area!

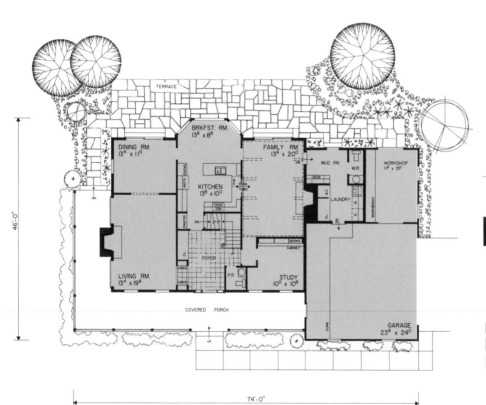

Design by
Home Planners,
Inc.

Design DD2946

First Floor: 1,581 square feet
Second Floor: 1,344 square feet;
Total: 2,925 square feet

● Here's a traditional design that's made for down-home hospitality, the pleasures of casual conversation, and the good grace of pleasant company. The star attractions are the large covered porch and terrace, perfectly relaxing gathering points for family and friends. Inside, though, the design is truly a hard worker; separate living room and family room, each with its own fireplace; formal dining room; large kitchen and breakfast area with bay windows; separate study; workshop with plenty of room to maneuver; mud room; and four bedrooms up, including a master suite. Not to be overlooked are the curio niches, the powder room, the built-in bookshelves, the kitchen pass-through, and pantry. For information on customizing the design, call 1-800-521-6797, ext. 800.

Design by
Home Planners,
Inc.

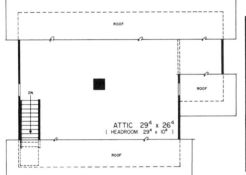

ATTIC 29⁴ x 26⁴
(HEADROOM 29⁴ x 10⁴)

BEDROOM/
STUDY
11⁰ x 13²

BATH

DRESS. RM.

VANITY

MASTER
BEDROOM
13⁰ x 13²

BATH

BEDROOM
10⁰ x 10⁶

BEDROOM
13⁰ x 10⁶

Design DD2774

First Floor: 1,366 square feet
Second Floor: 969 square feet
Total: 2,335 square feet

● This winning farmhouse adaption offers all the most up-to-date features expected in a new home. Beginning with the formal areas, there is the quiet corner living room which opens to the sizable dining room. This room enjoys an abundance of natural light from the delightful bay window overlooking the rear yard. The efficient U-shaped kitchen is conveniently located just a step away. The kitchen features many built-ins and a pass-through to the beamed-ceilinged breakfast room. Sliding glass doors to the terrace are located in both the sunken family room and breakfast room. The service entrance to the garage is flanked by a clothes closet and a large walk-in pantry. Recreational activities and hobbies may be pursued in the basement area. For information on customizing this design, call 1-800-521-6797, ext. 800.

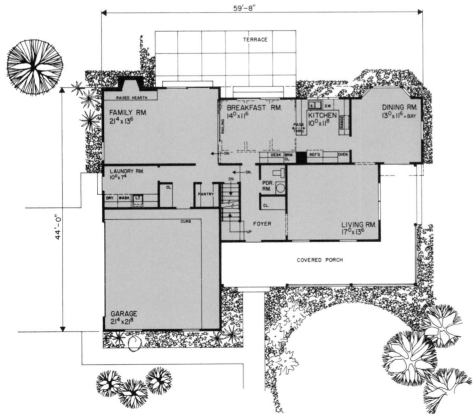

59'-8"

TERRACE

FAMILY RM.
21⁴ x 13⁶

RAISED HEARTH

BREAKFAST RM.
14⁰ x 11⁶

KITCHEN
10⁰ x 11⁸

RANGE

D.W.

DINING RM.
13⁰ x 11⁶ + BAY

PASS THRU

DESK

BRM. CL.

REF'G

OVEN

LAUNDRY RM.
10⁰ x 7⁶

DRY. WASH.

CL.

PANTRY

44'-0"

CURB

PDR. RM.

CL.

FOYER

LIVING RM.
17⁰ x 13⁶

UP

GARAGE
21⁴ x 21⁸

COVERED PORCH

QUOTE ONE™

Cost to build? See page 216
to order complete cost estimate
to build this house in your area!

Design DD3462

First Floor: 1,395 square feet
Second Floor: 813 square feet
Total: 2,208 square feet

● Get off to a great start with this handsome family farmhouse. Covered porches front and rear assure comfortable outdoor living while varied roof planes add visual interest. Inside, distinct formal and informal living zones provide the best accommodations for any occasion. The columned foyer opens to both the dining and living rooms. The central kitchen services the large family room with an island work counter and snack bar. For everyday chores, a laundry room is conveniently located and also provides access to the garage. On the first floor you'll find the master bedroom suite. It enjoys complete privacy and luxury with its double closets and master bath with double-bowl vanity, whirlpool tub and separate shower. Upstairs, three family bedrooms extend fabulous livability.

Design by
Home Planners, Inc.

Cost to build? See page 216 to order complete cost estimate to build this house in your area!

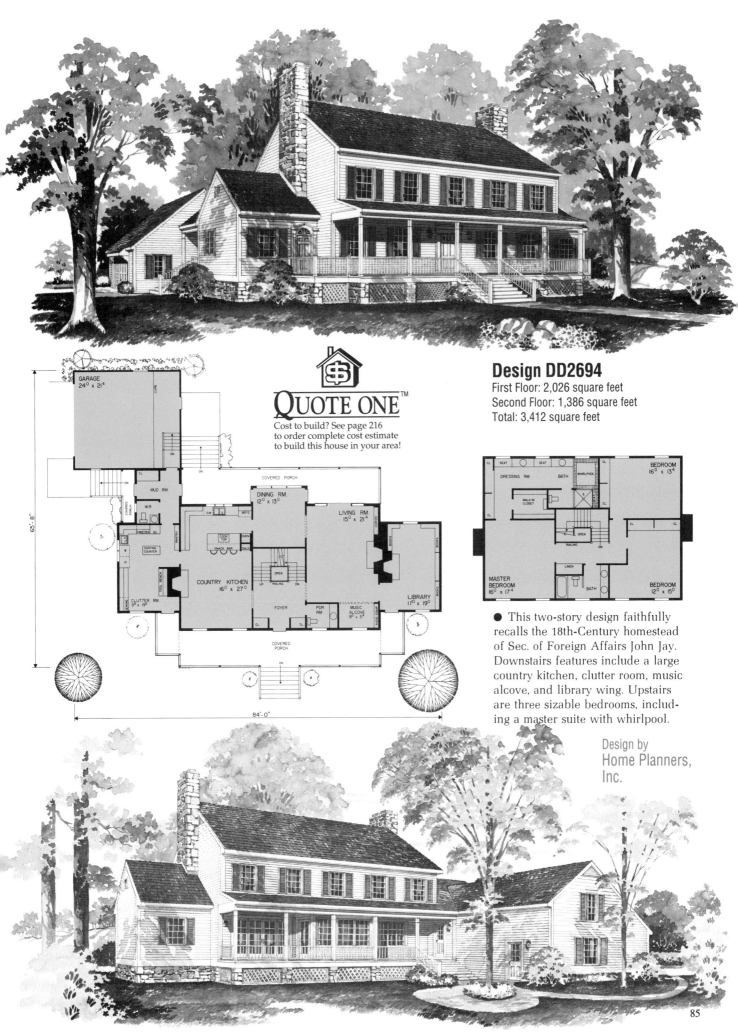

Design DD2694

First Floor: 2,026 square feet
Second Floor: 1,386 square feet
Total: 3,412 square feet

QUOTE ONE™

Cost to build? See page 216
to order complete cost estimate
to build this house in your area!

● This two-story design faithfully
recalls the 18th-Century homestead
of Sec. of Foreign Affairs John Jay.
Downstairs features include a large
country kitchen, clutter room, music
alcove, and library wing. Upstairs
are three sizable bedrooms, including a master suite with whirlpool.

Design by
Home Planners,
Inc.

Design DD9242

First Floor: 1,322 square feet
Second Floor: 1,272 square feet
Total: 2,594 square feet

● Here's the luxury you've been looking for—from the wraparound covered front porch to the bright sun room at the rear off the breakfast room. A sunken family room with fireplace serves everyday casual gatherings, while the more formal living and dining rooms are reserved for special entertaining situations. The kitchen has a central island with snack bar and is located most conveniently for serving and cleaning up. Upstairs are four bedrooms, one a lovely master suite with French doors into the master bath and a whirlpool tub in a dramatic bay window. A double vanity in the shared bath easily serves the three family bedrooms.

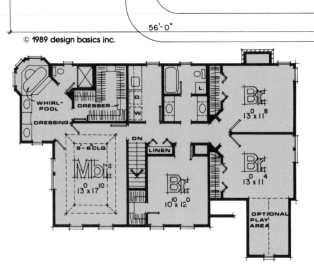

© 1989 design basics inc.

Design by
Design
Basics,
Inc.

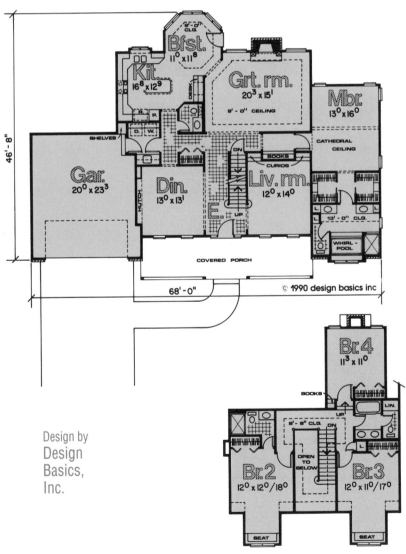

Design DD9274

First Floor: 1,780 square feet
Second Floor: 815 square feet
Total: 2,595 square feet

● A large covered front porch welcomes visitors to this home. The entrance hall opens to a formal dining room with hutch space and a living room with built-in curio cabinets. The volume great room features a handsome fireplace flanked by windows. A large kitchen provides an island counter, pantry, dual Lazy Susans and a desk. A private hall with built-in bookcase leads to the first-floor master suite. The extravagant master bath features two walk-in closets, His and Hers vanities and a whirlpool tub. Upstairs, two of the three bedrooms feature decorator window seats.

Design by
Design
Basics,
Inc.

Design DD9298

First Floor: 1,881 square feet
Second Floor: 814 square feet
Total: 2,695 square feet

● Oval windows and an appealing covered porch lend character to this 1½-story home. Inside, a volume entry views the formal living and dining rooms. Three large windows and a raised-hearth fireplace flanked by bookcases highlight a volume great room. An island kitchen with huge pantry and two Lazy Susans serves a captivating gazebo dinette. In the master suite, a cathedral ceiling, corner whirlpool and roomy dressing area deserve careful study. A gallery wall for displaying family mementos and prized heirlooms graces the upstairs corridor. Each secondary bedroom has convenient access to the bathrooms. This home's charm and blend of popular amenities will fit your lifestyle.

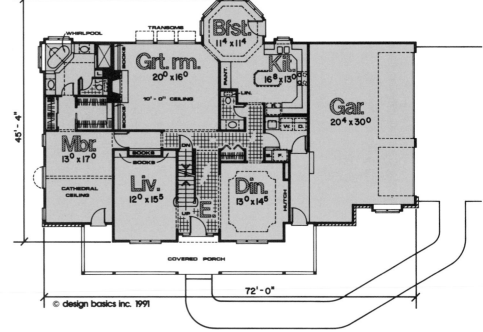

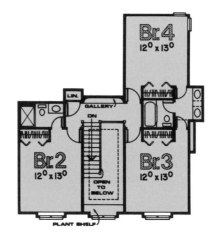

Design by
Design
Basics,
Inc.

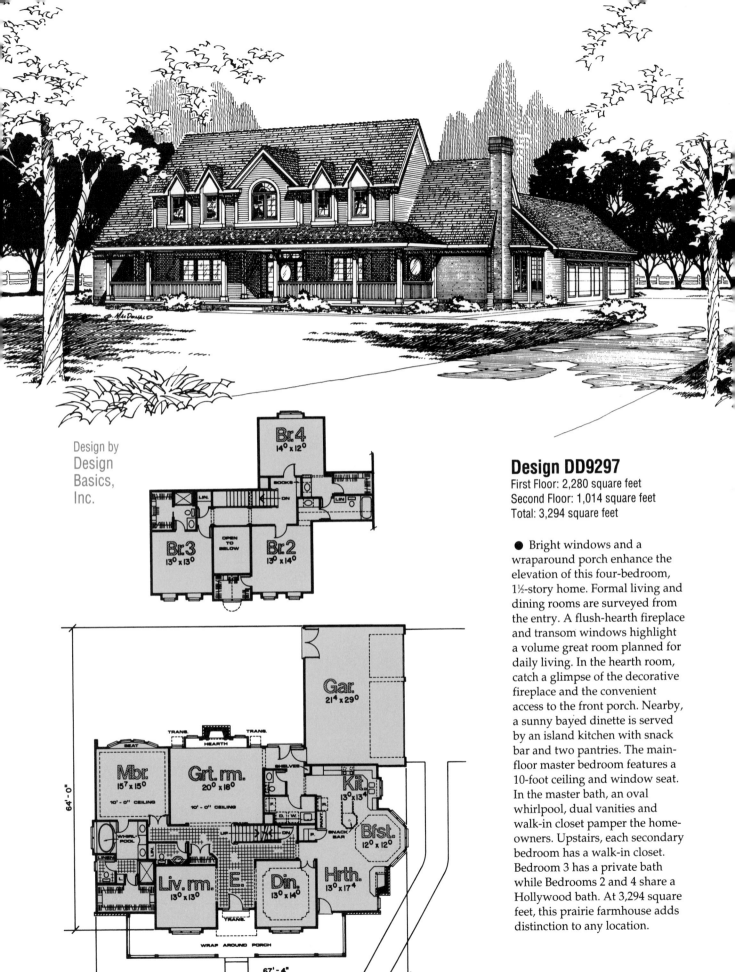

Design by
Design
Basics,
Inc.

Design DD9297

First Floor: 2,280 square feet
Second Floor: 1,014 square feet
Total: 3,294 square feet

● Bright windows and a
wraparound porch enhance the
elevation of this four-bedroom,
1½-story home. Formal living and
dining rooms are surveyed from
the entry. A flush-hearth fireplace
and transom windows highlight
a volume great room planned for
daily living. In the hearth room,
catch a glimpse of the decorative
fireplace and the convenient
access to the front porch. Nearby,
a sunny bayed dinette is served
by an island kitchen with snack
bar and two pantries. The main-
floor master bedroom features a
10-foot ceiling and window seat.
In the master bath, an oval
whirlpool, dual vanities and
walk-in closet pamper the homeowners. Upstairs, each secondary
bedroom has a walk-in closet.
Bedroom 3 has a private bath
while Bedrooms 2 and 4 share a
Hollywood bath. At 3,294 square
feet, this prairie farmhouse adds
distinction to any location.

© The Sater Group, Inc.

Jen King

Design DD6600
Square Footage: 1,795

● This engaging three-bedroom split plan promotes casual living both inside and out, offering contemporary amenities for convenient living. The foyer opens to the formal dining room on the right, and straight ahead, the great room complete with a fireplace and a built-in entertainment center. Double French doors unfold onto a large veranda. The kitchen includes a large walk-in pantry, an eating bar and a bayed breakfast nook. The relaxing master suite enjoys access to a screened porch, His and Hers walk-in closets and a private bath with a glass-enclosed shower. Two secondary bedrooms offer privacy and plenty of storage.

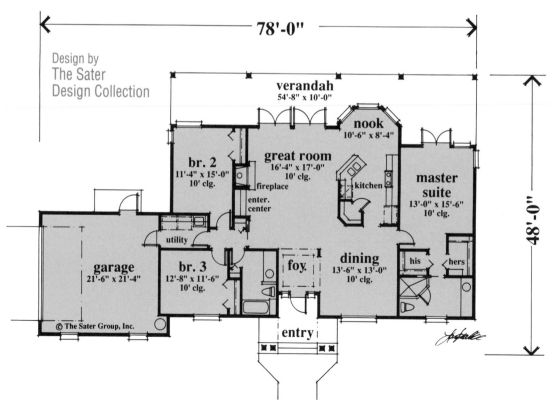

Design by
The Sater
Design Collection

78'-0"

48'-0"

verandah
54'-8" x 10'-0"

nook
10'-6" x 8'-4"

br. 2
11'-4" x 15'-0"
10' clg.

great room
16'-4" x 17'-0"
10' clg.

fireplace

enter. center

kitchen

master suite
13'-0" x 15'-6"
10' clg.

utility

garage
21'-6" x 21'-4"

br. 3
12'-8" x 11'-6"
10' clg.

foy.

dining
13'-6" x 13'-0"
10' clg.

his

hers

© The Sater Group, Inc.

entry

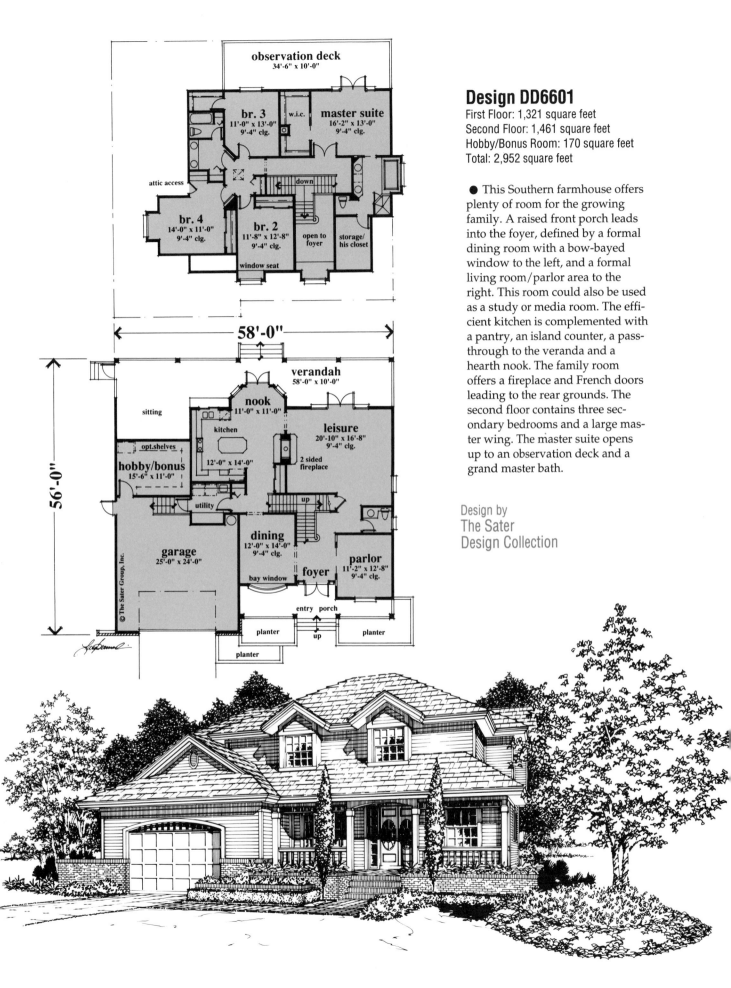

observation deck
34'-6" x 10'-0"

br. 3
11'-0" x 13'-0"
9'-4" clg.

w.i.c.

master suite
16'-2" x 13'-0"
9'-4" clg.

attic access

br. 4
14'-0" x 11'-0"
9'-4" clg.

down

br. 2
11'-8" x 12'-8"
9'-4" clg.

open to foyer

storage/ his closet

window seat

58'-0"

56'-0"

verandah
58'-0" x 10'-0"

sitting

nook
11'-0" x 11'-0"

kitchen

leisure
20'-10" x 16'-8"
9'-4" clg.

opt. shelves

2 sided fireplace

hobby/bonus
15'-6" x 11'-0"

12'-0" x 14'-0"

utility

up

© The Sater Group, Inc.

garage
25'-0" x 24'-0"

dining
12'-0" x 14'-0"
9'-4" clg.

foyer

bay window

parlor
11'-2" x 12'-8"
9'-4" clg.

entry porch

planter

up

planter

planter

Design DD6601

First Floor: 1,321 square feet
Second Floor: 1,461 square feet
Hobby/Bonus Room: 170 square feet
Total: 2,952 square feet

● This Southern farmhouse offers plenty of room for the growing family. A raised front porch leads into the foyer, defined by a formal dining room with a bow-bayed window to the left, and a formal living room/parlor area to the right. This room could also be used as a study or media room. The efficient kitchen is complemented with a pantry, an island counter, a pass-through to the veranda and a hearth nook. The family room offers a fireplace and French doors leading to the rear grounds. The second floor contains three secondary bedrooms and a large master wing. The master suite opens up to an observation deck and a grand master bath.

Design by
The Sater
Design Collection

91

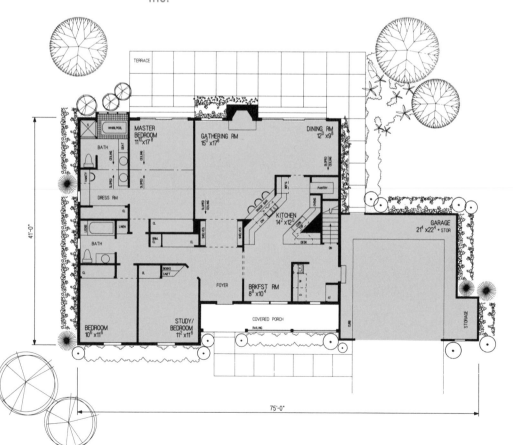

Design by
Home Planners,
Inc.

Quote One™
Cost to build? See page 216
to order complete cost estimate
to build this house in your area!

Design DD2947
Square Footage: 1,830

● This charming one-story traditional home greets visitors with a covered porch. A galley-style kitchen shares a snack bar with the spacious gathering room where a fireplace is the focal point. The dining room has sliding glass doors to the rear terrace as does the master suite. This bedroom area also includes a luxury bath with a whirlpool tub and a separate dressing room. Two additional bedrooms—one could double as a study—are located at the front of the home. For information on customizing this design, call 1-800-521-6797, ext. 800.

BEDROOM
9⁴ x 9⁴

BATH

MASTER
BEDROOM
10⁰ x 15⁰

BATH

LINEN

DN

BEDROOM
10⁰ x 10⁰

BEDROOM
11⁴ x 10⁰

4 BEDROOM PLAN

BATH

MASTER
BEDROOM
14⁸ x 11⁸

BATH

DN

LINEN

BEDROOM
10⁰ x 10⁰

BEDROOM
11⁴ x 13⁴

OPTIONAL 3 BEDROOM PLAN

Design by
Home Planners,
Inc.

Design DD1956 First Floor: 990 square feet
Second Floor: 728 square feet; Total: 1,718 square feet

● Simple, functional, and loaded with Colonial appeal, this versatile two-story plan includes details for both the three bedroom and four bedroom options. For information on customizing this design, call 1-800-521-6797, ext. 800.

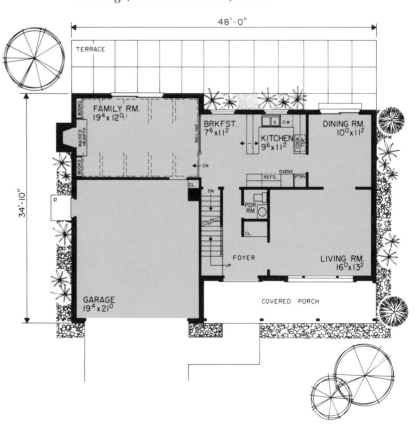

48'-0"

TERRACE

34'-10"

FAMILY RM.
19⁴ x 12⁰

RAISED HEARTH

BOOKS

BRKFST.
7⁶ x 11²

KITCHEN
9⁶ x 11²

DW

DINING RM.
10⁰ x 11²

OVENS

REF'G.

PTRY

DN

PDR RM.

CL

DN

FOYER

UP

LIVING RM.
16⁰ x 13²

GARAGE
19⁴ x 21⁰

COVERED PORCH

Design DD9711

First Floor: 1,271 square feet
Second Floor: 665 square feet
Total: 1,936 square feet

● Wood siding and a wraparound porch set the stage for a very charming country home. The great room features dormers that allow an influx of natural light. Both formal and family gatherings will be a joy in this room with its attention-getting center fireplace. The kitchen opens up into a bayed breakfast nook with back-porch access. A deck extends from the porch and supports a spa. The dining room is nestled off the kitchen and living room. You'll find even more livability in this design—it incorporates four bedrooms! One, at the front of the house, could serve as a study. Upstairs, the master bedroom acts as a nice retreat with its balcony overlooking the great room, and its full bath containing a whirlpool tub, a double-bowl vanity and a walk-in closet.

Design by
Donald A.
Gardner,
Architects, Inc.

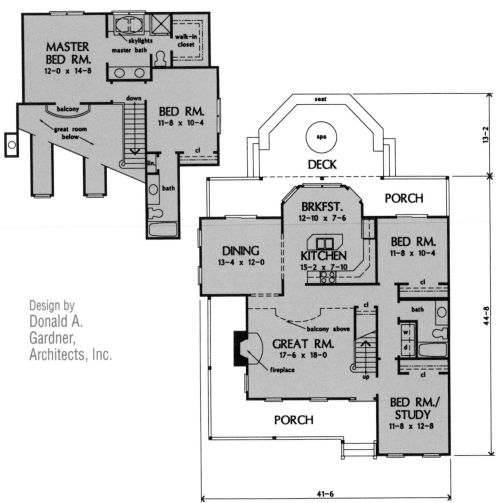

Design by
Donald A.
Gardner,
Architects, Inc.

Design DD9662
First Floor: 1,025 square feet
Second Floor: 911 square feet
Total: 1,936 square feet

● The exterior of this three-bedroom home is enhanced by its many gables, arched windows and wraparound porch. A large great room with impressive fireplace leads to both the dining room and screened porch with access to the deck. An open kitchen offers a country-kitchen atmosphere. The second-level master suite has two walk-in closets and an impressive bath. There is also bonus space over the garage. The plan is available with a crawl-space foundation.

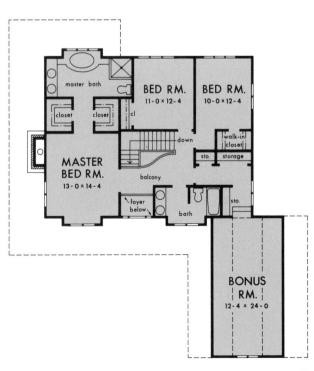

● This economical plan offers an impressive visual statement with its comfortable and well-proportioned appearance. The entrance foyer leads to all areas of the house. The great room, dining area and kitchen are all open to one another allowing visual interaction. The great room and dining area both have a cathedral ceiling. The fireplace is flanked by book shelves and cabinets. The master suite has a cathedral ceiling, walk-in closet and master bath with double-bowl vanity, whirlpool tub and shower. The plan is available with a crawl-space foundation.

Design by
Donald A.
Gardner,
Architects, Inc.

Design DD9664
Square Footage: 1,287

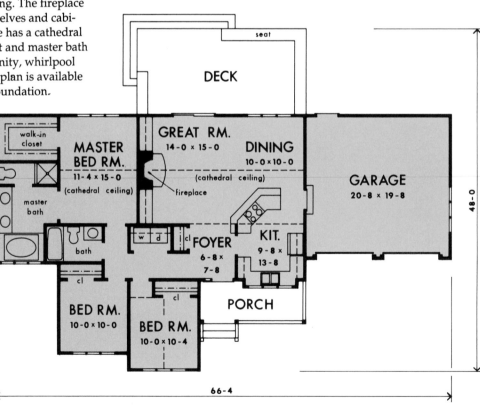

Texas Traditional and Brick Styles

YESTERYEAR'S TEXAS WAS ROUGH AND RUGGED, evoking images of wide-open spaces, blowing tumbleweeds, and cowboys rounding up cattle and huddling around a crackling campfire at day's end. Whether past or present, images of Texas always seem to be conceived on the grand scale. But how this region has developed over the years! Today's Texas is no stranger to luxury: consider Highland Park (part of the Park Cities) in Dallas, laid out by William David Cook, who also planned Beverly Hills! Or perhaps one of Houston's most exclusive areas, River Oaks. Different regions dictate different styles and textures. For example: San Antonio, with its limestone block exteriors and abundance of pecan wood interiors has originated a style all its own.

This section celebrates the old and the new, borrowing from historic details and the earlier architectural traditions and freely adapting them to our more contemporary shapes, materials and lifestyles. The result of this gentle blending is a style of American architecture that has emerged and unfolded from our nation's historic past, and yet provides a dominant theme in contemporary American design. Inspiration is provided by the Colonial, French and English styles combining to create one- and two-story designs that run the gamut from simple, comfortable residences to grand, opulent homes that satisfy even the most discriminating homeowners. Most of these Texas traditionals employ a brick exterior, valued not only for its beauty, but also for its practical insulating qualities.

The Mansard-style is first of the classic homes to combine the past with the contemporary styles of today. This design is easily identified by its dual-pitched hip roof. Not as common as its traditional counterparts, it features a symmetrical shape and high, narrow windows—often arched at the top—and a recessed entry.

Next comes an interesting style known as Neo-French, which offers a free interpretation of earlier, classic French designs. This home's most characteristic feature is its steeply-pitched hip roof. These homes are either one- or two-story and are often asymmetrical with high, arched windows and entries. Designs DD9156 and DD8006 both offer wonderful one-story examples, while DD9211 and DD9085 provide two-story models. To demonstrate how the combination of exterior textures enhance these traditional designs, see DD8014 and DD8021.

Not to be outdone by the French, the English make their own contribution to the Texas style with a traditional rendition called Neo-Tudor. These homes are characterized by dominant front-facing gables with a steeply-pitched roof as illustrated in Designs DD8010 and DD9741 and the half-timbered decorative detailing associated with classic Tudor style. In these homes, narrow windows are frequently found in groups of four or more.

Common to all these styles is the use of corner quoins, an abundance of windows, and a chimney located at the front exterior of the home.

The traditional versions represented in this section offer proof that these homes truly are designed as the best of the best, with plans that complement a wealth of lifestyles.

Design DD9097

Square Footage: 2,314

● This one-story traditional design incorporates open design with fine floor planning for one great home. The family room is the central focus around which radiate the formal dining room, the breakfast room, the kitchen and three bedrooms. The unique master suite is particularly notable with its octagon-shaped sitting room, French doors opening to a rear patio and relaxing corner whirlpool. Each bedroom contains a walk-in closet. Blueprints for this home include plans for a detached garage.

Design by
Larry W.
Garnett &
Associates, Inc.

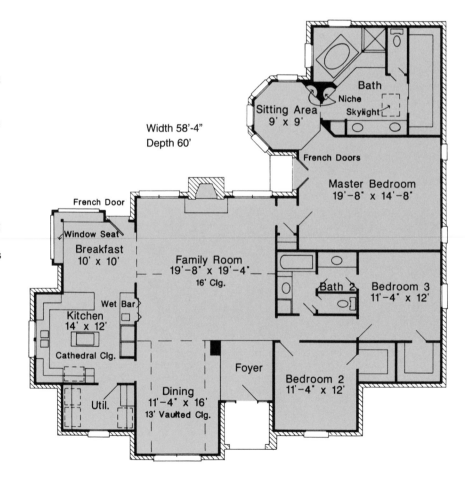

Width 58'-4"
Depth 60'

Bath

Sitting Area
9' x 9'

Niche
Skylight

French Doors

Master Bedroom
19'-8" x 14'-8"

French Door

Window Seat

Breakfast
10' x 10'

Family Room
19'-8" x 19'-4"
16' Clg.

Bath 2

Bedroom 3
11'-4" x 12'

Wet Bar

Kitchen
14' x 12'

Cathedral Clg.

Foyer

Util.

Dining
11'-4" x 16'
13' Vaulted Clg.

Bedroom 2
11'-4" x 12'

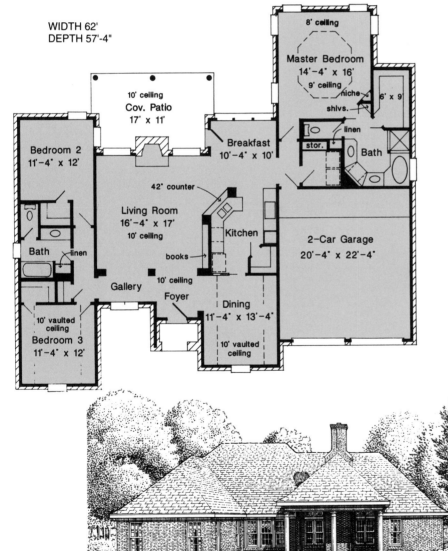

WIDTH 62'
DEPTH 57'-4"

8' ceiling

Master Bedroom
14'-4" x 16'
9' ceiling

niche
shlvs.

6' x 9'

10' ceiling
Cov. Patio
17' x 11'

Breakfast
10'-4" x 10'

linen

stor.

Bath

Bedroom 2
11'-4" x 12'

42" counter

Living Room
16'-4" x 17'
10' ceiling

Kitchen

2-Car Garage
20'-4" x 22'-4"

books

Bath

linen

Gallery

10' ceiling

Foyer

Dining
11'-4" x 13'-4"

10' vaulted
ceiling

Bedroom 3
11'-4" x 12'

10' vaulted
ceiling

Design by
Larry W.
Garnett &
Associates, Inc.

Design DD9161

Square Footage: 1,923

● Brick, shutters and graceful roof lines lend a timeless beauty in this traditional design. Greet guests in the ten-foot-high foyer, walk them through the gallery and into the impressive fireplace-graced living room which opens onto a covered patio. Dining is a delight beneath a ten-foot vaulted ceiling. The secluded master bedroom gives way to a glass-enclosed shower, spa bath, double-bowl vanity and dressing table. At the other end of the house, two family bedrooms—one with a ten-foot vaulted ceiling—share a full bath.

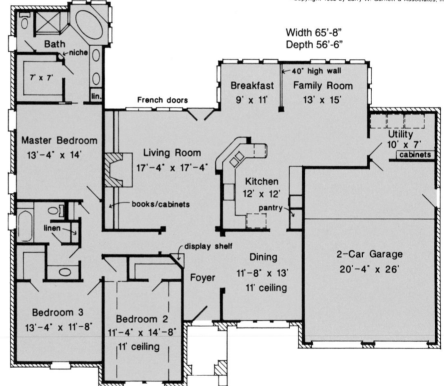

Width 65'-8"
Depth 56'-6"

Design by
Larry W.
Garnett &
Associates, Inc.

Bath

niche

7' x 7'

lin.

French doors

Breakfast
9' x 11'

Family Room
13' x 15'

40" high wall

Master Bedroom
13'-4" x 14'

Living Room
17'-4" x 17'-4"

Utility
10' x 7'

cabinets

Kitchen
12' x 12'

books/cabinets

pantry

linen

2-Car Garage
20'-4" x 26'

display shelf

Design DD9182
Square Footage: 2,185

● In a little over 2,000 square feet, this three-bedroom family plan offers lots of livability. A central kitchen overlooks the living room with built-in bookshelves, the breakfast nook and the family room. A utility area off this last room enjoys storage space and direct access to the two-car garage. For formal occasions, the dining room rises to an eleven-foot ceiling. A corner display shelf sits off the foyer. The sleeping zones of the house rest to the left of the plan. Two family bedrooms each enjoy a walk-in closet. The master bedroom furthers this with a sumptuous private bath that includes a 7' x 7' walk-in closet, a double-bowl vanity, a corner spa, a separate shower and a compartmented toilet.

Bedroom 3
13'-4" x 11'-8"

Bedroom 2
11'-4" x 14'-8"
11' ceiling

Foyer

Dining
11'-8" x 13'
11' ceiling

9' ceilings throughout unless otherwise noted

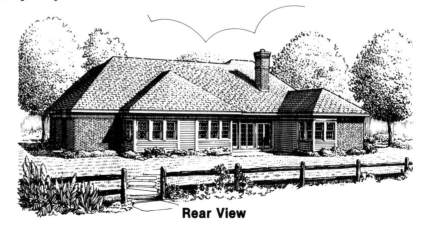

Rear View

Design DD9098
Square Footage: 1,996

● Living and working areas to the right, sleeping quarters to the left — that's the design of this home. To the rear is a long covered porch reached through the living room and master suite. The foyer is raised above the living room and dining room a few steps. A profusion of glass in the breakfast room and hall lights up these areas. Two family bedrooms share a full bath with double lavatories.

Design by
Larry W.
Garnett &
Associates, Inc.

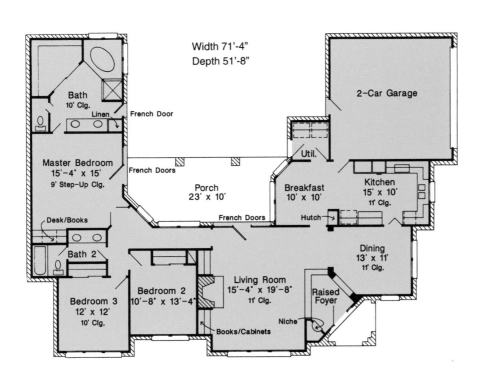

Width 71'-4"
Depth 51'-8"

2-Car Garage

Bath
10' Clg.

Linen

French Door

Master Bedroom
15'-4" x 15'
9' Step-Up Clg.

French Doors

Util.

Breakfast
10' x 10'

Kitchen
15' x 10'
11' Clg.

Porch
23' x 10'

Desk/Books

French Doors

Hutch

Bath 2

Dining
13' x 11'
11' Clg.

Bedroom 3
12' x 12'
10' Clg.

Bedroom 2
10'-8" x 13'-4"

Living Room
15'-4" x 19'-8"
11' Clg.

Raised Foyer

Books/Cabinets

Niche

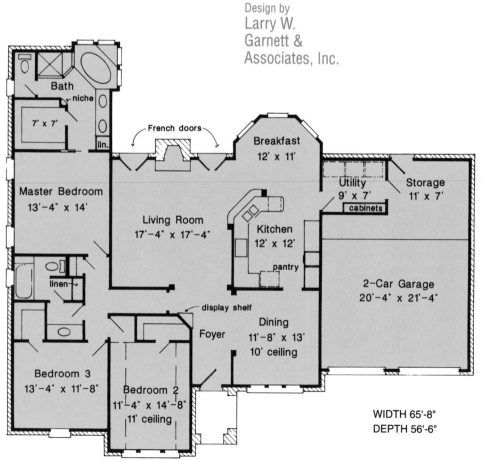

Design by
Larry W.
Garnett &
Associates, Inc.

Bath

niche

7' x 7'

lin.

French doors

Breakfast
12' x 11'

Master Bedroom
13'-4" x 14'

Living Room
17'-4" x 17'-4"

Kitchen
12' x 12'

pantry

Utility
9' x 7'

Storage
11' x 7'

cabinets

linen

display shelf

Foyer

Dining
11'-8" x 13'
10' ceiling

2-Car Garage
20'-4" x 21'-4"

Bedroom 3
13'-4" x 11'-8"

Bedroom 2
11'-4" x 14'-8"
11' ceiling

WIDTH 65'-8"
DEPTH 56'-6"

Design DD9088

Square Footage: 1,994

● This charming budget-conscious design provides an abundance of living space. Radiating around the roomy kitchen are the dining room with ten-foot ceiling and living room with French doors and fireplace. A glass-surrounded breakfast area near the kitchen provides space for casual eating. Three bedrooms, all with walk-in closets, dominate the left wing of the home. Bedroom 2 has an eleven-foot sloped ceiling. The master suite features a corner tub and a glass-enclosed shower with seat. Note the large utility room and storage space in the garage.

Design DD9089
Square Footage: 1,849

● A wonderful floor plan is found on the interior of this cozy one-story plan. The large living room and conveniently placed dining room both open from the raised foyer. In between is the galley kitchen with huge pantry and attached breakfast area. French doors flanking the fireplace in the living room open to the rear yard. To the right of the plan is the master bedroom with walk-in closet and double lavatories. To the left of the plan are two family bedrooms sharing a full bath in between.

Design by
Larry W.
Garnett &
Associates, Inc.

WIDTH 60'
DEPTH 57'-4"

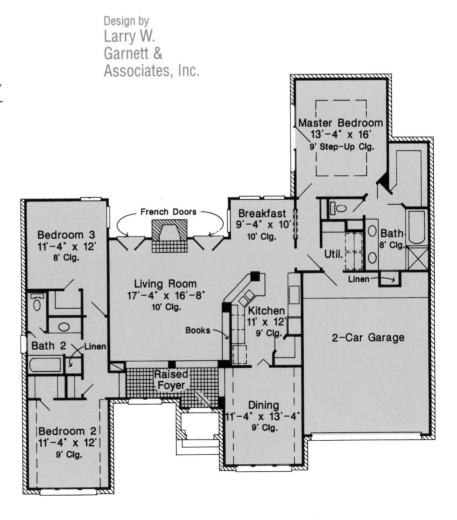

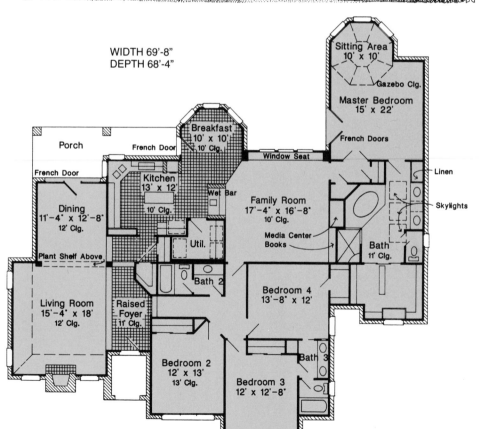

Design by
Larry W.
Garnett &
Associates, Inc.

Design DD9156
Square Footage: 2,885

● An entire wing on the right side of this house is dedicated to making the owners feel at home. The master bedroom includes an octagonal sitting area with gazebo ceiling and French doors to the rear yard. Three skylights illuminate a lavish master bath with tub, shower, and dual vanities, as well as abundant closet space. Three family bedrooms and two full baths complete the sleeping areas. A large family room features a wet bar and built-in media center and bookshelves. A breakfast bay is adjacent to the island kitchen. To the left of the home, formal areas include the dining room with French door and the living room with fireplace and plant shelf.

WIDTH 69'-8"
DEPTH 68'-4"

Porch

French Door

French Door

Dining
11'-4" x 12'-8"
12' Clg.

Plant Shelf Above

Living Room
15'-4" x 18'
12' Clg.

Raised
Foyer
11' Clg.

Kitchen
13' x 12'
10' Clg.

Breakfast
10' x 10'
10' Clg.

Wet Bar

Util.

Bath 2

Window Seat

Family Room
17'-4" x 16'-8"
10' Clg.

Media Center
Books

Bedroom 2
12' x 13'
13' Clg.

Bedroom 3
12' x 12'-8"

Bedroom 4
13'-8" x 12'

Bath 3

Sitting Area
10' x 10'

Gazebo Clg.

Master Bedroom
15' x 22'

French Doors

Linen

Skylights

Bath
11' Clg.

104

Design DD9025

Square Footage: 2,481

● Multiple gables, bay windows
and corner windows with tran-
soms above provide an exterior
reminiscent of English country-
side homes. A marble floor in
the foyer extends into the living
room as an elegant fireplace
hearth. The formal dining room
features an eleven-foot ceiling,
bay window, and French doors
that open onto a private dining
terrace. A spacious kitchen
overlooks the breakfast area and
the family room which has a
corner fireplace and dramatic
fourteen-foot ceiling with transom windows above triple French doors.
Another corner fireplace is located in the master bedroom, which also contains a built-in
desk and triple French doors. The luxurious
master bath features mirrored doors at the
large walk-in closet, a dressing table, and a
whirlpool tub inset in a bay window.

Design by
Larry W.
Garnett &
Associates, Inc.

Kitchen

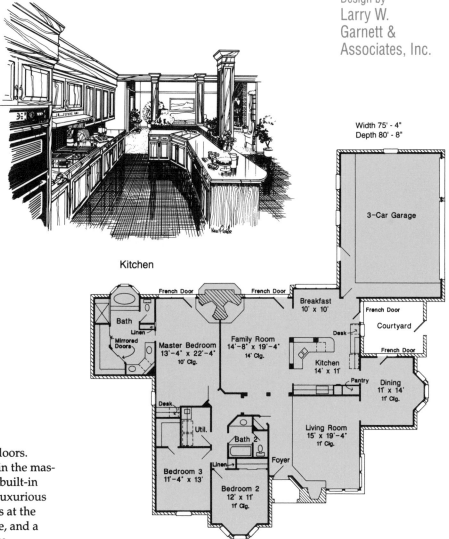

Width 75' - 4"
Depth 80' - 8"

Design DD8014

First Floor: 1,838 square feet
Second Floor: 844 square feet
Total: 2,682 square feet

● The traditional brick exterior of this home exudes a feeling of permanence and stability. The Palladian window over the foyer draws attention to the imposing two-story gable and invites entry to this flowing plan. Inside, columns with arches frame the living and dining room, lending an air of casual elegance. The addition of arched columns between the living and dining rooms complete this graceful picture, while plant ledges above the arches provide an additional feeling of spaciousness. Unobstructed views of the rear grounds are enjoyed from the living and dining rooms, the family room and the master bedroom. The master bedroom includes a luxury master bath with an enormous walk-in closet. A large kitchen with a built-in eating bar and a breakfast room are open to the family room and provide an ideal informal living area. The upstairs completes this lovely home with three large bedrooms and a gathering loft. This plan is available with either a crawlspace or slab foundation. Please specify when ordering.

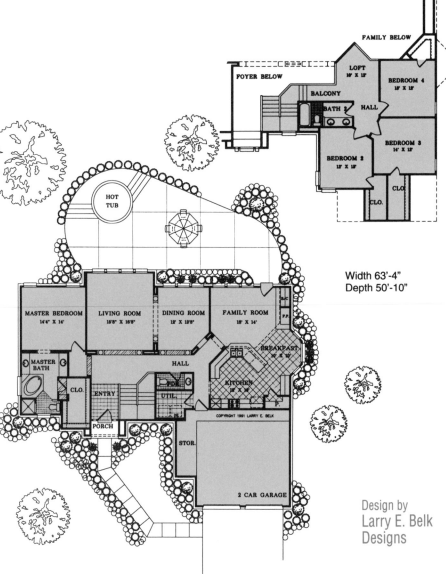

Width 63'-4"
Depth 50'-10"

Design by
Larry E. Belk
Designs

Width 55'-6"
Depth 52'

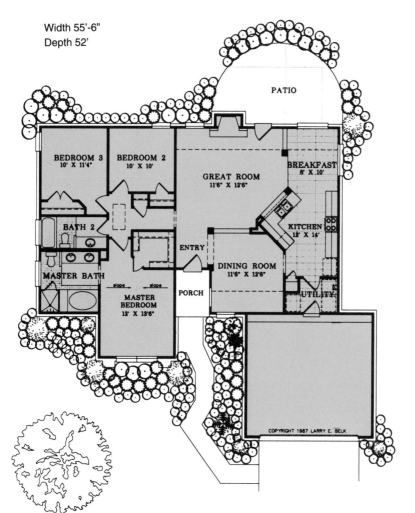

PATIO

BEDROOM 3
10' X 11'4"

BEDROOM 2
10' X 10'

GREAT ROOM
11'6" X 12'6"

BREAKFAST
8' X 10'

BATH 2

KITCHEN
12' X 14'

MASTER BATH

ENTRY

DINING ROOM
11'6" X 12'6"

slope   slope

MASTER
BEDROOM
12' X 13'6"

PORCH

UTILITY

Design DD8040
Square Footage: 1,575

● This homey traditional includes all the features of a large plan in a small package. Ten-foot ceilings in the entry, great room, breakfast room, kitchen and master bedroom give this home an open, expansive feel. An angled eating bar in the kitchen, with a plant ledge above, combines the great room with the kitchen/breakfast area. A dining room is provided for more formal entertaining. The utility room is large enough for an upright freezer, washer and dryer. The master bedroom includes an upscale master bath with a whirlpool and a separate shower. Two additional bedrooms and a bath complete this comfortable home.

Design by
Larry E. Belk
Designs

Design DD8010

First Floor: 1,902 square feet
Second Floor: 421 square feet
Total: 2,323 square feet

● Double French doors with a half-round transom make the entry to this home a real eye-catcher. A bay window on the front—repeating the door treatment—balances this pleasing elevation. Through the entry is the great room with a window wall to the rear yard. The dining room, kitchen and breakfast areas are all conveniently grouped. The kitchen is equipped with a large cooktop island and an eating bar. The corner sink and the windows above make the kitchen bright and add interest to the area. A sun room off the kitchen expands the breakfast area and makes a cozy place for gathering the family. The master bedroom located at the front of the house is notable for its large bay window. Two ample closets and a large master bath complete the master suite. Also included downstairs are two additional bedrooms, Bath 2 and the stairway to the game room upstairs. An expandable area is included for future use. This plan is available with either a crawlspace or slab foundation. Please specify when ordering.

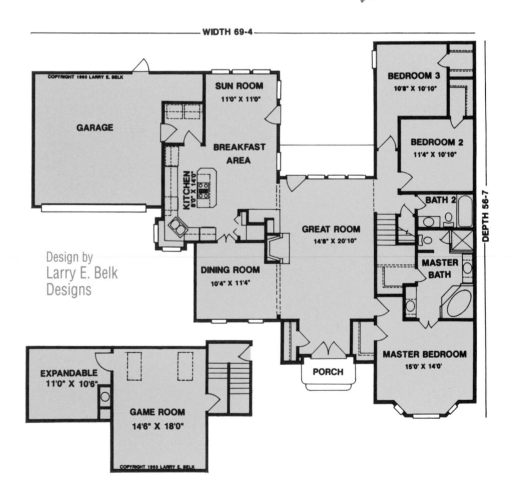

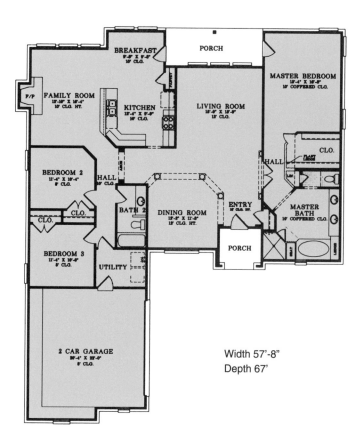

Width 57'-8"
Depth 67'

Design DD8006

Square Footage: 2,109

● A traditional exterior combined with an open design and amenities normally found in a larger home make this plan a popular choice. Inside, twelve-foot ceilings in the entry, the living room and the dining room open the house. The dining room is defined by three columns connected by arches and adds elegance to the home. The split bedroom plan separates the master bedroom from Bedrooms 2 and 3 to allow more privacy for the owner. With ten-foot ceilings and a luxury master bath, this suite offers it all. The family room, the breakfast area and the kitchen are designed together for informal, family use.

Design by
Larry E. Belk
Designs

109

Design DD8021

First Floor: 2,134 square feet
Second Floor: 858 square feet
Total: 2,992 square feet

Design by
Larry E. Belk
Designs

● An old-time metal roof forming the porch adds interest to this stucco-and-brick home. Upon entering, the eye is drawn to the two-story living room and dining room. Off the entry, a gallery effect is created with columns connected by arches into both the living room and dining room. The pattern is repeated with an opening between the living and dining rooms, flanked by columns and connected by an arch. Window walls in both rooms bring the outside into the home. The family room, the breakfast room and the kitchen are all adjacent and perfect for family gatherings after a busy day. The kitchen is equipped with an eating bar and a large pantry. The sink is situated toward the family room. A two-sided fireplace is visible from the kitchen, and the breakfast and family rooms. Ten-foot ceilings downstairs, in addition to the two-story entry, living and dining rooms, give this home a spacious and open feeling. The master suite includes a large master bedroom and a luxury bath with His and Hers walk-in closets. Upstairs, three bedrooms, a loft and a bath complete this plan. This plan is available with either a crawlspace or slab foundation. Please specify when ordering.

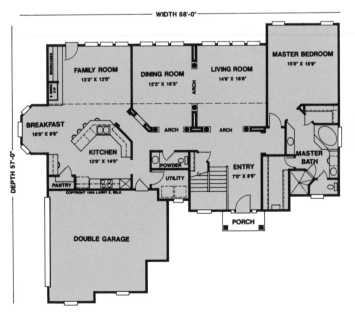

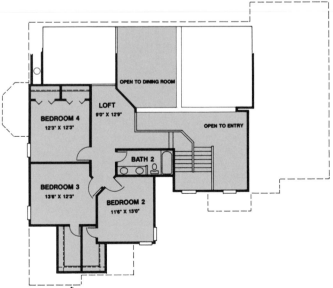

COPYRIGHT 1993

Design DD8049 First Floor: 1,764 square feet
Second Floor: 750 square feet; Total: 2,514 square feet; Bonus Room: 256 square feet

● Two distinctive pop-out dormers provide a chic image for this traditional home. This plan offers a wealth of livability in a compact layout. An efficient, spacious kitchen and breakfast area are located at the front of the house. The kitchen features a large walk-in pantry and a convenient pass-through to the dining room. The two-story great room, with a warming fireplace, is located to the rear of the plan, providing an unobstructed view of the rear grounds. The master bedroom, with large His and Hers walk-in closets, provides a private retreat. The pampering master bath is designed for self-indulgence with a corner whirlpool tub and an oversized shower. A split staircase leads to the second floor which contains two secondary bedrooms and a full bath. Stairs leading to the attic storage area are accessible from Bedroom 2 or the balcony. Area for a future game room with access to Bath 2 is conveniently located off the staircase. This plan is available with either a crawlspace or slab foundation. Please specify when ordering.

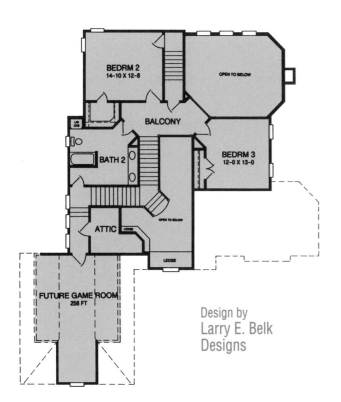

Design by
Larry E. Belk
Designs

Design by
Donald A.
Gardner,
Architects, Inc.

Design DD9728
Square Footage: 1,576

● This stately, three-bedroom, one-story home exhibits sheer elegance with its large, arched windows, round columns, covered porch and brick veneer. In the foyer, a multitude of natural light enters through arched windows in clerestory dormers. In the great room, a dramatic cathedral ceiling and a fireplace set the mood. Through gracious, round columns, the kitchen and breakfast room open up. For sleeping, turn to the master bedroom. Here, a large, walk-in closet and a well-planned master bath with a double-bowl vanity, a garden tub and a shower will pamper. Two additional bedrooms are located at the opposite end of the house for privacy.

DECK
spa

MASTER BED RM.
13-4 x 13-8

master bath
skylights

fireplace

BRKFST.
11-4 x 7-8

BED RM.
11-4 x 11-0

GREAT RM.
15-4 x 16-10
(cathedral ceiling)

w
d

walk-in closet

storage

cl

bath

KITCHEN
11-4 x 10-0

GARAGE
20-0 x 19-8

cl

FOYER
8-2 x 5-10

cl

50-9

BED RM./
STUDY
11-4 x 10-4

PORCH

DINING RM.
11-4 x 11-4

FLOOR PLAN

60-6

Design DD9734

Square Footage: 1,977
Bonus Room: 430 square feet

● A two-story foyer with a Palladian window above sets the tone for this sunlit home. Columns mark the passage from the foyer to the great room, where a centered fireplace and built-in cabinets are found. A screened porch with four sky-lights above and a wet bar pro-vides a pleasant place to start the day or wind down after work. The kitchen is flanked by the formal dining room and the breakfast room with sliding glass doors to the large, rear deck. Hidden quietly in the rear, the master suite includes a bath with dual vanities and skylights. Two family bedrooms (one an optional study) share a bath with twin sinks.

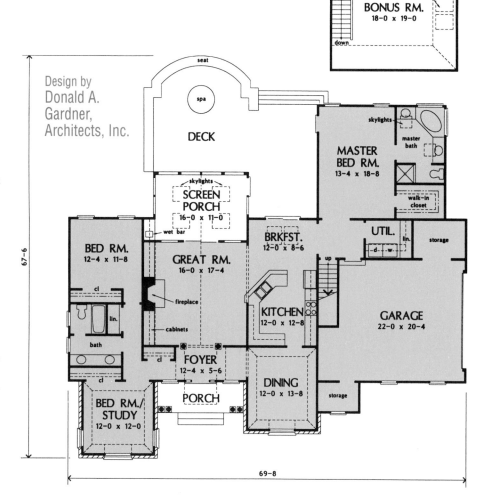

Design by
Donald A. Gardner, Architects, Inc.

Design DD9741

First Floor: 1,639 square feet
Second Floor: 662 square feet
Total: 2,301 square feet
Bonus Room: 336 square feet

● Multi-pane windows enhance the exterior and lend an air of casual elegance to this lovely traditional-style brick home. The great room features a cathedral ceiling, a fireplace and arched windows above doors leading to the rear deck, thus creating a space that will quickly become a favorite place for gatherings. Cooks will delight in the roomy kitchen and cheerful breakfast area. A gracious master suite is enhanced by His and Hers walk-in closets and a master bath complete with dual lavs, a separate shower and a skylit tub. Three secondary bedrooms, a full bath with a linen closet and a large bonus room complete the second floor.

DECK

spa

skylight

GREAT RM.
16-0 x 18-0

arched window above door

master bath

BRKFST.
11-4 x 11-8

fireplace

(cathedral ceiling)

walk-in closet

walk-in closet

KITCHEN
13-6 x 11-10

up   stor.

12-0

61-6

MASTER BED RM.
13-0 x 14-4

FOYER
7-8 x 7-0

DINING RM.
11-8 x 14-8

cl

pd. rm.

UTIL
8-4 x 9-6

porch

up

storage

GARAGE
20-0 x 20-8

54-11

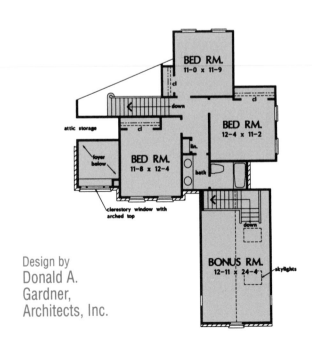

BED RM.
11-0 x 11-9

cl

attic storage

BED RM.
12-4 x 11-2

foyer below

BED RM.
11-8 x 12-4

lin.

bath

clerestory window with arched top

down

BONUS RM.
12-11 x 24-4

skylights

Design by
Donald A.
Gardner,
Architects, Inc.

114

Design DD9735

Square Footage: 2,625
Bonus Room: 447 square feet

● This stately brick facade features a columned, covered porch that ushers visitors in to the large foyer. An expansive great room with a fireplace and access to a covered rear porch awaits. The centrally located kitchen is within easy reach of the great room, the formal dining room and the skylit breakfast area. Split-bedroom planning places the master bedroom and elegant master bath to the right of the home. Two bedrooms with abundant closet space are placed to the left, while an optional bedroom or a study with a Palladian window faces the front. A large bonus room is located above the garage.

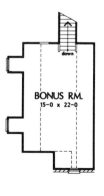

Design by
Donald A.
Gardner,
Architects, Inc.

DECK

spa

BED RM.
14-10 x 12-0

skylights

covered
porch

BRKFST.
12-0 x 9-10

MASTER
BED RM.
15-8 x 16-8

GREAT RM.
18-0 x 19-2

(cathedral ceiling)

bath

walk-in
closet

BED RM.
11-0 x 12-0

fireplace

KITCHEN
12-0 x 15-4

ln.

lin.

pd. rm.

master
bath

walk-in
closet

FOYER
15-2 x 5-10

d

skylight

BED RM./
STUDY
12-0 x 12-0

PORCH

DINING
12-0 x 13-8

UTIL.
7-8 x 9-0

up

storage

90-2

GARAGE
23-0 x 25-6

63-1

BONUS RM.
15-0 x 22-0

up

down

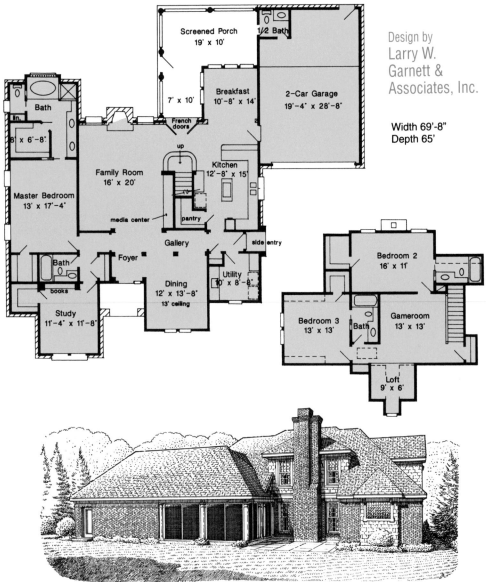

Design by
Larry W.
Garnett &
Associates, Inc.

Width 69'-8"
Depth 65'

Design DD9183
First Floor: 2,138 square feet
Second Floor: 842 square feet
Total: 2,980 square feet

● This plan abounds with all the amenities, starting with a columned foyer that leads to a spacious dining room and an even bigger family room. A study located at the front of the house will convert to the ideal guest room with its walk-in closet and nearby full bath. In the kitchen, an island cooktop sets the pace—along with an immense walk-in pantry. Off the breakfast area, a screened porch wraps around to the back of the house and even gains access to a wash room that connects to the garage. A utility room enjoys its own sunny spot as well as a helpful countertop. Three bedrooms include a first-floor master suite with two walk-in closets and a fabulous private bath. The secondary bedrooms on the second floor each feature walk-in closets and their own full bathrooms. A gameroom on this floor further enhances the plan.

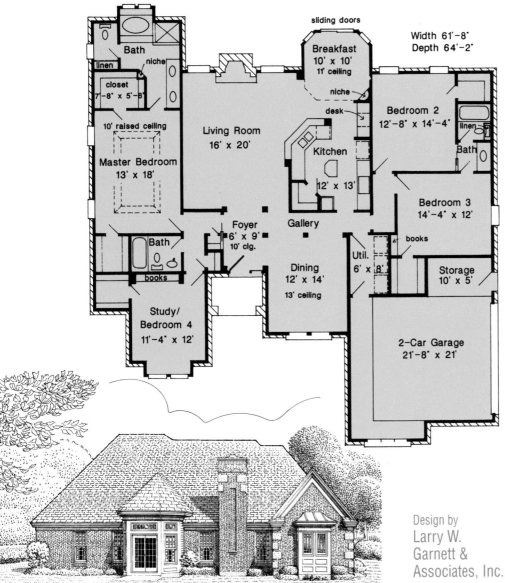

Bath

linen

niche

closet
7'-8" x 5'-8"

10' raised ceiling

Master Bedroom
13' x 18'

Bath

books

Study/
Bedroom 4
11'-4" x 12'

sliding doors

Breakfast
10' x 10'
11' ceiling

niche

desk

Living Room
16' x 20'

Kitchen

12' x 13'

Foyer
6' x 9'
10' clg.

Gallery

Dining
12' x 14'
13' ceiling

Util.
6' x 8'

Width 61'-8"
Depth 64'-2"

Bedroom 2
12'-8" x 14'-4"

linen

Bath

Bedroom 3
14'-4" x 12'

books

Storage
10' x 5'

2-Car Garage
21'-8" x 21'

Design DD8931

Square Footage: 2,397

● A steep-pitched roof and arched windows provide an elegant exterior to this house. A central kitchen overlooks the living and breakfast rooms—the latter has an eleven-foot ceiling and sliding doors to the back yard. Invite friends over for a glamorous dinner in the dining room; it's open to the gallery and has a thirteen-foot ceiling. This design also features an optional fourth bedroom, or use this room as a study. It'll be difficult to get out of bed in the morning—the master bedroom is a gem. Features include a ten-foot raised ceiling, a large walk-in closet, a double vanity, a spa bath and a shower. Bedrooms 2 and 3 share a full bath and both have large closets. Bedroom 3, like the study, makes use of built-in bookshelves.

Design by
Larry W.
Garnett &
Associates, Inc.

117

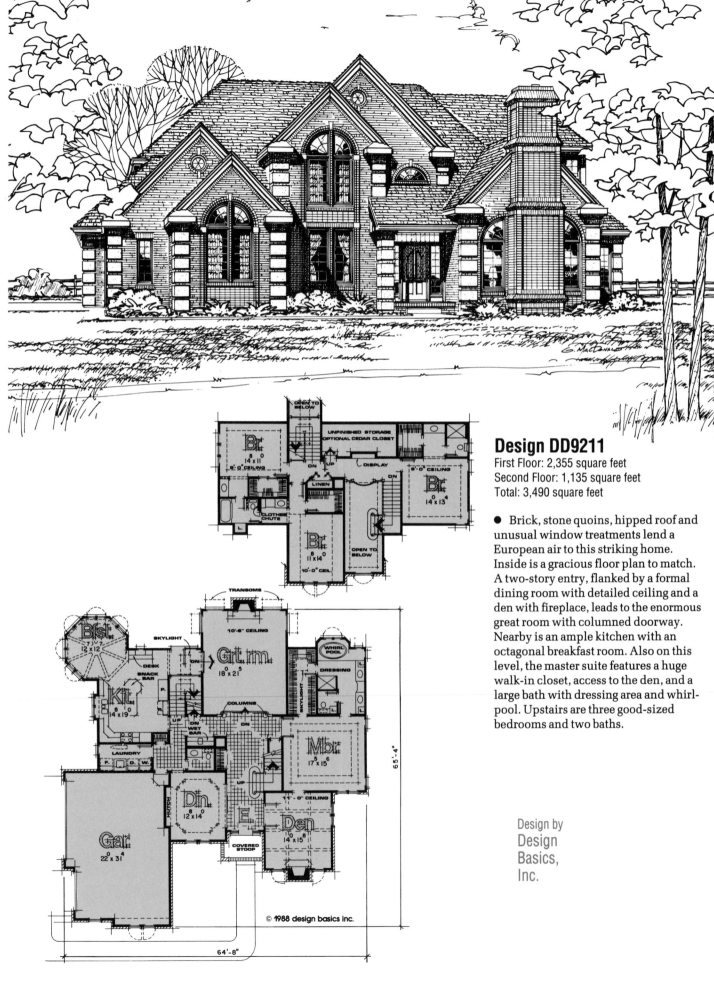

Design DD9211

First Floor: 2,355 square feet
Second Floor: 1,135 square feet
Total: 3,490 square feet

● Brick, stone quoins, hipped roof and unusual window treatments lend a European air to this striking home. Inside is a gracious floor plan to match. A two-story entry, flanked by a formal dining room with detailed ceiling and a den with fireplace, leads to the enormous great room with columned doorway. Nearby is an ample kitchen with an octagonal breakfast room. Also on this level, the master suite features a huge walk-in closet, access to the den, and a large bath with dressing area and whirlpool. Upstairs are three good-sized bedrooms and two baths.

Design by
Design
Basics,
Inc.

© 1990 design basics inc.

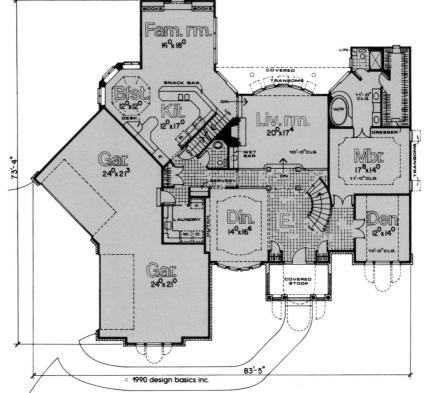

© 1990 design basics inc.

83'-5"

73'-4"

Design DD9346

First Floor: 2,617 square feet
Second Floor: 1,072 square feet
Total: 3,689 square feet

● A spectacular volume entry
with a curving staircase features
columns to the formal areas of this
home. The living room contains a
fireplace, bowed window and a
wet bar. The formal dining room
contains hutch space and a nearby
servery. All main-level rooms have
nine-foot ceilings. To the rear of the
plan is the family room. It has
bookcases surrounding a fireplace.
French doors lead into the den with
a stunning window. The master
suite is located on the first floor
and has a most elegant bath and a
huge walk-in closet. Second-floor
bedrooms also have walk-in closets
and private baths.

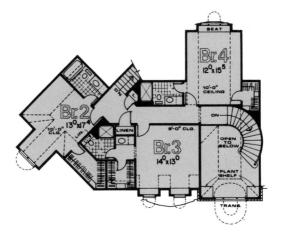

Design by
Design
Basics,
Inc.

119

Design by
Larry W.
Garnett &
Associates, Inc.

Design DD9085

First Floor: 2,467 square feet
Second Floor: 710 square feet
Total: 3,177 square feet

● With dramatic transitional appeal this brick two-story home has a floor plan that is impressive. From the central foyer, go left to a sunken living room with a view of the formal dining room. A gameroom adjoins the U-shaped kitchen with attached breakfast nook. To the right is the master bedroom suite with twelve-foot ceiling and luxury bath. Note the access to the courtyard from this room as well as from the gameroom. Guest quarters lie to the rear of the first-floor plan. A curving staircase to the second floor leads to two additional bedrooms which share a full bath. The upstairs balcony overlooks the foyer below.

Guest
Quarters
11' x 13'

Bath 2

3-Car Garage

Breakfast
10' x 10'

French Door

Util.

Wet Bar

Kitchen
14' x 13'

Gameroom
20'-4" x 14'-8"
Volume Clg.

Courtyard

Pantry

French Doors

Dining
13'-4" x 11'-4"

42" High Wall

Porch

French Doors

Foyer

Bath
Barrel
Vaulted
Clg.

Sunken
Living Room
17' x 17'-4"
14' Clg.

Master Bedroom
14' x 21'
12' Clg.

Mirrored
Doors

10' Clg. Throughout First Floor
Unless Otherwise Noted

Bedroom 3
16' x 14'

Stor.

Gameroom Below

Bath 3

Bedroom 2
11' x 14'

Foyer Below

WIDTH 55'
DEPTH 78'-8"

9' Clg. Throughout Second Floor

SAN FRANCISCO VICTORIAN *and* FOLK DESIGNS

IN THE LATE 19TH CENTURY, America's industrialization had a dramatic impact on home construction and design. The introduction of "balloon framing," using light two-inch boards held together with wire nails, and the expanded availability of building materials opened a whole world of style possibilities for those romantic homes we know as Victorians. There must be something in all of us that identifies with these classic American beauties, much like the sense of familiarity and recognition we experience when browsing through antique family scrapbooks, studying the sepia photographs of our ancestors.

Touted as the Gilded Age, the Victorian era was one of enormous energy. Perhaps it is that fresh energy that found its elaboration in these dwellings of larger scale, freer design and more elaborate details.

The Victorian cycle was officially begun with the Second Empire style. These homes were designed with a dual-pitched hip roof and featured dormer windows on the steep lower slope. Molded cornices and decorative brackets beneath the eaves provided its ornamentation.

The Stick style, actually the transitional style which linked the early Gothic Revival with the Queen Anne style, was noted for its steeply pitched gable roof and stickwork raised from the surface of the walls as shown in Design DD3385.

Perhaps the most popular and enduring style was the Queen Anne, introduced to America by architect Henry Hobson Richardson. Designs DD9012 and DD9014 help to define the characteristics of this delightful style. These unique, multi-story houses are irregular in shape, have a steeply pitched roof also of irregular shape, and usually employ a dominant front-facing gable. They have a variety of surface textures, materials and colors including patterned shingles. Bay windows and windows of various shapes are common, as are turrets and big chimneys. A one-story partial or full-width porch that wraps around one or both side walls is common. San Francisco's "painted ladies" offer some of the most imaginative examples of Queen Anne Victorians.

The Shingle style layered the exterior wall and roof with continuous wood shingles; or sometimes the shingled wall appeared on the second story only. These designs were uniquely American adaptions, usually a free-form and variable style with a steeply pitched roof, and cross gables. Designs DD9420 and DD9277 provide a contemporary spin to such unique shingle detailing.

Folk Victorians made new use of the spindlework and jigsaw-cut trims of other Victorians. These pre-railroad folk houses "dressed up in the clothes" of the Italianate or Queen Anne designs and sported fancy fretwork and newly added appendages to a basic folk cottage. The charming accents of the Folk Victorian are demonstrated in Designs DD9009 and DD2974.

The Victorian versions in this section are reminiscent of yesteryear, but with the modern amenities and sophistication of the best interior designs. Thankfully, we need not say farewell to that golden era.

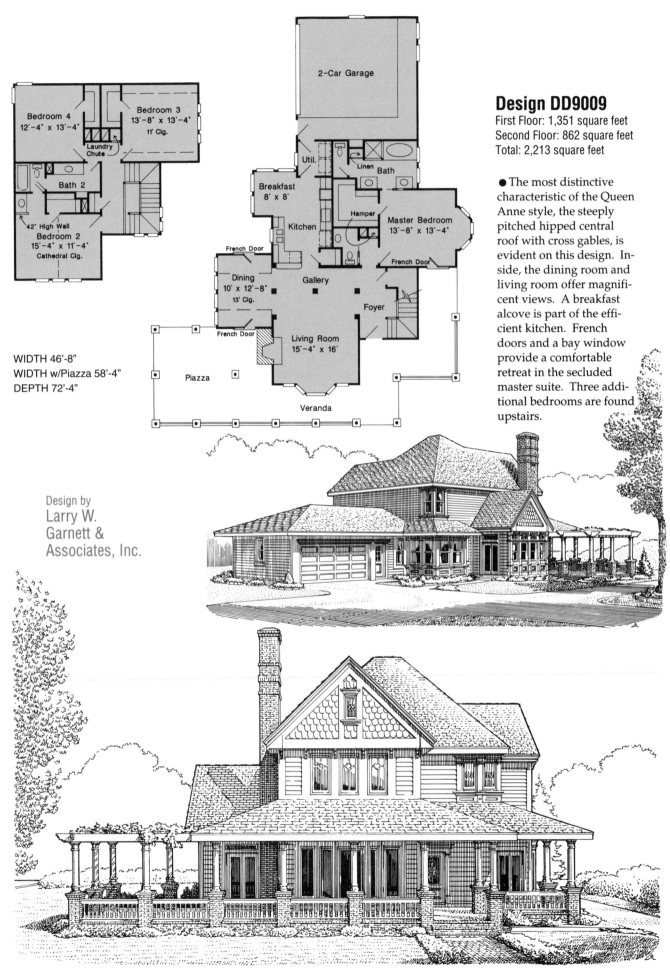

Bedroom 4
12'-4" x 13'-4"

Bedroom 3
13'-8" x 13'-4"
11' Clg.

Laundry Chute

Bath 2

42" High Wall

Bedroom 2
15'-4" x 11'-4"
Cathedral Clg.

2-Car Garage

Util.

Linen   Bath

Breakfast
8' x 8'

Kitchen

Hamper

Master Bedroom
13'-8" x 13'-4"

French Door

French Door

Dining
10' x 12'-8"
13' Clg.

Gallery

Foyer

French Door

Living Room
15'-4" x 16'

Piazza

Veranda

WIDTH 46'-8"
WIDTH w/Piazza 58'-4"
DEPTH 72'-4"

Design by
Larry W.
Garnett &
Associates, Inc.

Design DD9009

First Floor: 1,351 square feet
Second Floor: 862 square feet
Total: 2,213 square feet

● The most distinctive characteristic of the Queen Anne style, the steeply pitched hipped central roof with cross gables, is evident on this design. Inside, the dining room and living room offer magnificent views. A breakfast alcove is part of the efficient kitchen. French doors and a bay window provide a comfortable retreat in the secluded master suite. Three additional bedrooms are found upstairs.

Design DD9067

First Floor: 1,999 square feet
Second Floor: 933 square feet
Total: 2,932 square feet

● The wraparound veranda and simple lines give this home an unassuming elegance that is characteristic of its Folk Victorian heritage. Opening directly to the formal dining room, the two-story foyer offers extra space for large dinner parties. Double French doors lead to the study with raised paneling and a cozy fireplace. Built-in bookcases conceal a hidden security vault. The private master suite features a corner garden tub, glass-enclosed shower and a walk-in closet. Overlooking the family room and built-in breakfast nook is the central kitchen. A rear staircase provides convenient access to the second floor from the family room. The balcony provides a view of the foyer below and the Palladian window. Three additional bedrooms complete this exquisite home.

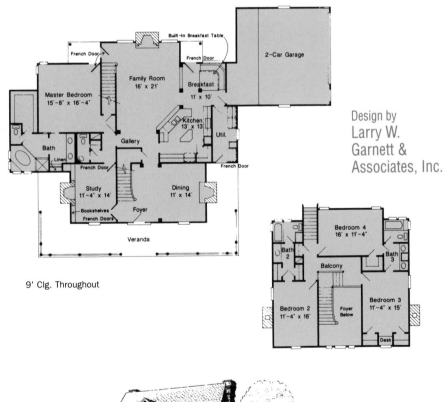

9' Clg. Throughout

Design by
Larry W.
Garnett &
Associates, Inc.

REAR VIEW

WIDTH 79' 8"
DEPTH 59'

Design DD9012

First Floor: 1,357 square feet
Second Floor: 1,079 square feet
Total: 2,436 square feet

● An inviting wraparound veranda with delicate spindlework and a raised turret with leaded-glass windows recall the grand Queen Anne Victorians of the late 1880s. Double doors open from the dramatic two-story foyer to a private study with built-in bookcases and a bay window. The gallery, with decorative wood columns and an arched ceiling, overlooks both the large formal dining and living rooms. French doors open from the living room to the front veranda and to the screened porch. A fireplace adds warmth to the breakfast area and the island kitchen. Above the two-car garage is an optional area that is perfect for a home office or guest quarters. Upstairs, the master suite, with His and Hers walk-in closets, leads to a luxurious bath with a garden tub and glass-enclosed shower. An optional exercise loft and plant shelves complete this elegant master bath. Two additional bedrooms, one with a private deck and the other with a cathedral ceiling, share a dressing area and bath.

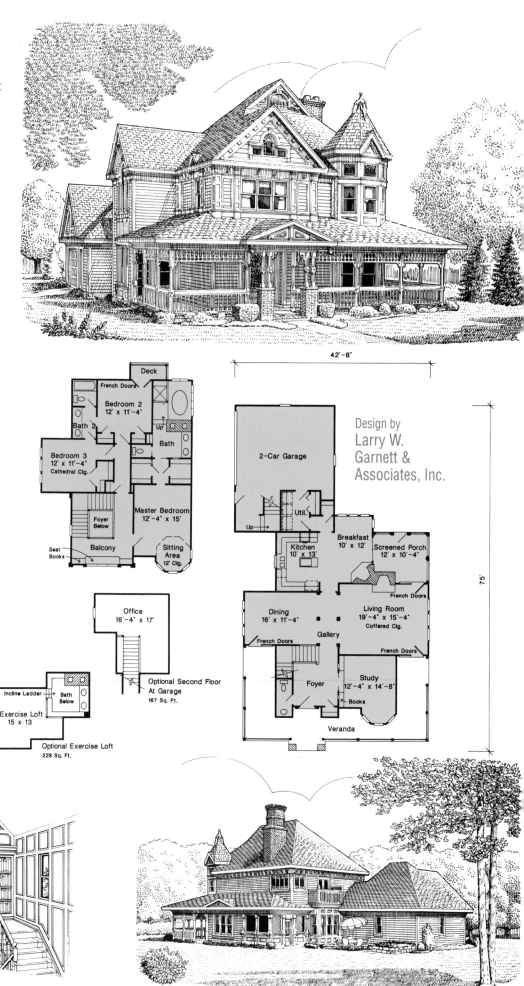

Deck

French Doors

Bedroom 2
12' x 11'-4"

Bath 2

Bath

Bedroom 3
12' x 11'-4"
Cathedral Clg.

Master Bedroom
12'-4" x 15'

Foyer Below

Balcony

Seat
Books

Sitting Area
12' Clg.

Office
16'-4" x 17'

Optional Second Floor At Garage
167 Sq. Ft.

Incline Ladder

Bath Below

Exercise Loft
15 x 13

Optional Exercise Loft
228 Sq. Ft.

42'-8"

Design by
Larry W. Garnett & Associates, Inc.

2-Car Garage

Util.

Up

Kitchen
10' x 13'

Breakfast
10' x 12'

Screened Porch
12' x 10'-4"

French Doors

Dining
16' x 11'-4"

Living Room
19'-4" x 15'-4"
Coffered Clg.

Gallery

French Doors

French Doors

Foyer

Study
12'-4" x 14'-8"

Books

Veranda

75'

124

Design DD9015

First Floor: 1,948 square feet
Second Floor: 1,891 square feet
Total: 3,839 square feet

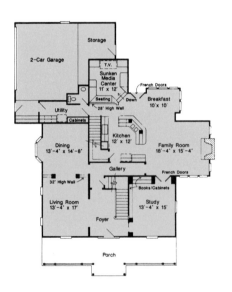

Width 59' - 4"
Depth 72' - 8"

Design by
Larry W.
Garnett &
Associates, Inc.

● As authentic as the exterior of this design is, the interior offers all the luxury and elegance that today's homeowners could desire. The formal living and dining rooms are separated by detailed wood columns. Built-in bookcases and cabinets highlight the block-paneled study. The centrally located kitchen becomes the focal point of a truly outstanding family living center which includes a sunken media area, breakfast alcove, and a family room with a fireplace. Adjacent to the kitchen is a large hobby room with a built-in desk, a space for a freezer, and generous cabinet storage. A rear staircase provides convenient access to the second floor. The secluded master suite is beyond compare, with such extras as a fireplace with flanking window seats and cabinets, an enormous walk-in closet, and a private deck. The luxurious bath features a dressing table, a whirlpool tub with a gazebo-shaped ceiling above, and an oversized shower. Finally, there is a private exercise room with a bay-window seat. Three additional bedrooms and a laundry room complete the second floor. A staircase leads to an optional third floor area.

2-Car Garage

Porch

French Door

Storage

Breakfast
10' x 10'

Util.

Pantry

Media Center

Kitchen
16' x 10'

Family Room
18'-4" x 14'-8"

Desk Below
Landing

Seating

Dining
11'-4" x 13'

Study
12'-8" x 10'

Foyer

French Door

Living Room
14'-8" x 12'-8"

Porch

Arbor

WIDTH 46'-6"
DEPTH 65'-8"

10' Ceilings Throughout
First Floor

Bedroom 4
12' x 11'

Bedroom 3
13' x 11'

Bath 3

32" High
Cabinet

Linen

Bath 2

Seat

Bedroom 2
12' x 13'

Bath

Linen

Alcove
10' x 7'

Master Bedroom
20'-4" x 14'-4"

9' Ceilings Throughout Second Floor

Design by
Larry W.
Garnett &
Associates, Inc.

Design DD9056

First Floor: 1,354 square feet
Second Floor: 1,418 square feet
Total: 2,772 square feet

● Inside this charming turn-of-the-century design, classical columns separate the foyer and dining room. A French door opens from the living room to a lattice-covered side arbor. Double doors in both the living and family rooms provide access to a bay-windowed study with built-in bookcases and desk. The large family room contains a fireplace, media cabinet and a serving bar open from the kitchen. A six-foot curved picture window offers a full view of the rear porch from the breakfast and kitchen areas. Upstairs, the master suite features an elegant bath with a garden tub inset in a bay window, and a walk-in closet. Bedrooms 3 and 4 share a bath, while Bedroom 2 has a private bath and a bay-windowed alcove.

Design DD9014

First Floor: 1,565 square feet
Second Floor: 1,598 square feet
Total: 3,163 square feet

● The angled entry of this home opens to a grand foyer and a formal parlor with expansive windows and a French door leading to the side yard. The formal dining area features a built-in hutch. Double French doors open from the foyer to the large study with bookcases and full-length windows. The spacious family room with a fireplace and wet bar is a superb entertainment area. The kitchen with its work island and abundant cabinet space overlooks the octagon-shaped breakfast room. Upstairs, the master bedroom has French doors which open onto a rear deck. The distinctive bath features a bay-windowed tub area and glass enclosed shower. Three additional bedrooms each have walk-in closets. Plans for two-car detached garage are included.

Design by
Larry W.
Garnett &
Associates, Inc.

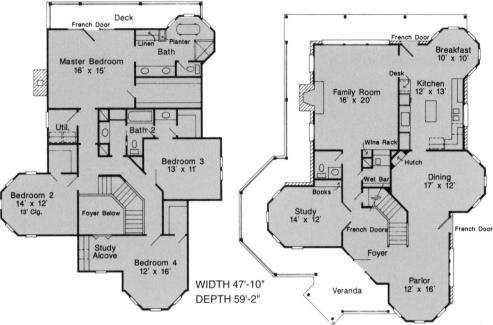

Deck

French Door

Master Bedroom
16' x 15'

Linen   Planter
Bath

Util.

Bath 2

Bedroom 3
13' x 11'

Bedroom 2
14' x 12'
13' Clg.

Foyer Below

Study
Alcove

Bedroom 4
12' x 16'

WIDTH 47'-10"
DEPTH 59'-2"

French Door

Breakfast
10' x 10'

Desk

Family Room
16' x 20'

Kitchen
12' x 13'

Wine Rack

Hutch

Wet Bar

Dining
17' x 12'

Books

Study
14' x 12'

French Doors

Foyer

French Door

Veranda

Parlor
12' x 16'

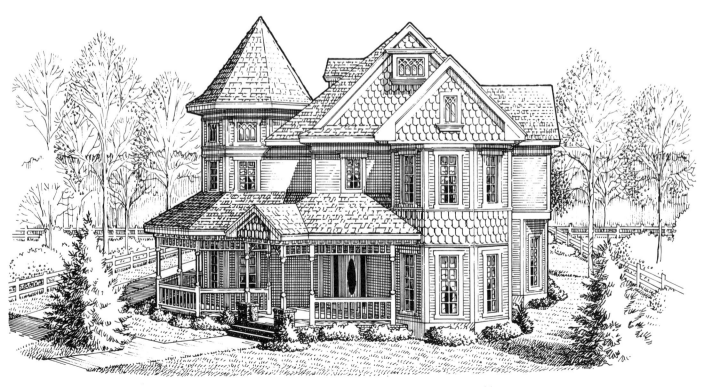

127

Design DD2973

First Floor: 1,269 square feet
Second Floor: 1,227 square feet
Total: 2,496 square feet

● A most popular feature of the Victorian house has always been its covered porches. These finely detailed outdoor living spaces may be found on the front, the side, the rear or even in all three locations at once. The two designs on these two pages show just that. In addition to being an appealing exterior design feature, covered porches have their practical side, too. They provide wonderful indoor-outdoor living relationships. This home has a myriad of features to cater to the living requirements of the growing, active family. For information on customizing this design, call 1-800-521-6797, ext. 800.

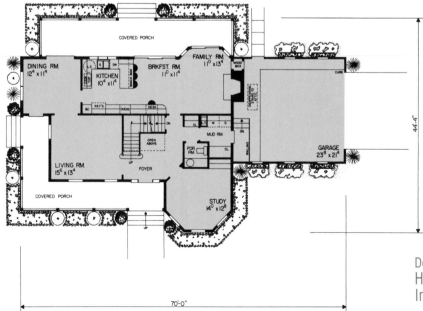

QUOTE ONE™

Cost to build? See page 216 to order complete cost estimate to build this house in your area!

Design by
Home Planners,
Inc.

Design DD2974 First Floor: 911 square feet
Second Floor: 861 square feet; Total: 1,772 square feet

● Victorian houses are well known for their orientation on narrow building sites. And when this occurs nothing is lost to captivating exterior styling. This house is but 38 feet wide. Its narrow width belies the tremendous amount of livability found inside. And, of course, the ubiquitous porch/veranda contributes mightily to style as well as livability. The efficient, U-shape kitchen is flanked by the informal breakfast room and formal dining room. The rear living area is spacious and functions in an exciting manner with the outdoor areas. Bonus recreational, hobby and storage space is offered by the basement and the attic.

QUOTE ONE™

Cost to build? See page 216 to order complete cost estimate to build this house in your area!

Design by
Home Planners, Inc.

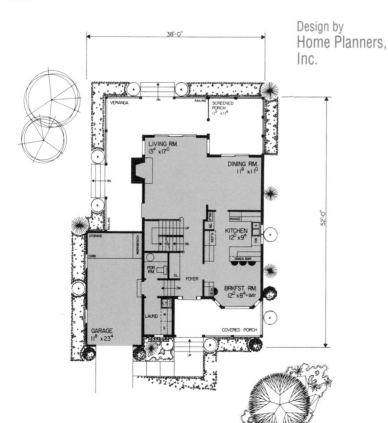

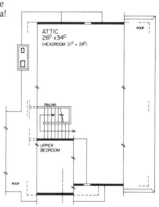

● Covered porches front and rear are the first signal that this is a fine example of Folk Victorian styling. Complementing the exterior is a grand plan for family living. A formal living room and attached dining room provide space for entertaining guests. The large family room with fireplace is a gathering room for everyday. Both areas have access to outdoor spaces. Four bedrooms occupy the second floor. The master suite features two lavatories, a window seat and three closets. One of the family bedrooms has its own private balcony and could be used as a study. Note the open staircase and convenient linen storage.

Design DD3385

First Floor: 1,096 square feet
Second Floor: 900 square feet
Total: 1,996 square feet

QUOTE ONE™

Cost to build? See page 216 to order complete cost estimate to build this house in your area!

Width 56'
Depth 44'

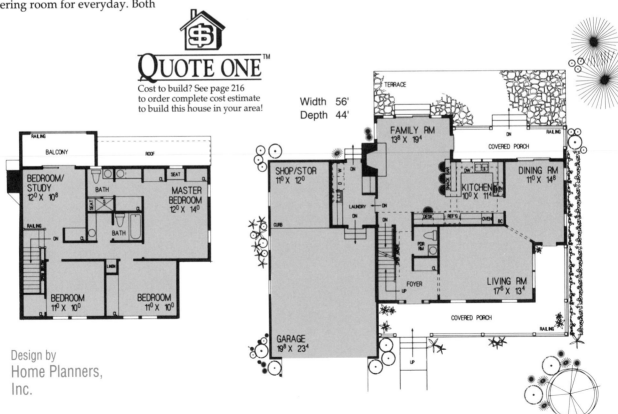

Design by
Home Planners,
Inc.

Design DD3309

First Floor: 1,375 square feet
Second Floor: 1,016 square feet
Total: 2,391 square feet

QUOTE ONE™

Cost to build? See page 216
to order complete cost estimate
to build this house in your area!

● Covered porches, front and back, are
a fine preview to the livable nature of
this Victorian. Living areas are defined
in a family room with fireplace, formal
living and dining rooms, and a kitchen
with breakfast room. An ample laundry
room, garage with storage area, and
powder room round out the first floor.
Three second floor bedrooms are joined
by a study and two full baths.

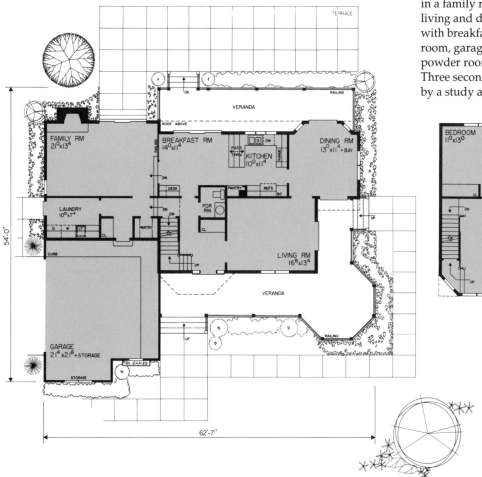

Design by
Home Planners,
Inc.

131

Design DD2970 First Floor: 1,538 square feet
Second Floor: 1,526 square feet; Third Floor: 658 square feet
Total: 3,722 square feet

● A porch, is a porch, is a porch. But, when it wraps around to a side, or even two sides, of the house, we have called it a veranda. This charming Victorian features a covered outdoor living area on all four sides! It even ends at a screened porch which features a sun deck above. This interesting plan offers three floors of livability. And what livability it is! Plenty of formal and informal living facilities to go along with the potential of five bedrooms. The master suite is just that. It is adjacent to an interesting sitting room. It has a sun deck and excellent bath/personal care facilities. The third floor will make a wonderful haven for the family's student members.

QUOTE ONE™

Cost to build? See page 216 to order complete cost estimate to build this house in your area!

Design by
Home Planners, Inc.

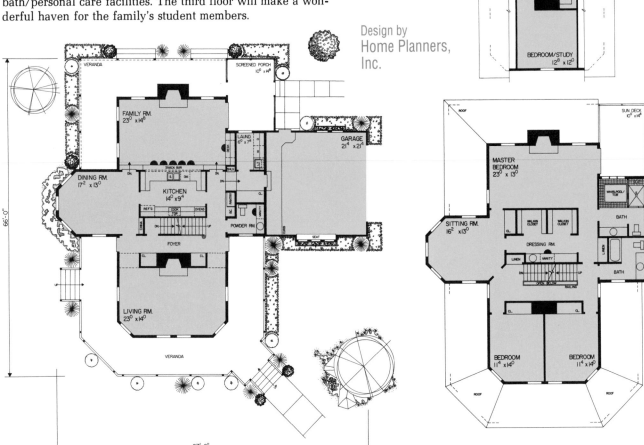

● A magnificent, finely wrought covered porch wraps around this impressive Victorian estate home. The gracious two-story foyer provides a direct view past the stylish bannister and into the great room with large central fireplace. To the left of the foyer is a bookshelf-lined library and to the right is a dramatic, octagonal-shaped dining room. The island cooktop completes a convenient work triangle in the kitchen, and a pass-through connects this room with the Victorian-style morning room. A butler's pantry, walk-in closet, and broom closet offer plenty of storage space. A luxurious master suite is located on the first floor and opens to the rear covered porch. A through-fireplace warms the bedroom, sitting room, and dressing room, which includes His and Hers walk-in closets. The step-up whirlpool tub is an elegant focal point to the master bath. Four uniquely designed bedrooms, three full baths, and a restful lounge with fireplace are located on the second floor. Who says you can't combine the absolute best of today's amenities with the quaint styling and comfortable warmth of the Victorian past!

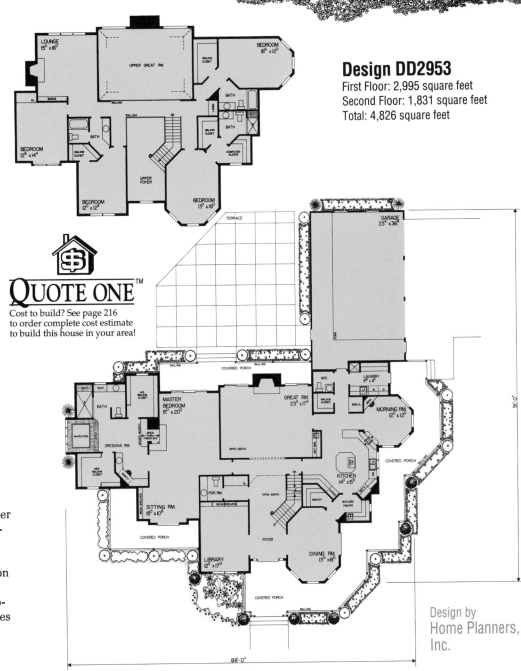

Design DD2953
First Floor: 2,995 square feet
Second Floor: 1,831 square feet
Total: 4,826 square feet

QUOTE ONE™
Cost to build? See page 216 to order complete cost estimate to build this house in your area!

Design by
Home Planners, Inc.

Design DD9420

First Floor: 1,587 square feet
Second Floor: 716 square feet
Bonus Room: 427 square feet
Total: 2,730 square feet

Design by
Alan Mascord
Design Associates, Inc.

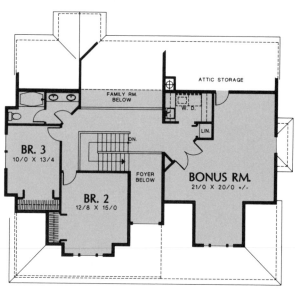

◄ 54' ►

▲
49'
▼

● This compact Victorian home has its fully featured master bedroom on the main floor. A wraparound porch with a pair of French doors leading from the dining room complements the facade. The upper hallway overlooks the vaulted family room on one side and the two-story foyer on the other. A bonus room over the garage allows some expansion space to either add another bedroom or a game room.

Design by
Alan Mascord
Design Associates, Inc.

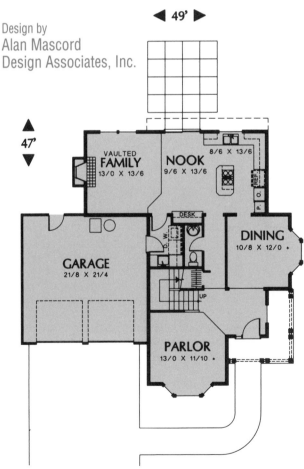

◀ 49' ▶

▲
47'
▼

VAULTED
FAMILY
13/0 X 13/6

NOOK
9/6 X 13/6

8/6 X 13/6

REF.

P. O.

DESK

DINING
10/8 X 12/0

GARAGE
21/8 X 21/4

UP

PARLOR
13/0 X 11/10

Design DD9475

First Floor: 1,085 square feet
Second Floor: 1,110 square feet
Total: 2,195 square feet

● Farmhouse design is popular throughout the country—this plan is an outstanding example. The corner entry leads to a formal parlor on the left and dining room on the right. To the rear of the first floor are the family room with fireplace and island kitchen with nook. The stairs are centrally located and a nearby powder room will be appreciated by guests. Upstairs are four bedrooms (or three and a den). The master bedroom has a vaulted ceiling and lovely private bath.

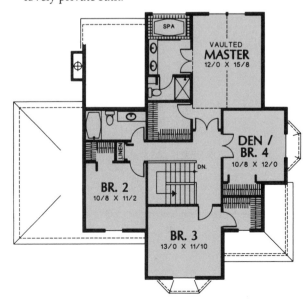

SPA

VAULTED
MASTER
12/0 X 15/8

LINEN

DEN /
BR. 4
10/8 X 12/0

BR. 2
10/8 X 11/2

DN.

BR. 3
13/0 X 11/10

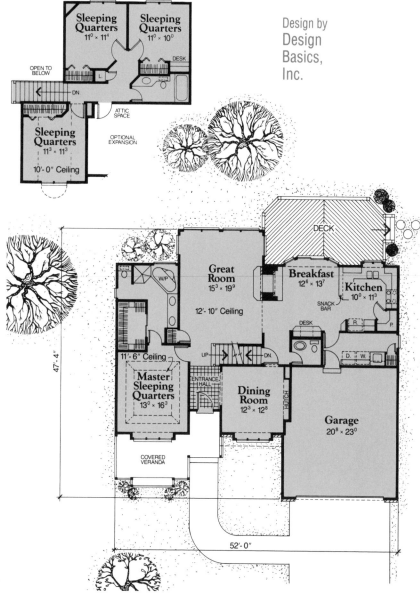

Sleeping Quarters
11⁰ × 11⁴

Sleeping Quarters
11⁰ × 10⁰

OPEN TO BELOW

DESK

DN.

ATTIC SPACE

Sleeping Quarters
11³ × 11³

OPTIONAL EXPANSION

10'- 0" Ceiling

Design by
Design Basics, Inc.

Design DD9288

First Floor: 1,421 square feet
Second Floor: 578 square feet
Total: 1,999 square feet

● Victorian details and a covered veranda lend peaceful flavor to the elevation of this popular home. A volume entry hall views the formal dining room and luxurious great room. Imagine the comfort of relaxing in the great room which features a 12'-10" ceiling and abundant windows! The kitchen/breakfast area includes a through fireplace, snack bar, walk-in pantry and wrapping counters. The secondary sleeping quarters have special amenities unique to each. A secluded main-floor master sleeping quarters features a vaulted ceiling, luxurious dressing/bath area and corner whirlpool tub. At 1,999 square feet, this home truly captures the simpler lifestyle of yesteryear!

DECK

Great Room
15³ × 19⁹

12'- 10" Ceiling

W/P

Breakfast
12⁶ × 13⁷

Kitchen
10⁰ × 11³

SNACK BAR

DESK

R

P

11'- 6" Ceiling

Master Sleeping Quarters
13⁰ × 16³

UP

DN.

D W.

ENTRANCE HALL

Dining Room
12³ × 12⁸

HUTCH

Garage
20⁸ × 23⁰

47'- 4"

COVERED VERANDA

52'- 0"

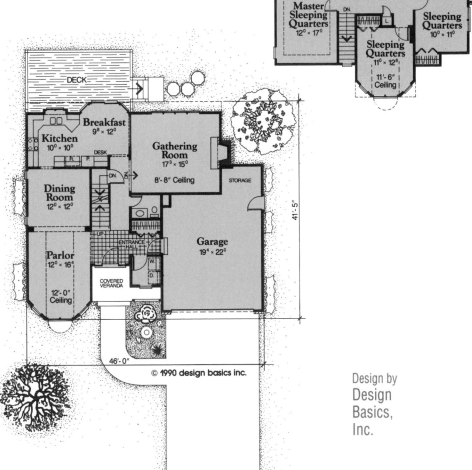

Design DD9270

First Floor: 1,113 square feet
Second Floor: 965 square feet
Total: 2,078 square feet

● Elegant detail, a charming veranda and the tall brick chimney create a pleasing facade on this four-bedroom Victorian home. Yesterday's simpler lifestyle is reflected throughout this plan. A large bayed parlor with sloped ceiling is visible from the entry. Step down to enter the gathering room with a fireplace and plenty of windows. Note the pantry cabinet and built-in desk in the kitchen and breakfast area. The formal dining room opens to the parlor for entertaining ease. The second-floor master suite is segregated for privacy and provides a dressing and bath area with double lavatories, skylight and whirlpool tub.

Design by
**Design
Basics,
Inc.**

Design DD9251

First Floor: 1,653 square feet
Second Floor: 700 square feet
Total: 2,353 square feet

● Beautiful arches and elaborate detail give the elevation of this four-bedroom, 1½-story home an unmistakable elegance. Inside the floor plan is equally appealing. Note the formal dining room with bay window, visible from the entrance hall. The large great room has a fireplace and a wall of windows out the back. A hearth room, with bookcase, adjoins the kitchen area with walk-in pantry. The master suite on the first floor features His and Hers wardrobes, a large whirlpool and double lavatories. Upstairs quarters share a full bath with compartmented sinks.

Design by
Design Basics, Inc.

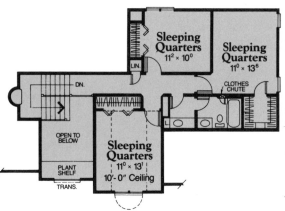

© 1990 design basics inc.

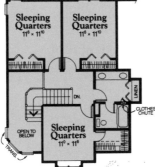

Design DD9277

First Floor: 1,553 square feet
Second Floor: 725 square feet
Total: 2,278 square feet

● The intricate detailing, tall brick chimney and stately veranda on the elevation of this four-bedroom, 1½-story home blend effortlessly into Victorian elegance. Other preferred features include: two-story entrance hall, bay window in formal dining room, open island kitchen with pantry and desk, private master suite with vaulted ceiling, two-person whirlpool in master bath. This versatile plan is designed for practical living with guest rooms or children's bedrooms located on the upper level. One of these second-story bedrooms has a walk-in closet.

Design by
Design
Basics,
Inc.

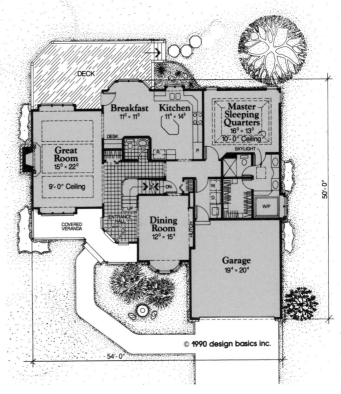

Design DD9268

First Floor: 1,308 square feet; Second Floor: 1,107 square feet; Total: 2,415 square feet

Design by
Design
Basics,
Inc.

● Embellished with interesting detail, this four-bedroom, two-story home offers an alternative to the ordinary. The covered veranda welcomes all to a marvelous floor plan. Thoughtful amenities include a dining room with added hutch space, a bay window in the parlor, a large gathering room with fireplace and plenty of windows and a featured-filled kitchen. The luxurious master bedroom has a vaulted ceiling and pampering bath with whirlpool, double lavatories and two closets. Three secondary bedrooms share a full bath with double lavatories.

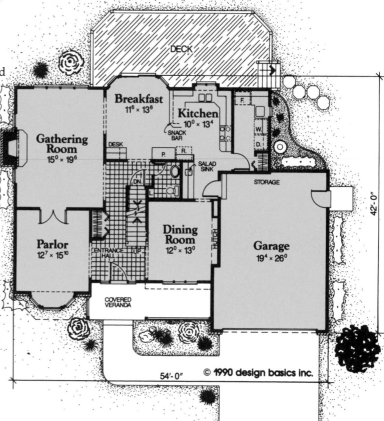

CALIFORNIA CRAFTSMAN *and* REGIONAL BUNGALOWS

THE EARLY 20TH CENTURY promised the American family a new style of living, thus the homeowner's revolution was born. This new form of construction allowed for the expression of the modern American spirit as well as the realization of the American Dream. The ground-breaking practice of relating interior and exterior space was being discovered, along with a new understanding of the nature of building materials.

From sea to shining sea, one of America's most enduring home styles—the bungalow—gained popularity in the shore communities of both the East and West coasts. There were several reasons why this style was so largely favored, but primarily it was due to its smaller size (making it more affordable) and the unadorned versatility that characterized its exterior.

Details helped transform the bungalow from log-cabin rustic to continental-looking Swiss chalet, but the form was fairly consistent—a small, one-story home exhibiting either an open or enclosed porch. Design DD3314 provides a glimpse of the Tudor influence, while two-story Design DD9666 exhibits the rustic feel of a cabin in the woods. The bungalow provided an ideal answer to the milder climates and informal lifestyle of both coasts. Design DD9131 displays the shingled exterior of the bungalows often found in resort regions. Throughout construction, the natural quality of materials was emphasized. Evidence of the more conventional features of the bungalow is found in Design DD3496, while Design DD9898 exhibits a more formal approach in its styling.

The Craftsman-style bungalows that were designed from the late 1800s through the early 1900s were essentially the brainchildren of two brothers from Pasadena, California, Charles Sumner and Henry Mather Greene. Their homes exemplified simplicity of design and the true integrity of craftsmanship. The clean, simple lines of the Arts and Crafts movement greatly influenced their development. The styles produced by these two brothers received a great deal of attention through a series of pattern books which offered pre-cut packages of lumber and details. These early kits made it easy to have homes assembled by local labor, and the distribution and broad exposure of pattern books soon made the Craftsman style the most popular and fashionable of the smaller homes in the country.

For the most part, classic Craftsman-style homes have a low-pitched gable roof and exposed roof rafters. Decorative beams and full or partial porches are supported by short, square upper columns with bases or pedestals extending to the ground. Designs DD3316 and DD3313 offer excellent examples of traditional Craftsman-style architecture, while DD8065 yields a contemporary twist to this classic favorite.

The designs displayed in this section represent the "spirit" of the American Bungalow and Craftsman Home—now made ultimately more livable and comfortable by contemporary interiors and amenities.

Design DD3314

Square Footage: 1,951

● Formal living areas in this
plan are joined by a sleeping
wing that holds three bedrooms.
Two verandas and a screened
porch enlarge the plan and
enhance indoor/outdoor livability. Notice the abundant storage
space.

Design by
Home Planners,
Inc.

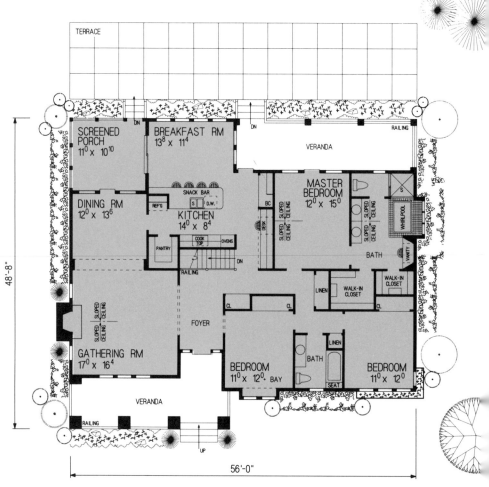

QUOTE ONE™

Cost to build? See page 216
to order complete cost estimate
to build this house in your area!

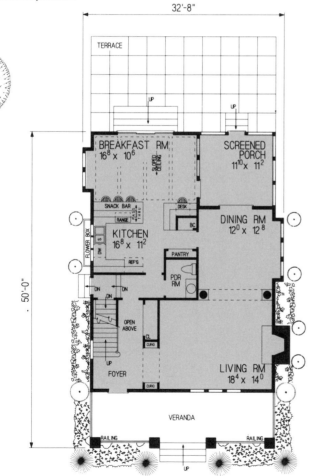

TERRACE

UP   UP

BREAKFAST RM.
16⁸ x 10⁶

SCREENED PORCH
11¹⁰ x 11²

SNACK BAR

RANGE

DESK

BC

DINING RM.
12⁰ x 12⁸

KITCHEN
16⁸ x 11²

DW

REF'G

FLOWER BOX

PANTRY

PDR RM

S

DN   DN

OPEN ABOVE

CL

CURIO

FOYER

LIVING RM.
18⁴ x 14⁰

CURIO

DN

UP

VERANDA

RAILING   RAILING

UP

32'-8"

50'-0"

Design DD3316

First Floor: 1,111 square feet
Second Floor: 886 square feet
Total: 1,997 square feet

● Don't be fooled by a small-looking exterior. This
plan offers three bedrooms and plenty of living space.
Notice that the screened porch leads to a rear terrace
with access to the breakfast room. A living room/dining
room combination adds spaciousness to the first floor.

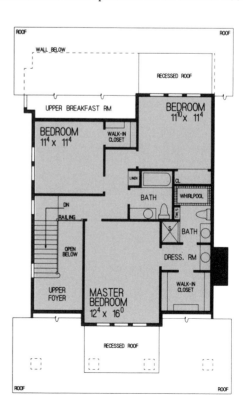

ROOF   ROOF

WALL BELOW

RECESSED ROOF

UPPER BREAKFAST RM.

BEDROOM
11¹⁰ x 11⁴

BEDROOM
11⁴ x 11⁴

WALK-IN CLOSET

LINEN   CL

BATH

WHIRLPOOL

DN

RAILING

BATH

S

OPEN BELOW

DRESS. RM.

UPPER FOYER

MASTER BEDROOM
12⁴ x 16⁰

WALK-IN CLOSET

RECESSED ROOF

ROOF   ROOF

Design by
Home Planners,
Inc.

Design DD3496
Square Footage: 2,033

Design by
Home Planners,
Inc.

● Get more out of your homebuilding dollars with this unique one-story bungalow. A covered front porch provides sheltered entry into a spacious living room. Here, glass block accents and a wet bar shared with the living area provide special touches. The dining room enjoys a cathedral ceiling and an eight-foot wall with a plant shelf separating the kitchen. An island workspace with a cooktop is included to make kitchen tasks easy, as is a ceiling-mounted swivel TV that may be enjoyed from the breakfast area or the morning room. A rear deck provides outdoor enjoyment and can be accessed from the morning room as well as the master bedroom. The large master suite pampers with a sitting area and a luxurious bath which features a corner tub, a separate shower and dual lavatories. Glass block and clerestory glass add finishing touches. The first floor contains two additional bedrooms sharing a full bath. For information on customizing this design, call 1-800-521-6797, ext. 800.

Width 47'-6"
Depth 65'-6"

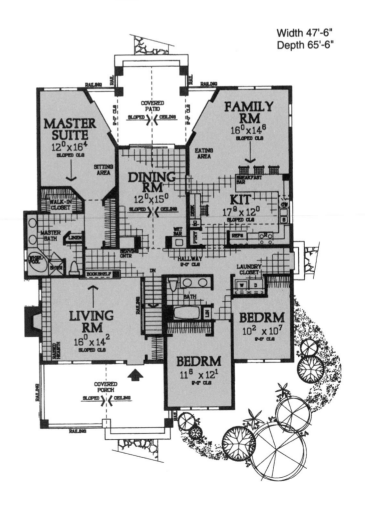

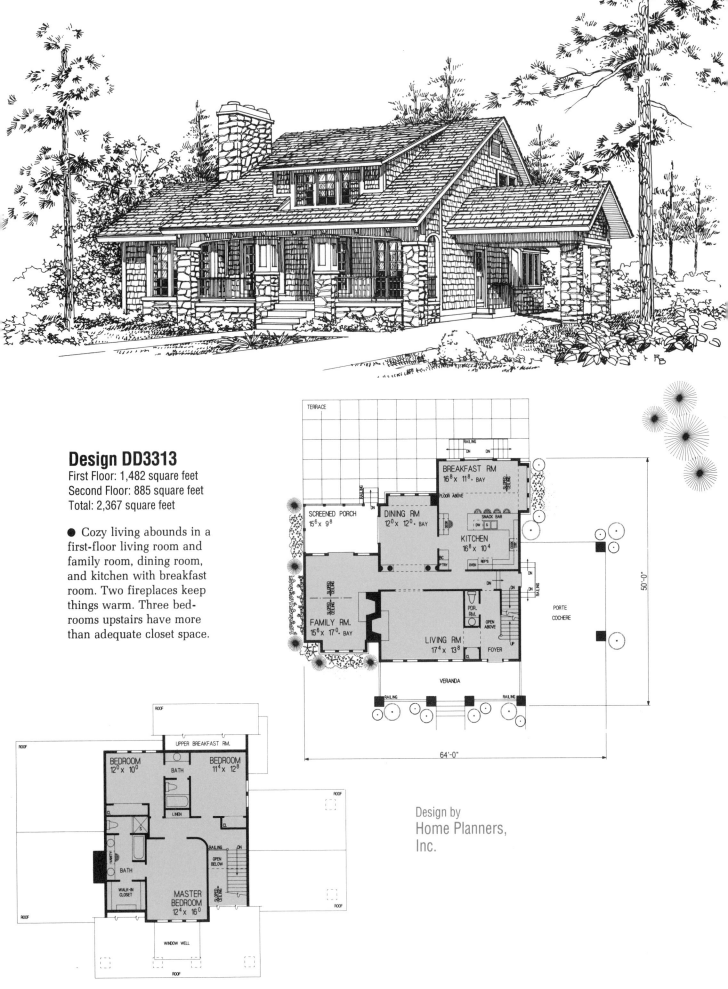

Design DD3313

First Floor: 1,482 square feet
Second Floor: 885 square feet
Total: 2,367 square feet

● Cozy living abounds in a
first-floor living room and
family room, dining room,
and kitchen with breakfast
room. Two fireplaces keep
things warm. Three bed-
rooms upstairs have more
than adequate closet space.

Design by
Home Planners,
Inc.

145

Design DD9185

Square Footage: 1,567

● Square columns supported by brick pedestals and a low-pitched roof are reminiscent of the Craftsman style brought to popularity in the early 1900s. Livability is the foremost consideration in this well-designed plan. To the left of the foyer is the cozy living room, warmed by an inviting fireplace. Straight ahead, the dining room shares space with an efficient, step-saving kitchen. A French door provides access to a covered porch for outdoor meals and entertaining. To the rear of the plan rests the master suite. The master bath is highlighted by a tub and a separate shower, a double-bowl vanity, a compartmented toilet and a large walk-in closet. Two family bedrooms, a full bath and a utility room with a linen closet complete this marvelous plan.

Design by
Larry W.
Garnett &
Associates, Inc.

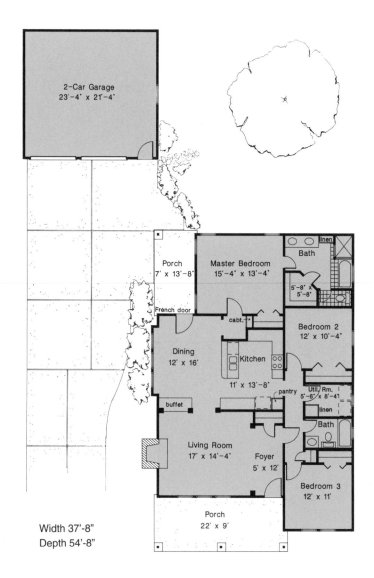

Width 37'-8"
Depth 54'-8"

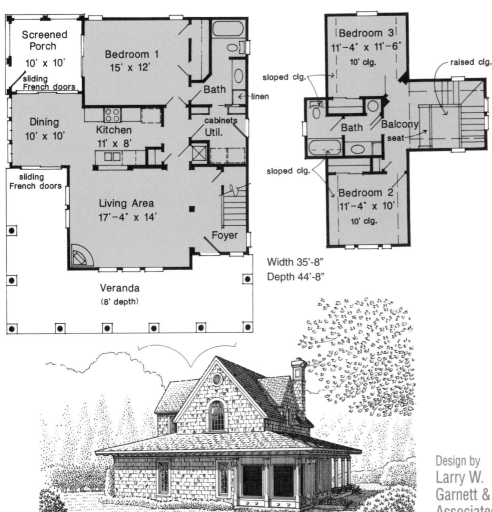

Screened Porch
10' x 10'

sliding French doors

Bedroom 1
15' x 12'

Bath

linen

Dining
10' x 10'

cabinets

Kitchen
11' x 8'

Util.

sliding French doors

Living Area
17'-4" x 14'

Foyer

Veranda
(8' depth)

Bedroom 3
11'-4" x 11'-6"
10' clg.

raised clg.

sloped clg.

Bath

Balcony
seat

sloped clg.

Bedroom 2
11'-4" x 10'
10' clg.

Width 35'-8"
Depth 44'-8"

Design DD9131

First Floor: 978 square feet
Second Floor: 464 square feet
Total: 1,442 square feet

● From the covered front veranda to the second-story Palladian window, this home exudes warmth and grace. Though smaller in square footage, the floor plan offers plenty of room. The living area is complemented by a cozy corner fireplace and is attached to a dining area with French doors to a screened porch and the front veranda. The galley-style kitchen is the central hub of the first floor. A large bedroom on this floor has an attached full bath and serves equally well as guest bedroom or master bedroom. The second floor holds two bedrooms and another full bath. An open balcony area here overlooks the foyer below.

Design by
Larry W.
Garnett &
Associates, Inc.

147

◀ 48' ▶

COVERED PATIO

VAULTED NOOK
7/0 X 10/0

VAULTED MASTER
14/8 X 14/0 +/-

8/0 X 14/0

DINING
12/0 X 10/0

LINEN

BR. 2
12/0 X 10/0

VAULTED LIVING
12/0 X 13/0

BR. 3
9/6 X 12/8

GARAGE
19/4 X 21/8

▲ 48' ▼

P. REF.

Design by
Alan Mascord
Design Associates, Inc.

Design DD9439
Square Footage: 1,338

● This classic single-story home invites a second look—particularly for those who are planning to build for affordability. Special features make it attractive while budget-worthy: the living room, nook and master suite all contain vaulted ceilings; the covered patio provides outdoor enjoyment even in inclement weather. Notice that the living and dining areas remain open to each other—this creates a friendly atmosphere for entertaining. Of course, the fireplace in the living room adds additional warmth to the setting. Each of the family bedrooms enjoys ample closet space as well as lots of privacy. The master bedroom, opening through double doors, spotlights its own bath.

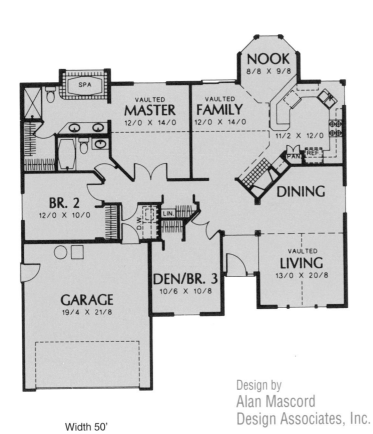

Width 50'
Depth 52'-10"

Design by
Alan Mascord
Design Associates, Inc.

Design DD9403
Square Footage: 1,565

● If you're looking for a traditional-styled ranch, this one with front-facing gables and a combination of cedar shingles and vertical cedar siding may be just right for you. The vaulted living room faces the street and is set off with a gorgeous Palladian window. The family room (note angled fireplace here) and master bedroom also have vaulted ceilings. Look for a spa tub, large shower and walk-in closet in the master bedroom. Through French doors in the entry is a den that could be used as a third bedroom.

Design DD9518

First Floor: 944 square feet
Second Floor: 1,013 square feet
Total: 1,957 square feet

● The true meaning of "less is more" is apparent in this two-story narrow lot home. Creative use of space makes this home appear much larger than it actually is. Enter the formal living areas—a bayed living room and a columned dining room—to the right of the foyer. Informal living areas occupy the rear of the plan. A family room with a warming fireplace shares space with an efficient, L-shaped kitchen with a cooktop island and a sunny eating nook that provides access to the rear grounds. The second floor contains the sleeping zone with three family bedrooms and the master suite. The master bedroom is highlighted by a vaulted ceiling and a walk-in closet. The master bath features a shower and a double-bowl vanity.

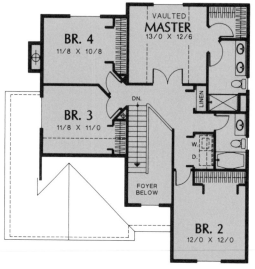

BR. 4
11/8 X 10/8

VAULTED
MASTER
13/0 X 12/6

BR. 3
11/8 X 11/0

DN.

LINEN

FOYER
BELOW

BR. 2
12/0 X 12/0

◄ 40' ►

Design by
Alan Mascord
Design Associates, Inc.

42'

FAMILY
14/0 X 12/8

NOOK
10/0 X 10/6

10/4 X 12/6

DESK

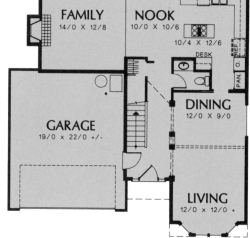

GARAGE
19/0 x 22/0 +/-

DINING
12/0 X 9/0

LIVING
12/0 x 12/0 +

◀ 36' ▶

NOOK
9/0 X 9/0

FAMILY
14/0 X 15/8

VAULTED
DINING
10/6 X 10/4

11/0 X 12/0

VAULTED
LIVING
14/8 X 14/0

UP

50'

GARAGE
19/4 X 21/8

PORCH

Design DD9519

First Floor: 913 square feet
Second Floor: 813 square feet
Total: 1,726 square feet

● Columns and pedestals form the inviting porch on this charming Craftsman-style home. The decorative styling of the pedestals is also extended to the garage and the dormered window above. Vaulted ceilings in the formal living room and dining room create a spacious, open feeling. Completing the first floor, a step-saving kitchen with a bumped-out nook and a family room with a fireplace offer the perfect space for informal family gatherings. Upstairs, the amenity-filled master suite provides a welcoming retreat. A soothing spa, dual lavs and a compartmented toilet with a shower complete the master bath. Two secondary bedrooms share a full bath, completing the second floor.

Design by
Alan Mascord
Design Associates, Inc.

BR. 3
11/10 X 10/0

BR. 2
11/10 X 10/0

DN.

VAULTED
MASTER
13/0 X 14/8 +/-

SPA

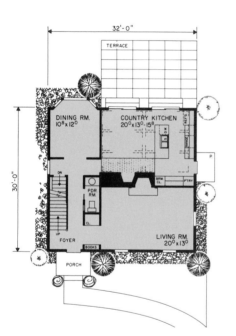

TERRACE

DINING RM.
10⁸ x 12⁰

COUNTRY KITCHEN
20⁰ x 13⁰-15⁸

32'-0"

30'-0"

DN

PDR.
RM.

BRM.
CL.

PTRY.

P

UP

FOYER

CL

BOOKS

LIVING RM.
20⁰ x 13⁰

PORCH

ROOF

BEDROOM
12¹⁰ x 9⁸

BEDROOM
12¹⁰ x 9⁸

CL

CL

DN

LINEN

BATH

BATH

CL

MASTER
BEDROOM
11¹⁰ x 14⁰

ROOF

QUOTE ONE™

Cost to build? See page 216
to order complete cost estimate
to build this house in your area!

Design DD2682

First Floor (Basic Plan): 976 square feet
First Floor (Expanded Plan): 1,230 square feet
Second Floor (Both Plans): 744 square feet
Total (Basic Plan): 1,720 square feet
Total (Expanded Plan): 1,974 square feet

● Here is an expandable
design that offers a full measure of charm. For those who
wish to build the basic house,
there is an abundance of livability. Twin fireplaces serve
the formal living room and
the informal country kitchen.
Upstairs, three bedrooms
and two full baths complete
the plan. For information on
customizing this design, call
1-800-521-6797, ext. 800.

Design by
Home Planners,
Inc.

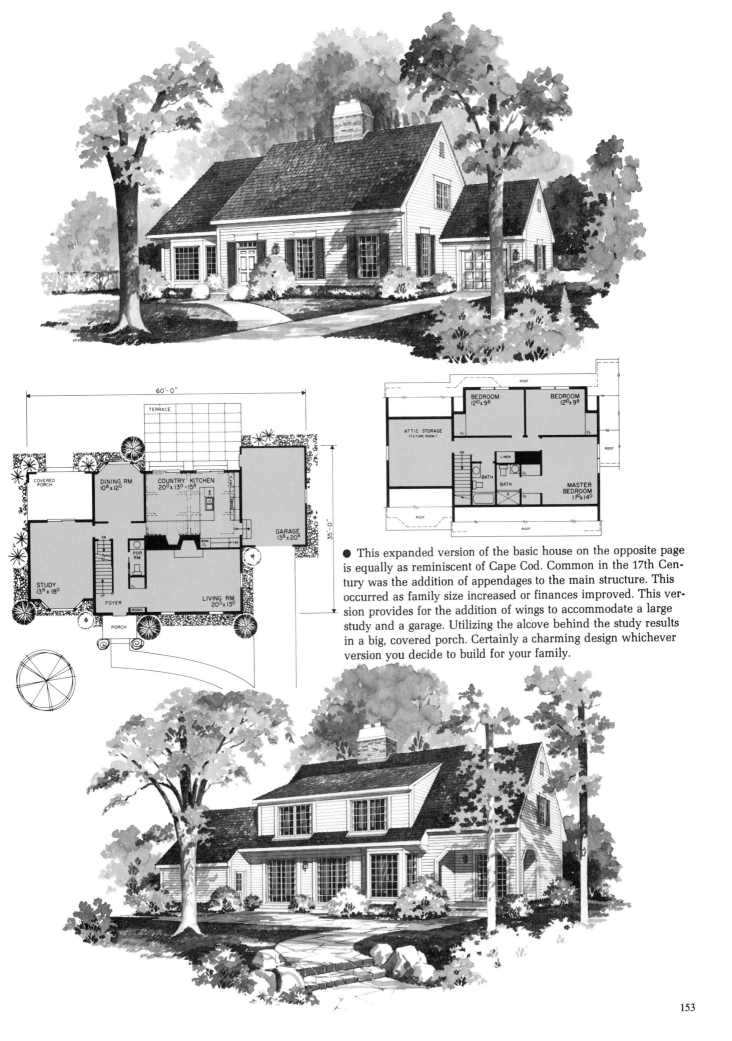

60'-0"

TERRACE

COVERED PORCH

DINING RM
10⁸ x 12⁰

COUNTRY KITCHEN
20⁰ x 13⁰ - 15⁸

GARAGE
13⁸ x 20⁴

DN
PDR RM
BRM CL
PTRY

STUDY
13⁶ x 18⁰

FOYER

BOOKS

LIVING RM
20⁰ x 13⁰

PORCH

35'-0"

ROOF

BEDROOM
12¹⁰ x 9⁸

BEDROOM
12¹⁰ x 9⁸

ATTIC STORAGE
(FUTURE ROOM)

ROOF

DN

LINEN

BATH

CL

BATH

MASTER BEDROOM
11⁶ x 14⁰

ROOF

ROOF

● This expanded version of the basic house on the opposite page is equally as reminiscent of Cape Cod. Common in the 17th Century was the addition of appendages to the main structure. This occurred as family size increased or finances improved. This version provides for the addition of wings to accommodate a large study and a garage. Utilizing the alcove behind the study results in a big, covered porch. Certainly a charming design whichever version you decide to build for your family.

Design DD9666

First Floor: 1,027 square feet
Second Floor: 580 square feet;
Total: 1,607 square feet

● This economical, rustic three-bedroom plan
sports a relaxing country image with both front
and back covered porches. The openness of the
expansive great room to kitchen/dining areas
and loft/study areas is reinforced with a shared
cathedral ceiling for impressive space. The first
level allows for two bedrooms, a full bath and a
utility area. The master suite on the second level
has a walk-in closet and a master bath with
whirlpool tub, shower and double-bowl vanity.
The plan is available with a crawl-space
foundation.

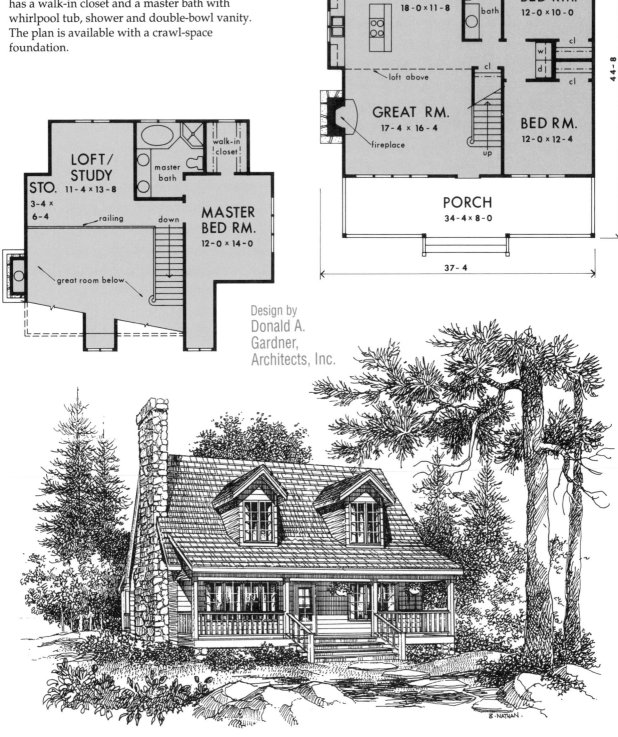

Design by
Donald A.
Gardner,
Architects, Inc.

Design DD4061

First Floor: 1,008 square feet
Second Floor: 323 square feet
Total: 1,331 square feet

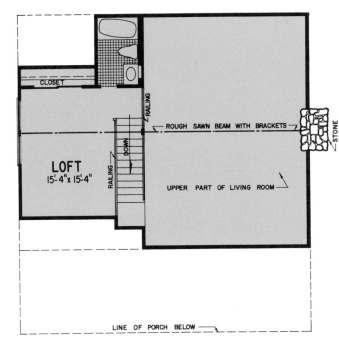

CLOSET

LOFT
15'-4" x 15'-4"

DOWN

RAILING

ROUGH SAWN BEAM WITH BRACKETS

STONE

UPPER PART OF LIVING ROOM

RAILING

LINE OF PORCH BELOW

36'-0"

WASH TUB DRY

LAUNDRY
ROOM

D.W. RANGE

SINK

KITCHEN & DINING
20'-0" x 8'-0"

SHOWER
BATH

REFRIG.

CLOSET

WH
STORAGE

FIREPLACE

STONE

CLOSET CLOSET

RAILING

38'-0"

BEDROOM
11'-8" x 13'-0"

LIVING ROOM
20'-0" x 19'-0"

UP

COATS

DN.

PORCH
36'-0" x 10'-0"

WOOD POSTS & RAILING

Design by
Home Planners,
Inc.

L
LIFESTYLE
HOME PLANS

● This charming farmhouse design will be economical to build and a pleasure to occupy. Like most vacation homes, this design features an open plan. The large living area includes a living room and dining room and a massive stone fireplace. A partition separates the kitchen from the living room. Also downstairs are a bedroom, full bath, and laundry room. Upstairs is a spacious sleeping loft overlooking the living room. Don't miss the large front porch — this will be a favorite spot for relaxing.

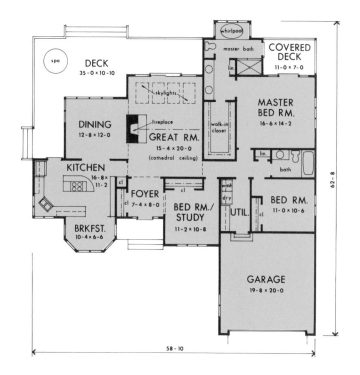

Floor plan labels:

DECK
35-0 × 10-10

spa

DINING
12-8 × 12-0

skylights

fireplace

GREAT RM.
15-4 × 20-0
(cathedral ceiling)

KITCHEN
16-8 ×
11-2

cl

FOYER
7-4 × 8-0

cl

BRKFST.
10-4 × 6-6

BED RM./
STUDY
11-2 × 10-8

whirlpool

master bath

lin.

COVERED
DECK
11-0 × 7-0

MASTER
BED RM.
16-6 × 14-2

walk-in
closet

lin.

bath

wash

dry

UTIL.

BED RM.
11-0 × 10-6

cl

GARAGE
19-8 × 20-0

58 - 10

62 - 8

Design DD9611

Square Footage: 1,817

● This inviting ranch offers many special features uncommon to the typical house this size. A large entrance foyer leads to the spacious great room with cathedral ceiling, fireplace, and operable skylights that allow for natural ventilation. A bedroom just off the foyer doubles nicely as a study. The large master suite contains a walk-in closet and a pampering master bath with double-bowl vanity, shower and whirlpool tub. For outdoor living, look to the open deck with spa at the great room and kitchen, as well as the covered deck at the master suite.

Design by
Donald A.
Gardner,
Architects, Inc.

spa

DECK

MASTER BED RM.
13-4 x 13-8

master bath
skylights

storage

fireplace

BRKFST.
11-4 x 7-4

w
d

walk-in closet

BED RM.
11-4 x 11-4

cl

GREAT RM.
15-4 x 16-10
(cathedral ceiling)

bath

KITCHEN
11-4 x 10-0

GARAGE
20-0 x 19-8

cl

FOYER
8-2 x 6-6

cl

cl

BED RM./ STUDY
11-4 x 10-4

PORCH

DINING RM.
11-4 x 11-4

50-8

59-8

Design by
Donald A.
Gardner,
Architects, Inc.

Design DD9726

Square Footage: 1,498

● This charming one-story home utilizes multi-pane windows, columns, dormers and a covered porch to offer a welcoming front exterior. Inside, the great room with a dramatic cathedral ceiling commands attention; the kitchen and breakfast room are just beyond a set of columns. The tiered ceilinged dining room presents a delightfully formal atmosphere for dinner parties or family gatherings. A tray ceiling in the master bedroom will please, as will a large walk-in closet and a gracious master bath with dual lavatories, a garden tub, and a separate shower. The secondary bedrooms are located at the opposite end of the house for privacy. This plan is available with a crawlspace foundation.

Design DD9898

First Floor: 2,070 square feet
Second Floor: 790 square feet
Total: 2,860 square feet

● Wood shingles add a cozy touch to the exterior of this home; the arched covered front porch adds its own bit of warmth. Interior rooms include a great room with a bay window and a fireplace, a formal dining room and a study with another fireplace. A guest room on the first floor contains a full bath and a walk-in closet. The relaxing master suite is also on the first floor and features a pampering master bath with His and Hers walk-in closets, dual vanities, a separate shower and a whirlpool tub just waiting to soothe and rejuvenate. The second floor holds two additional bedrooms, a loft area and a gallery which overlooks the central hall. This home is designed with a basement foundation.

Width 57'-6"
Depth 54'

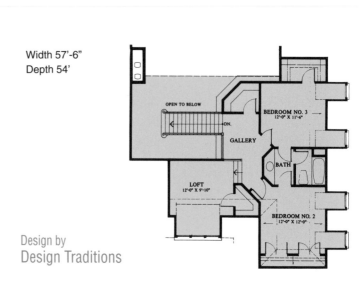

Design by
Design Traditions

Design DD9862

Square Footage: 2,170

● This classic cottage features a stone and wooden exterior with an arch-detailed porch and a box-bay window. From the foyer, double doors open to the den with built-in bookcases and a fireplace. A full bath is situated next to the den, allowing for an optional guest room. The family room is centrally located, just beyond the foyer. Its hearth is framed by windows overlooking the porch at the rear of the home. The master bedroom opens onto the rear porch. The master bath, with a large walk-in closet, double vanities, a corner tub and a separate shower, completes this relaxing retreat. Left of the family room awaits a sun room with access to the covered porch. A breakfast area complements the attractive and efficiently designed kitchen. Two secondary bedrooms with large closets share a full bath featuring double vanities. This home is designed with a basement foundation.

Design by
Design Traditions

Width 62'-4"
Depth 62'-2"

Design DD8065

First Floor: 1,482 square feet
Second Floor: 631 square feet
Total: 2,113 square feet

● Four square design reminiscent of the 1940s gives this home its landmark look. An inviting porch opens to a two-story foyer. Straight ahead, the living room is visible through two columns mounted on pedestals and connected by a graceful arch. Dormers located in the living room's vaulted ceiling flood the area with natural light. The dining room is situated nearby and entered through another arched opening. A large kitchen and a sunny breakfast room invite casual conversations and unhurried meals. The master bedroom includes a luxuri-ous master bath with His and Hers walk-in closets, a soothing whirlpool tub and a separate shower. Two additional bedrooms (one with a balcony) and a full bath share the second floor. This plan is available with either a crawlspace or slab foundation. Please specify when ordering.

Design by
Larry E. Belk
Designs

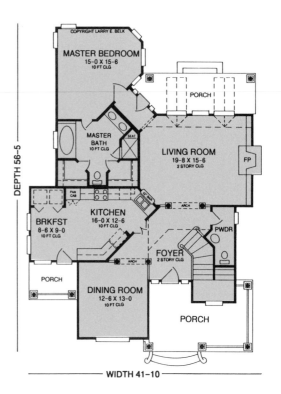

FLORIDA, ARIZONA and SUN-COUNTRY DESIGNS

IT STANDS TO REASON that the early architectural details of the homes constructed in the sun-country regions of America were strongly influenced by the Spanish culture. A vast portion of what is now the southwestern United States was controlled by the Spanish from the 17th Century until 1821, when Mexico gained its independence, and was thereafter a part of Mexico until the late 1840s, following the Mexican-American War.

One of the earliest dwellings in these regions was the Spanish Colonial. Originally, these homes were one-story, occasionally two, designed with a low-pitched or flat roof with a parapet. Because of the intense desert climate, these colonial homes were constructed of thick, adobe brick walls which provided not only excellent insulation, but an integral alliance with the surrounding landscape. Very few windows existed in these homes and for the ones that did, glass was seldom used. The preference was for bars, wrought-iron grilles or covered openings, often protected with the spiny ribs of the ocotillo cactus or other trees and shrubs indigenous to the area. From the interior, wooden shutters offered protection against the outside elements.

Because of the warm climate, long porches were built that opened onto courtyards and functioned as sheltered passageways between rooms, which usually lacked interior connecting doorways. Design DD9083 tenders a bird's-eye view of just such a courtyard. Designed with broad overhanging porches and roofs, these areas offered protection not only as sunshade, but as an umbrella to the pounding monsoon rains of the summer. The more detailed of these outdoor porches took the form of

graceful, colonnaded arcades with elaborate masonry arches.

In the late 1800s the Mission-style home came into prominence, designed with a stucco exterior, and built as either a one- or two-story dwelling. Typically, these homes had wide, overhanging eaves and were easily recognized by a mission-type dormer or parapet, traditional elements featured in Design DD3437. Porches are supported by large square piers and are most commonly arched above.

By the early 1900s, the Pueblo Revival that took its cue from the ancient Indian dwellings of the Southwest was well underway. This style was characterized by a stucco exterior and a flat roof with a parapet above irregular rounded edges. Projecting wooden roof beams called *vigas* extended through the walls. The stepped-back roof line of the original Native American pueblos was often imitated, with window lintels and porches carrying out the hand-crafted theme. Designs DD3433 and DD3405 provide modern examples of the Pueblo Revival style with a Santa Fe flavor.

Between 1915 and 1940, the Spanish Eclectic home made its appearance. Asymmetrical in shape, these homes were most often built with a stucco exterior and a red tile roof. The most telling features of these homes are the arches above the windows and/or doors, and the decorative details inspired by Moorish or Byzantine cultures. Designs DD6603 and DD6608 establish these traits while Design DD6602 takes a more contemporary approach.

The plans in this section are representative of the finest designs for easy, informal sun-country living with accommodating floor plans to suit every need.

Design DD9740

Square Footage: 1,838

● Arched windows and a dramatic arched entry enhance this exciting Southwestern home. The expansive great room, highlighted by a cathedral ceiling and a fireplace, offers direct access to the rear patio and the formal dining room—a winning combination for both formal and informal gettogethers. An efficient U-shaped kitchen provides plenty of counter space and easily serves both the dining room and the great room. Sunlight floods the master bedroom and affords views of the rear grounds with its wall of windows. The master bath invites relaxation with its soothing corner tub and separate shower. Two secondary bedrooms (one serves as an optional den) share an adjacent bath.

Design by
Donald A.
Gardner,
Architects, Inc.

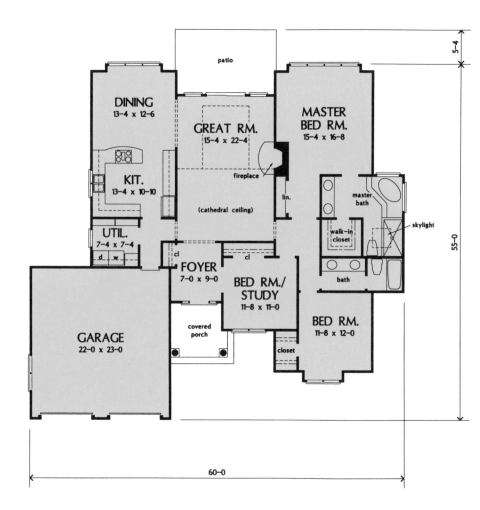

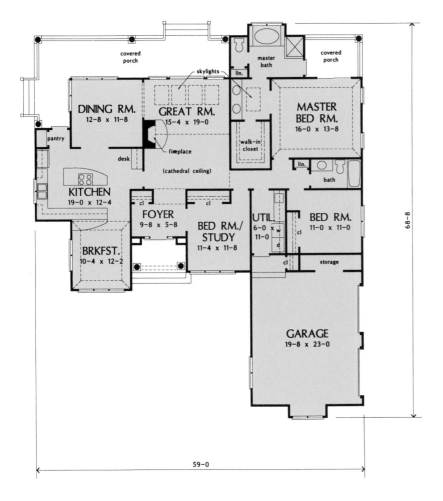

Design DD9737

Square Footage: 1,929

● Make the most of warmer climes in this striking three-bedroom home. A grand entry gives way to a great room with skylights and a fireplace. A cathedral ceiling furthers the open feeling of this room. A large dining room surveys views on two sides. Nearby, the kitchen will delight with its large island work space and abundance of counter and cabinet space. Facing the front, the breakfast room offers ample space along with elegant ceiling detail. Three bedrooms—or two with a study—make up the sleeping quarters of this plan. In the master bedroom, large proportions include a private bath with dual lavs, a walk-in closet and a bumped-out garden tub. A secluded covered porch provides the opportunity for outdoor enjoyment.

Design by
Donald A.
Gardner,
Architects, Inc.

Design DD6607

Square Footage: 2200

● A joyful marriage of indoor outdoor living relationships endures in this spirited stucco home. An abundance of windows to the front of the plan allows bright, warming sunlight to flood the rooms. All rooms to the rear offer access to a full-length veranda and a screened porch—perfect for enjoying evening's cooling breezes and beautiful sunsets. An airy, open feeling is created by the combination of the formal dining room (divided from the foyer by a half-wall), the spacious great room and the charming kitchen. The latter is complete with a walk-in pantry and a bayed breakfast nook. Split sleeping quarters contain the master wing to the left and two secondary bedrooms to the right. The secluded master suite is highlighted by a double walk-in closet, a relaxing garden tub with a privacy wall, a separate shower and a double-bowl vanity.

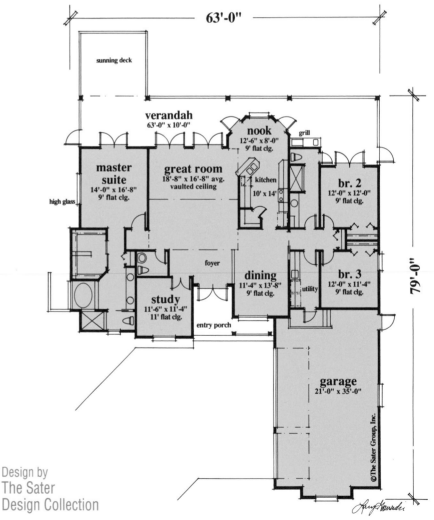

Design by
The Sater
Design Collection

© The Sater Group, Inc.

Design DD6614

Square Footage: 2,282

● Two elevations are yours to choose from in this stunning sun country home. An octagonal-shaped dining room with a tray ceiling and a living room opening to the lanai make up the formal living areas. Pass through an arched doorway and enter the informal living area comprised of an efficient kitchen, a sunlit breakfast nook and a comfortable leisure room with a fireplace and built-ins to one side. There is access to the lanai here. The far right side of the plan contains two family bedrooms and a full bath. To the far left, is a private master suite with a sitting area opening to the lanai. His and Hers walk-in closets, a compartmented toilet, a calming corner tub and a separate shower and a double-bowl vanity complete this pampering suite.

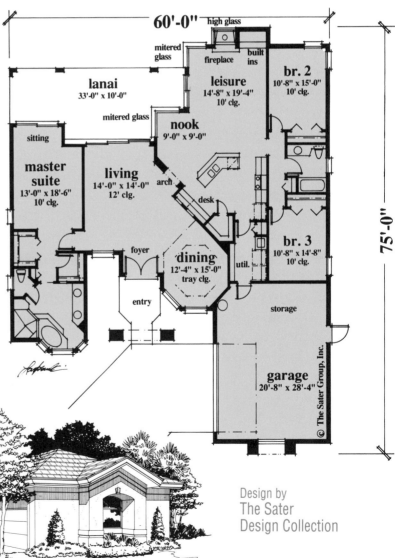

60'-0"

high glass

mitered glass

fireplace   built ins

leisure
14'-8" x 19'-4"
10' clg.

br. 2
10'-8" x 15'-0"
10' clg.

lanai
33'-0" x 10'-0"

mitered glass

nook
9'-0" x 9'-0"

sitting

master suite
13'-0" x 18'-6"
10' clg.

living
14'-0" x 14'-0"
12' clg.

arch

desk

util.

br. 3
10'-8" x 14'-8"
10' clg.

foyer

dining
12'-4" x 15'-0"
tray clg.

entry

storage

garage
20'-8" x 28'-4"

75'-0"

© The Sater Group, Inc.

Design by
The Sater
Design Collection

© The Sater Group, Inc.

© The Sater Group, Inc.

Design DD6612

Square Footage: 1,487

● Here's an offer too good to pass up! Two elevations and a wealth of modern livability is presented in this compact one-story home. Inside, a great room with a vaulted ceiling opens to the lanai, offering wonderful options for either formal or informal entertaining. Step out onto the lanai and savor the outdoors from the delightful kitchen with its bay-windowed breakfast nook. Two secondary bedrooms (each with its own walk-in closet) share a full bath. Finally, enjoy the lanai from the calming master suite and pampering bath featuring a corner tub, a separate shower and a large walk-in closet.

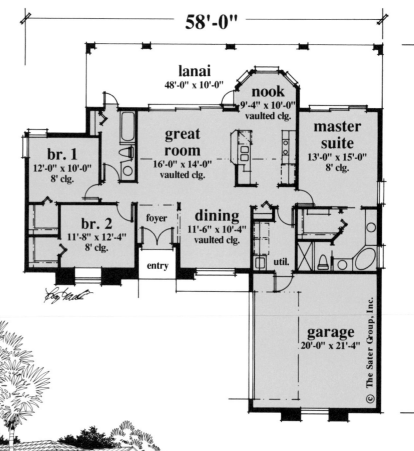

58'-0"

58'-0"

lanai
48'-0" x 10'-0"

nook
9'-4" x 10'-0"
vaulted clg.

master
suite
13'-0" x 15'-0"
8' clg.

great
room
16'-0" x 14'-0"
vaulted clg.

br. 1
12'-0" x 10'-0"
8' clg.

br. 2
11'-8" x 12'-4"
8' clg.

foyer

dining
11'-6" x 10'-4"
vaulted clg.

util.

entry

garage
20'-0" x 21'-4"

© The Sater Group, Inc.

© The Sater Group, Inc.

Design by
The Sater
Design Collection

The Sater Group, Inc.

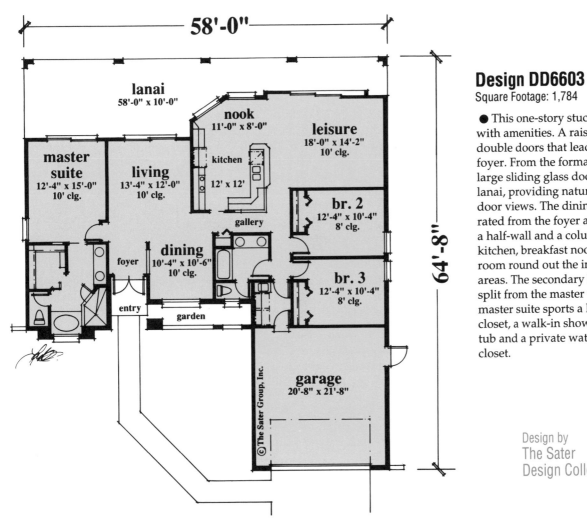

58'-0"

lanai
58'-0" x 10'-0"

nook
11'-0" x 8'-0"

leisure
18'-0" x 14'-2"
10' clg.

master suite
12'-4" x 15'-0"
10' clg.

living
13'-4" x 12'-0"
10' clg.

kitchen
12' x 12'

br. 2
12'-4" x 10'-4"
8' clg.

gallery

foyer

dining
10'-4" x 10'-6"
10' clg.

br. 3
12'-4" x 10'-4"
8' clg.

entry

garden

64'-8"

© The Sater Group, Inc.

garage
20'-8" x 21'-8"

Design DD6603
Square Footage: 1,784

● This one-story stucco home is filled with amenities. A raised entry features double doors that lead to the grand foyer. From the formal living room, large sliding glass doors open to the lanai, providing natural light and outdoor views. The dining room is separated from the foyer and living area by a half-wall and a column. The large kitchen, breakfast nook and leisure room round out the informal gathering areas. The secondary bedrooms are split from the master wing. The cozy master suite sports a large walk-in closet, a walk-in shower, a whirlpool tub and a private water closet.

Design by
The Sater
Design Collection

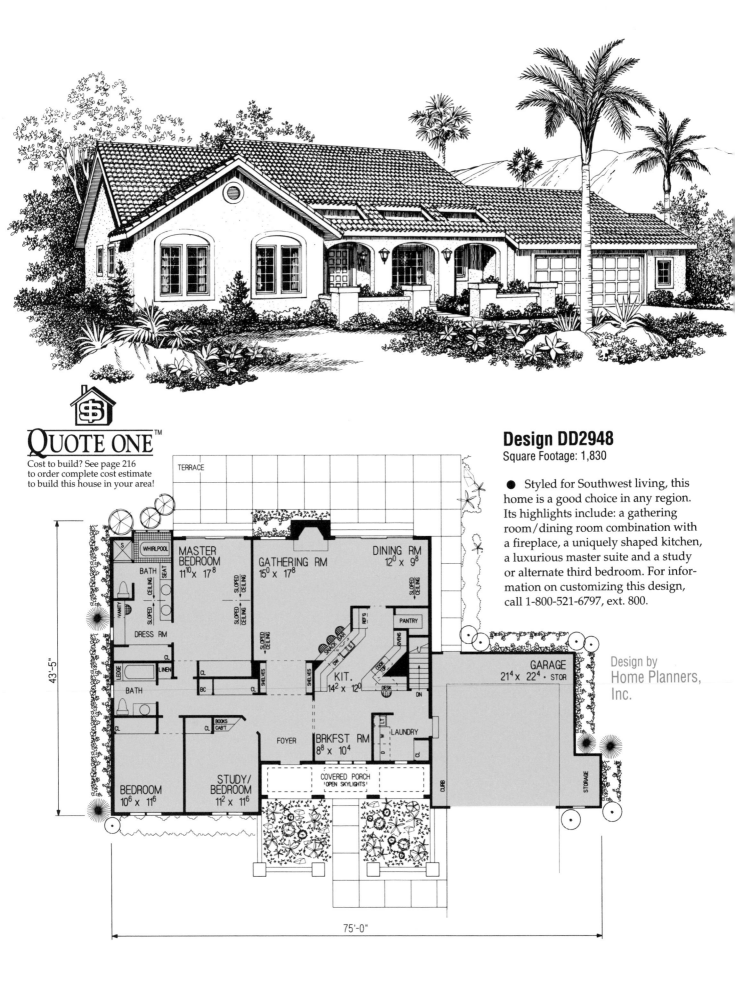

Design DD2948
Square Footage: 1,830

● Styled for Southwest living, this
home is a good choice in any region.
Its highlights include: a gathering
room/dining room combination with
a fireplace, a uniquely shaped kitchen,
a luxurious master suite and a study
or alternate third bedroom. For information on customizing this design,
call 1-800-521-6797, ext. 800.

Design by
Home Planners,
Inc.

© The Sater Group, Inc.

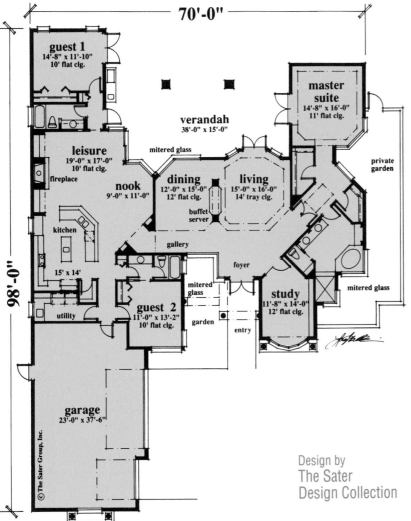

70'-0"

guest 1
14'-8" x 11'-10"
10' flat clg.

master suite
14'-8" x 16'-0"
11' flat clg.

verandah
38'-0" x 15'-0"

mitered glass

leisure
19'-0" x 17'-0"
10' flat clg.

fireplace

nook
9'-0" x 11'-0"

dining
12'-0" x 15'-0"
12' flat clg.

living
15'-0" x 16'-0"
14' tray clg.

private garden

kitchen
15' x 14'

buffet server

gallery

foyer

mitered glass

utility

guest 2
11'-0" x 13'-2"
10' flat clg.

garden

entry

study
11'-8" x 14'-0"
12' flat clg.

mitered glass

98'-0"

garage
23'-0" x 37'-6"

© The Sater Group, Inc.

Design by
The Sater
Design Collection

Design DD6602

Square Footage: 2,794

● Classic columns, circle-head windows and a bay-windowed study give this stucco home a wonderful street presence. The foyer leads into the formal living and dining areas. An arched buffet server separates these rooms and contributes an open feeling. The kitchen, nook and leisure room are grouped for informal living. A desk/message center in the island kitchen, art niches in the nook and a fireplace with an entertainment center and shelves add custom touches. Two secondary suites have guest baths and offer full privacy from the master wing. The master suite hosts a private garden area, while the master bath features a walk-in shower that overlooks the garden, and a water closet room with space for books or a television. Large His and Hers walk-in closets complete these private quarters.

Design DD9082
Square Footage: 2,360

● Reminiscent of the homes built long ago in the Southwest, this Spanish adaptation has many components to draw attention to it. Note the long entry porch leading to an angled foyer flanked by a huge living room with cathedral ceiling and dining room with sloped ceiling. Across the gallery is a long porch with skylights that over-looks the tiled courtyard. The kitchen features plenty of counter space and a large pantry. To the rear, in privacy is the master bedroom suite. It has a tub area with raised gazebo ceiling and transom windows. There are also two family bed-rooms sharing a full bath with double vanities.

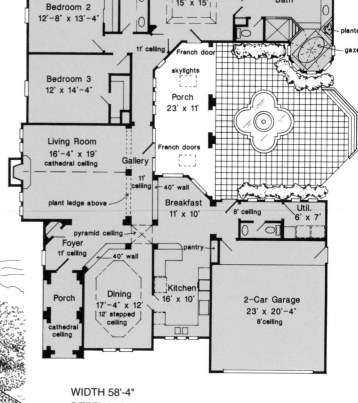

Bath

11' stepped ceiling

Master Bedroom
15' x 15'

planter

Bedroom 2
12'-8" x 13'-4"

Bath

planter

gazebo ce

11' ceiling

French door

Bedroom 3
12' x 14'-4"

skylights

Porch
23' x 11'

Living Room
16'-4" x 19'
cathedral ceiling

Gallery

French doors

11' ceiling

40' wall

Breakfast
11' x 10'

8' ceiling

Util.
6' x 7'

plant ledge above

pyramid ceiling

Foyer
11' ceiling

40' wall

pantry

Dining
17'-4" x 12'
12' stepped ceiling

Kitchen
16' x 10'

2-Car Garage
23' x 20'-4"
8' ceiling

Porch

cathedral ceiling

WIDTH 58'-4"
DEPTH 73'-4"

Design by
Larry W.
Garnett &
Associates, Inc.

170

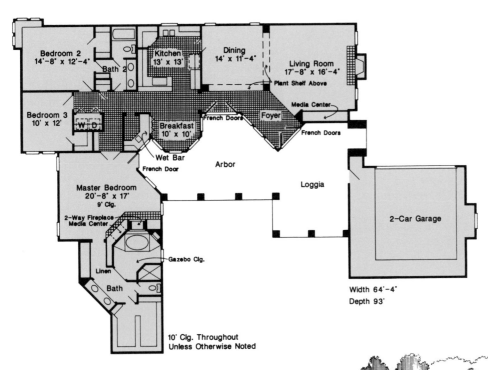

Bedroom 2
14'-8" x 12'-4"

Bath 2

Kitchen
13' x 13'

Dining
14' x 11'-4"

Living Room
17'-8" x 16'-4"

Plant Shelf Above

Media Center

Bedroom 3
10' x 12'

W. D.

Breakfast
10' x 10'

French Doors

Foyer

French Doors

Wet Bar

Arbor

French Door

Master Bedroom
20'-8" x 17'
9' Clg.

Loggia

2-Way Fireplace
Media Center

2-Car Garage

Gazebo Clg.

Linen

Bath

Width 64'-4"
Depth 93'

10' Clg. Throughout
Unless Otherwise Noted

Design DD9083
Square Footage: 2,176

● This grand Southwestern design caters to outdoor lifestyle with areas that invite visitation. The front entry opens to a beautiful and characteristic Spanish courtyard with loggia, arbor and spa area. The foyer runs the length of the home and leads from open living and dining areas to convenient kitchen and breakfast nook, then back to the sleeping quarters. The master suite is especially notable with its luxurious bath and ample closet space. Note the many extras in the plan: fireplace and media center in the living room and in the master bedroom, wet bar at the breakfast nook, oversized pantry in the kitchen.

Design by
Larry W.
Garnett &
Associates, Inc.

© The Sater Group, Inc.

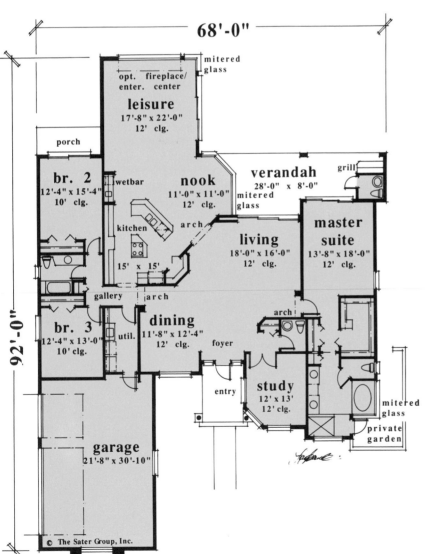

© The Sater Group, Inc.

Design DD6606

Square Footage: 2,984

● Glass surrounds the entry of this appealing stucco home. Arched doorways lead from the formal living and dining rooms to the sleeping zones and the informal living area. The study is situated to the right of the entry and will make a wonderful home office. Ideally suited for informal entertaining, the gourmet kitchen shares space with a sunny breakfast nook and a spacious leisure room which offers access to the rear grounds and a covered veranda. The leisure room provides optional space for a fireplace and entertainment center. The master suite sports two closets: an oversized walk-in closet and a smaller closet nearby. Treat yourself to a relaxing soak in the garden tub or enter the private garden through an adjacent door. A separate shower, dual vanities and a compartmented toilet complete the master sleeping quarters. On the opposite side of the plan, two secondary bedrooms share a full bath.

Design by
The Sater
Design Collection

172

Design DD6611

Square Footage: 3,104

● Brick accents warm the exterior of this captivating Floridian home. A feeling of elegance makes a fine first impression upon entering the grand foyer. It opens to the formal living and dining room through columns and archways. Step out onto the verandah and enjoy the cooling breezes. It is accessible from the formal living area, the private master suite or the cheerful breakfast nook. The spacious kitchen is a cook's delight with its large pantry, an island cooktop and garden greenhouse window. The leisure room hosts a fireplace with built-in shelves and convenient access to an outdoor patio and grill, making it a favorite for informal gatherings. The sumptuous master wing features a bayed study and a master suite with a stepped ceiling, a huge walk-in closet and plenty of space for a sitting area. The master bath enjoys a relaxing tub with a private garden view, a separate shower and a compartmented toilet. This home will please even the most discriminating homeowner.

Design by
The Sater
Design Collection

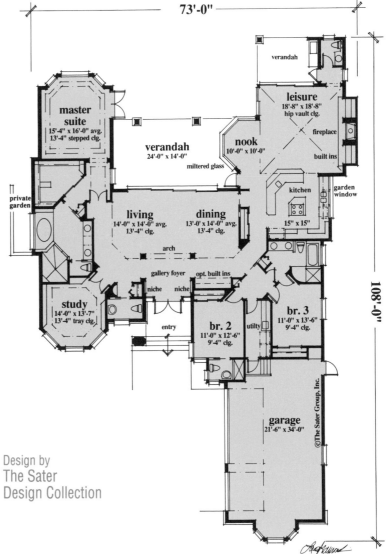

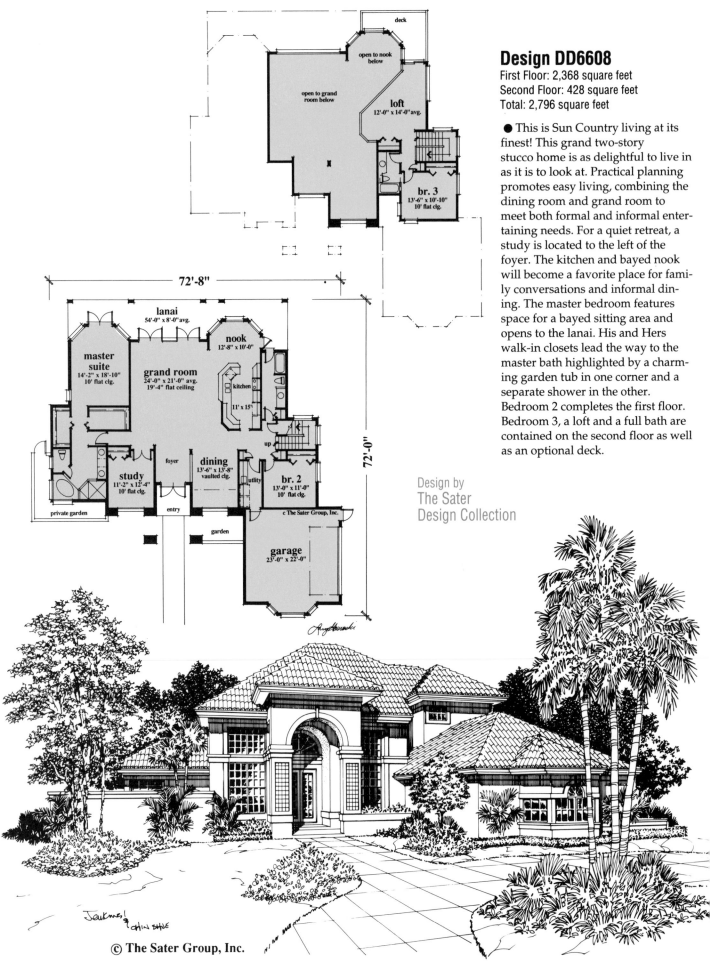

deck

open to nook
below

open to grand
room below

loft
12'-0" x 14'-0" avg.

br. 3
13'-6" x 10'-10"
10' flat clg.

72'-8"

lanai
54'-0" x 8'-0" avg.

nook
12'-8" x 10'-0"

master
suite
14'-2" x 18'-10"
10' flat clg.

grand room
24'-0" x 21'-0" avg.
19'-4" flat ceiling

kitchen
11' x 15'

72'-0"

foyer

dining
13'-6" x 13'-8"
vaulted clg.

up

utility

study
11'-2" x 12'-4"
10' flat clg.

br. 2
13'-0" x 11'-0"
10' flat clg.

private garden

entry

garden

garage
23'-0" x 22'-0"

c The Sater Group, Inc.

Design DD6608

First Floor: 2,368 square feet
Second Floor: 428 square feet
Total: 2,796 square feet

● This is Sun Country living at its finest! This grand two-story stucco home is as delightful to live in as it is to look at. Practical planning promotes easy living, combining the dining room and grand room to meet both formal and informal entertaining needs. For a quiet retreat, a study is located to the left of the foyer. The kitchen and bayed nook will become a favorite place for family conversations and informal dining. The master bedroom features space for a bayed sitting area and opens to the lanai. His and Hers walk-in closets lead the way to the master bath highlighted by a charming garden tub in one corner and a separate shower in the other. Bedroom 2 completes the first floor. Bedroom 3, a loft and a full bath are contained on the second floor as well as an optional deck.

Design by
The Sater
Design Collection

© The Sater Group, Inc.

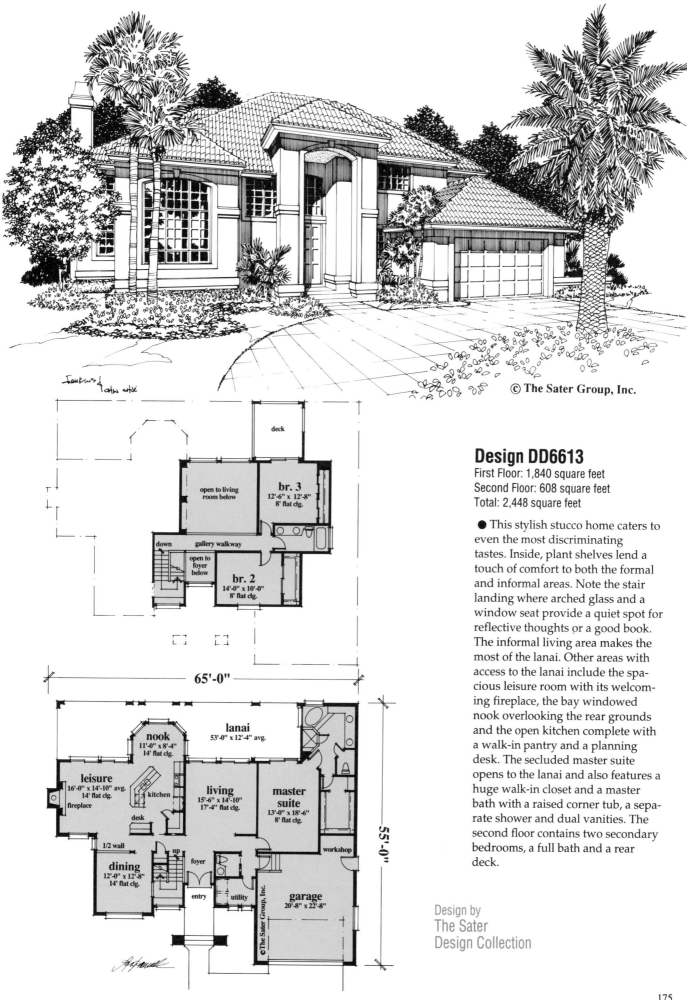

© The Sater Group, Inc.

deck

open to living room below

br. 3
12'-6" x 12'-8"
8' flat clg.

down   gallery walkway

open to foyer below

br. 2
14'-0" x 10'-0"
8' flat clg.

65'-0"

nook
11'-0" x 8'-4"
14' flat clg.

lanai
53'-0" x 12'-4" avg.

leisure
16'-0" x 14'-10" avg.
14' flat clg.

fireplace

kitchen

desk

living
15'-6" x 14'-10"
17'-4" flat clg.

master suite
13'-0" x 18'-6"
8' flat clg.

1/2 wall

up

dining
12'-0" x 12'-8"
14' flat clg.

foyer

entry

utility

workshop

garage
20'-8" x 22'-8"

© The Sater Group, Inc.

55'-0"

Design DD6613

First Floor: 1,840 square feet
Second Floor: 608 square feet
Total: 2,448 square feet

● This stylish stucco home caters to even the most discriminating tastes. Inside, plant shelves lend a touch of comfort to both the formal and informal areas. Note the stair landing where arched glass and a window seat provide a quiet spot for reflective thoughts or a good book. The informal living area makes the most of the lanai. Other areas with access to the lanai include the spacious leisure room with its welcoming fireplace, the bay windowed nook overlooking the rear grounds and the open kitchen complete with a walk-in pantry and a planning desk. The secluded master suite opens to the lanai and also features a huge walk-in closet and a master bath with a raised corner tub, a separate shower and dual vanities. The second floor contains two secondary bedrooms, a full bath and a rear deck.

Design by
The Sater
Design Collection

175

Design DD3563

First Floor: 1,023 square feet
Second Floor: 866 square feet
Total: 1,889 square feet

● Practical to build, this wonderful transitional plan combines the best of contemporary and traditional styling. Its stucco exterior is enhanced by arched windows and a recessed arched entry plus a lovely balcony off the second-floor master bedroom. A walled entry court extends the living room to the outside. The double front doors open to a foyer with a hall closet and a powder room. The service entrance is just to the right and accesses the two-car garage. The large living room adjoins directly to the dining room. The family room is set off behind the garage and features a sloped ceiling and a fireplace. Sleeping quarters consist of two secondary bedrooms with a shared bath and a generous master suite with a well-appointed bath.

Design by
Home Planners, Inc.

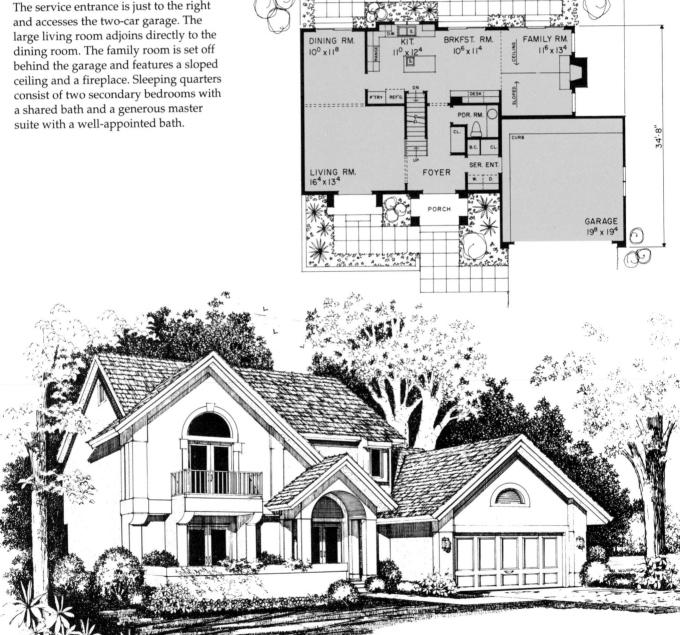

Design DD3562

First Floor: 1,182 square feet
Second Floor: 927 square feet
Total: 2,109 square feet

● Interesting detailing marks the exterior of this home as a beauty. Its interior makes it a livable option for any family. Entry occurs through double doors to the left side of the plan. A powder room with curved wall is handy to the entry. Living areas of the home are open and well-planned. The formal living room shares a through fireplace with the large family room. The dining room is adjoining and has a pass-through counter to the L-shaped kitchen. Special details on this floor include a wealth of sliding glass doors to the rear terrace and built-ins throughout. Upstairs are three bedrooms with two full baths.

Design by
Home Planners,
Inc.

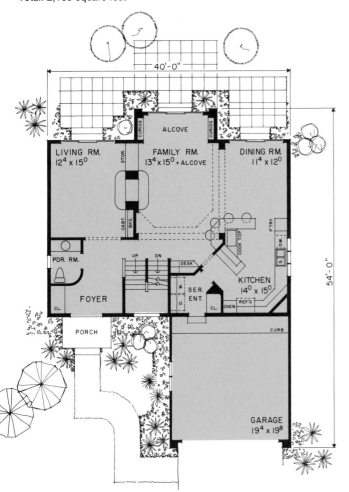

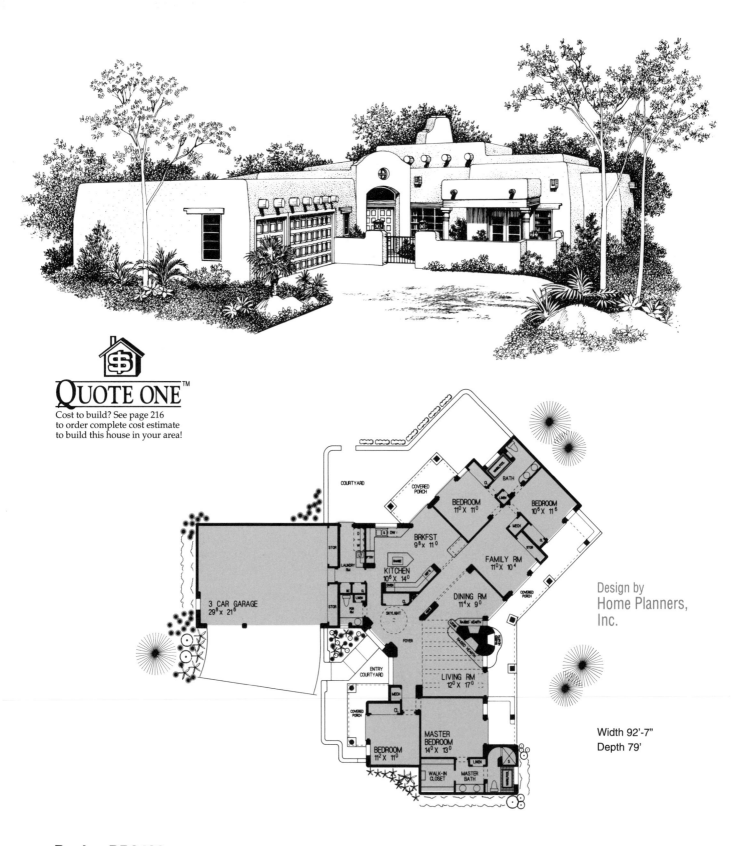

Design by
Home Planners,
Inc.

Width 92'-7"
Depth 79'

Design DD3433

Square Footage: 2,350

● Santa Fe styling creates interesting angles in this one-story home. A grand entrance leads through a courtyard into the foyer with circular skylight, closet space and niches, and convenient powder room. Turn right to the master suite with deluxe bath and a bedroom close at hand, perfect for a nursery, home office or exercise room. Two more family bedrooms are placed quietly in the far wing of the house. Fireplaces in the living room, dining room and covered porch create various shapes. Make note of the island range in the kitchen, extra storage in the garage, and covered porches on two sides. For information on customizing this design, call 1-800-521-6797, ext. 800.

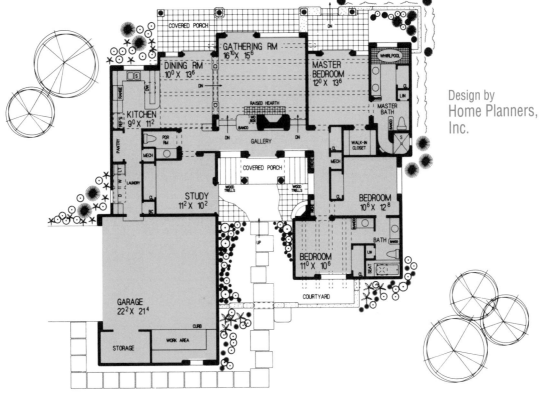

Quote One™

Cost to build? See page 216
to order complete cost estimate
to build this house in your area!

Width 61'-6"
Depth 67'-4"

Design by
Home Planners,
Inc.

Design DD3431
Square Footage: 1,907

● Graceful curves welcome you into the courtyard of this Santa Fe home. Inside, a gallery directs the work zone to the left and the sleeping zone to the right. Straight ahead lies a sunken gathering room with a beamed ceiling and a raised-hearth fireplace. The covered rear porch is accessible from the dining room, the gathering room and the master bedroom. Luxury awaits in the master bath featuring a whirlpool tub, a separate shower, double vani- ties and a walk-in closet. Two family bedrooms share a compartmented bath. The study could serve as a guest room, media room or home office. For information on customizing this design, call 1-800-521-6797, ext. 800.

QUOTE ONE™

Cost to build? See page 216
to order complete cost estimate
to build this house in your area!

Design by
Home Planners,
Inc.

Design DD3405

Square Footage: 3,144

● In classic Santa Fe style, this home strikes a beautiful combination of historic exterior detailing and open floor planning on the inside. A covered porch running the width of the facade leads to an entry foyer that connects to a huge gathering room with a fireplace and a formal dining room. The family kitchen allows special space for casual gatherings. The right wing of the home holds two family bedrooms and a full bath. The left wing is devoted to the master suite and guest room or study. For information on customizing this design, call 1-800-521-6797, ext. 800.

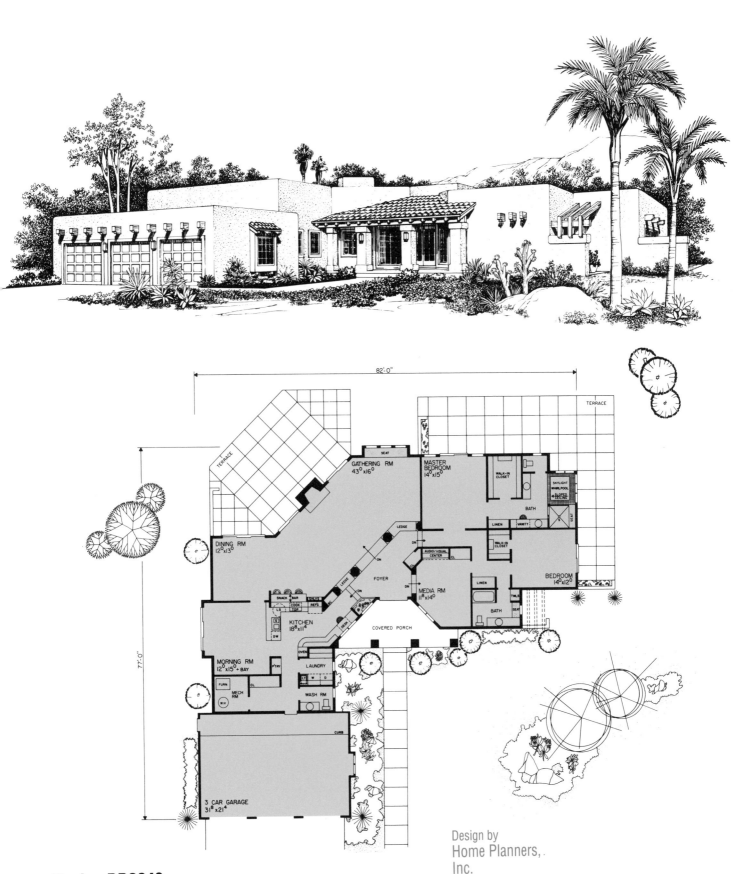

Design DD2949

Square Footage: 2,922

● Spanish and western influences take center stage in a long, low stucco design. You'll enjoy the Texas-sized gathering room that opens to a formal dining area and has a snack bar through to the kitchen. More casual dining is accommodated in the nook. A luxurious master suite is graced by plenty of closet space and a soothing whirlpool spa. Besides another bedroom and full bath, there is a media room that could easily double as a third bedroom or guest room.

Width 69'-6"
Depth 61'

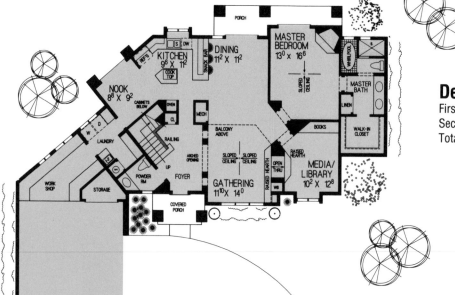

Design DD3437

First Floor: 1,522 square feet
Second Floor: 800 square feet
Total: 2,322 square feet

Design by
Home Planners,
Inc.

● This two-story Spanish Mission-style home has character inside and out. The first-floor master suite features a fireplace and a gracious bath with a walk-in closet, a whirlpool, a shower, dual vanities and linen storage. The kitchen, with an island cooktop, includes a snack bar and an adjoining breakfast nook. Three bedrooms and two full baths occupy the second floor. For information on customizing this design, call 1-800-521-6797, ext. 800.

QUOTE ONE™

Cost to build? See page 216
to order complete cost estimate
to build this house in your area!

Design DD3432

First Floor: 1,966 square feet
Second Floor: 831 square feet
Total: 2,797 square feet

● Unique in nature, this two-story
Santa Fe-style home is as practical as it
is lovely. The large entry court is overlooked by windows in the dining
room and a covered patio from one of
two family bedrooms. The entry foyer
leads to living areas at the back of the
plan. These include a living room with
a corner fireplace and a family room
connected to the kitchen via a built-in
eating nook. Upstairs, the master suite
features a grand bath and a large
walk-in closet. Every room in this
home has its own outdoor area. For
information on customizing this
design, call 1-800-521-6797, ext. 800.

Design by
Home Planners,
Inc.

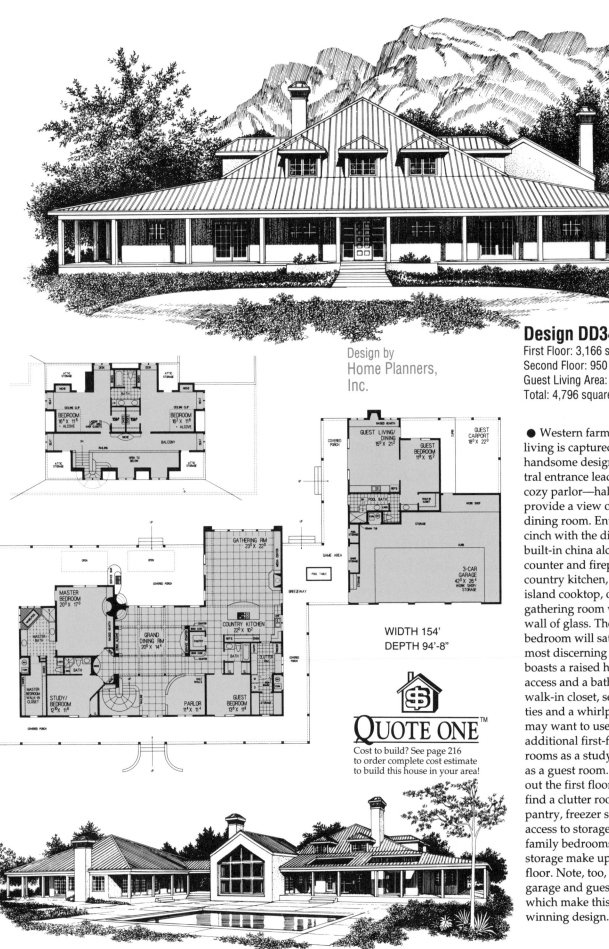

Design by
Home Planners,
Inc.

WIDTH 154'
DEPTH 94'-8"

Design DD3471

First Floor: 3,166 square feet
Second Floor: 950 square feet
Guest Living Area: 680 square feet
Total: 4,796 square feet

● Western farmhouse-style living is captured in this handsome design. The central entrance leads into a cozy parlor—half walls provide a view of the grand dining room. Entertaining's a cinch with the dining room's built-in china alcove, service counter and fireplace. The country kitchen, with a large island cooktop, overlooks the gathering room with its full wall of glass. The master bedroom will satisfy even the most discerning tastes. It boasts a raised hearth, porch access and a bath with a walk-in closet, separate vanities and a whirlpool. You may want to use one of the additional first-floor bedrooms as a study, the other as a guest room. To round out the first floor, you'll also find a clutter room with a pantry, freezer space and access to storage space. Two family bedrooms and attic storage make up the second floor. Note, too, the separate garage and guest house which make this such a winning design.

QUOTE ONE™

Cost to build? See page 216
to order complete cost estimate
to build this house in your area!

CONTEMPORARY
and
TRANSITIONAL STYLES

WEBSTERS DEFINES TRANSITIONAL AS "an act, process, or instance of changing from one state, form, activity, or place to another." Nowhere in America's changing home styles have these characteristics been as significant as what we see in the transitional designs of today.

Contemporary styling was first initiated in America during the 1920s by architects who had come to this country to escape the chaos in Europe. The concepts they introduced had a profound influence on the earliest contemporary styles of American homes, namely Modernist and International. The decorative, traditional elements of yesterday's home design were discarded, with new emphasis being placed on more geometric and functional elements.

Frank Lloyd Wright, a key figure in the evolution of contemporary design, said, "Organic architecture can live and let live because it can never express mere style." The primary function of the contemporary form was to enclose a portion of the living area with carefully chosen building materials—those which integrate the indoor and outdoor space into one, instituted through the extensive use of glass and lack of ornamentation. Although contemporary design harmonizes well with all regions, it was, and is still, perhaps at its best in the wide open spaces of the West, particularly the lush, wooded landscape of the Pacific Northwest.

International homes were asymmetrical in shape with a flat roof. Window treatment was most often glass block or metal casement windows set flush with smooth exterior walls. There was no evidence of decorative detailing at the windows or doors. An excellent model of this style is found in Design DD3403.

The flat-roofed contemporary styles introduced in the 1940s were descendants of their predecessor, the International style. When the first gable designs were introduced, they were borrowed from the functional Craftsman and Prairie styles. These homes relied heavily on texture, and often used combinations of wood, brick and/or stone, with the integration of the landscape once again as the key factor.

Subsequently, the Shed Contemporary emerged. The fundamentally distinctive feature of this design was its multi-directional shed roof—whose intersecting planes ultimately resulted in different geometric shapes. Commonly, wood shingles or board siding were used in a vertical, horizontal or diagonal pattern. The entrances were generally recessed and windows remained small and asymmetrically placed. The overall effect resulted in bold diagonals, counterpointed shapes and multiple massing as observed in Designs DD2711 and DD2781.

The development of contemporary styling continues to grow today, evident in multi-storied homes with stucco exteriors, hipped roofs, and high, recessed entrances as noted in Designs DD9520 and DD9498. Other two-story examples, such as the contemporary farmhouse styles of DD3466 and DD3467, trace their roots to yesterday's farmhouses and sport steeply-pitched, metal-seamed roofs. These and other bold designs exhibit the progress made by today's contemporary styling and assure us that the opportunities for evolution in the future are endless.

The homes presented in this section represent the vast choices in contemporary design, with an excellent variety of plans sure to appeal to all devotees of modern styling.

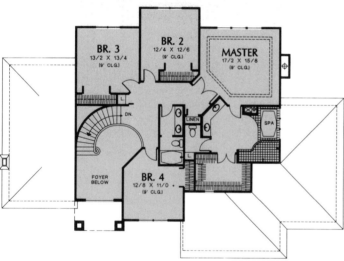

◄ 70' ►

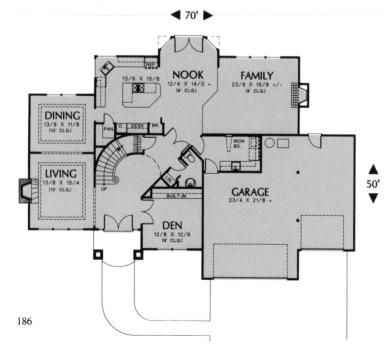

▲
50'
▼

Design DD9513

First Floor: 1,764 square feet
Second Floor: 1,393 square feet
Total: 3,157 square feet

● A volume entry gives way to an elegant curving stairway. The formal living and dining rooms with 13-foot-high tray ceilings are to the left, while a den with built-ins is to the right. An angled powder room with linen storage is placed conveniently near the foyer. Double doors lead to the spacious kitchen, breakfast nook and family room combination. Fireplaces are located in both the living and family rooms. The laundry room includes a sink and a built-in ironing board. Four bedrooms occupy the second floor, including a master bedroom with 9-foot tray ceiling. The master bath features a spa tub, separate shower, dual vanities, walk-in closet and a wide dressing area.

Design by
Alan Mascord
Design Associates, Inc.

Design DD9520 First Floor: 2,375 square feet; Second Floor: 762 square feet; Total: 3,137 square feet

● Clean lines, a hipped roof and a high, recessed entry define this sleek contemporary home. Inside, curved lines add a twist to the well-designed floor plan. For informal entertaining, gather in the multi-windowed family room with its step-down wet bar and warming fireplace. The open kitchen will delight everyone with its center cooktop island, a corner sink and an adjacent breakfast nook. A formal dining room enjoys views of the rear grounds and separates the informal living area from the master wing. Enter the grand master suite through double doors and take special note of the see-through fireplace between the bedroom and bath. A large walk-in closet, a relaxing spa and dual vanities complete the master bath. An additional see-through fireplace is located between the living room and den. Upstairs, two family bedrooms (each with walk-in closets) share a full bath.

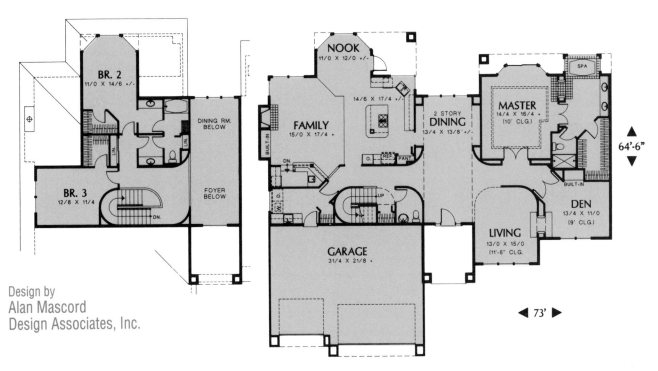

Design by
Alan Mascord
Design Associates, Inc.

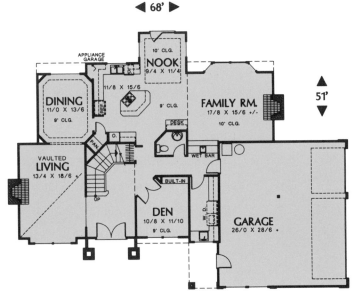

◀ 68' ▶

▲
51'
▼

APPLIANCE GARAGE

10' CLG.
NOOK
9/4 X 11/4

11/8 15/6

DINING
11/0 X 13/6
9' CLG.

9' CLG.

FAMILY RM.
17/8 X 15/6 +/-
10' CLG.

DESK

VAULTED
LIVING
13/4 X 18/6

WET BAR

PAN.

UP

BUILT-IN

DEN
10/8 X 11/10
9' CLG.

W. D.

GARAGE
26/0 X 28/6 +

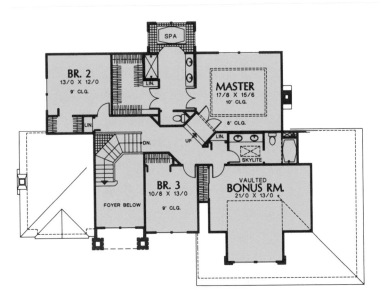

SPA

BR. 2
13/0 X 12/0
9' CLG.

LIN.

LIN.

MASTER
17/8 X 15/6
10' CLG.

LIN.

8' CLG.

DN.

UP

LIN.

SKYLITE

BR. 3
10/8 X 13/0
9' CLG.

FOYER BELOW

VAULTED
BONUS RM.
21/0 X 13/0

Design DD9400

First Floor: 1,618 square feet
Second Floor: 1,212 square feet
Bonus Room: 376 square feet
Total: 3,206 square feet

● This attractive European-styled plan
has a stucco finish and arched windows
complementing the facade. Nine-foot
ceilings are standard throughout both
levels with some areas, such as the
nook, family room and master bedroom,
having ten-foot ceilings. From the two-
story foyer with its angled stair, look to
the dramatically vaulted living room on
one side and den with French doors on
the other. Upstairs a sumptuous master
suite includes spa tub, shower and large
walk-in closet. Over the garage is a
vaulted bonus room, perfect as a game
or hobby room.

Design by
Alan Mascord
Design Associates, Inc.

Design DD9477

First Floor: 1,308 square feet
Second Floor: 1,141 square feet
Total: 2,449 square feet
Bonus Room: 266 square feet

Design by
Alan Mascord
Design Associates, Inc.

◀ 56' ▶

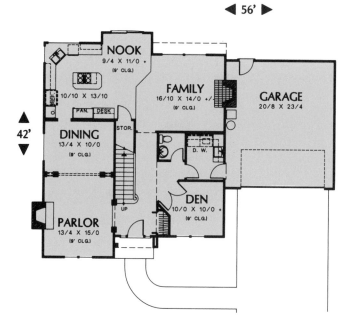

◀ 42' ▶

NOOK
9/4 X 11/0 +
(9' CLG.)

10/10 X 13/10

PAN. DESK

STOR.

DINING
13/4 X 10/0
(9' CLG.)

FAMILY
16/10 X 14/0 +/-
(9' CLG.)

GARAGE
20/8 X 23/4

D. W.

UP

DEN
10/0 X 10/0
(9' CLG.)

PARLOR
13/4 X 15/0
(9' CLG.)

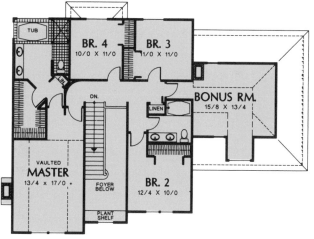

TUB

BR. 4
10/0 X 11/0

BR. 3
11/0 X 11/0

DN.

BONUS RM.
15/8 X 13/4

LINEN

**VAULTED
MASTER**
13/4 x 17/0 +

FOYER
BELOW

PLANT
SHELF

BR. 2
12/4 X 10/0

● Quietly stated elegance is the key to this home's attraction. Its floor plan allows plenty of space for formal and informal occasions. Note that the rear of the first floor is devoted to an open area serving as family room, breakfast nook and island kitchen. This area is complemented by a formal parlor/dining room combination. A private den could function as a guest room with the handy powder room nearby. There are four bedrooms on the second floor. Bonus room over the garage could become an additional bedroom or study.

Design DD3450

First Floor: 1,801 square feet
Second Floor: 1,086 square feet
Total: 2,887 square feet

● A striking facade includes a covered front porch with four columns. To the left of the foyer is a large gathering room with a fireplace and a bay window. The adjoining dining room leads to a covered side porch. The kitchen includes a snack bar, a pantry, a planning desk and a bayed eating area with French doors opening to the rear terrace. The first-floor master suite provides a spacious bath with a walk-in closet, a whirlpool and a separate shower. Also on the first floor are a study and a garage workshop. Two bedrooms and a lavish guest suite share the second floor. For information on customizing this design, call 1-800-521-6797, ext. 800.

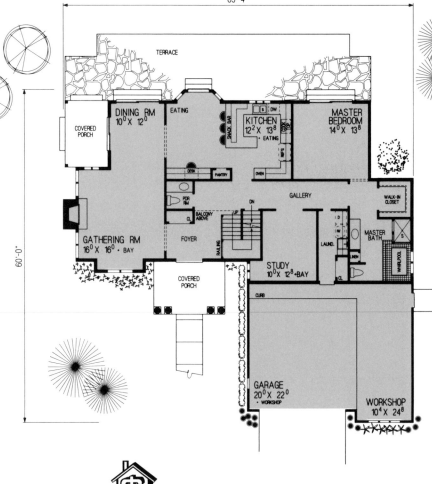

QUOTE ONE™

Cost to build? See page 216
to order complete cost estimate
to build this house in your area!

Design by
**Home Planners,
Inc.**

Design DD3439

First Floor: 1,424 square feet
Second Floor: 995 square feet
Total: 2,419 square feet

● Featuring a facade of wood and window glass, this home presents a striking first impression. It's floor plan is equally as splendid. Formal living and dining areas flank the entry foyer—both are sunken two steps down. Also sunken from the foyer is the family room with attached breakfast nook. A fireplace in this area sits adjacent to a built-in audio-visual center. A nearby study with adjacent full bath doubles as a guest room. Upstairs are three bedrooms including a master suite with whirlpool spa and walk-in closet. Plant shelves adorn the entire floor plan. For information on customizing this design, call 1-800-521-6797, ext. 800.

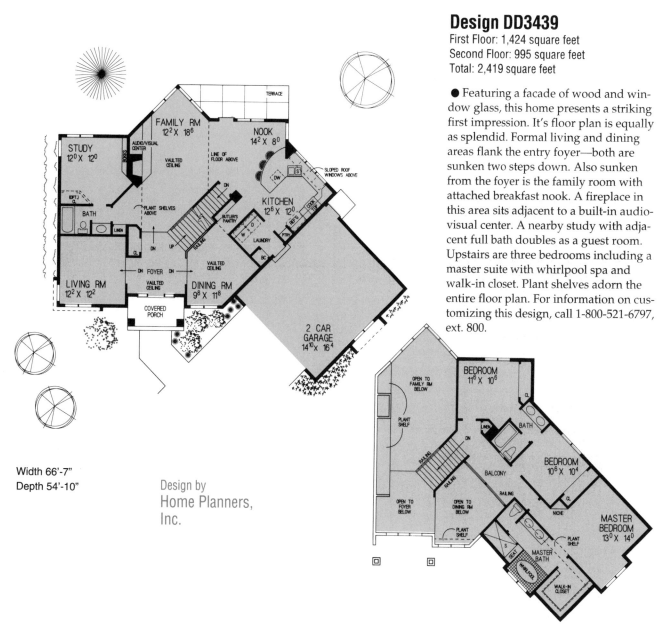

Width 66'-7"
Depth 54'-10"

Design by
Home Planners,
Inc.

BALCONY

MASTER
BED RM.
18⁰ x 13⁶

VANITY

DRESSING RM.

BATH

WALK IN
CLOSET

S

CL

CL

Design DD2711

First Floor: 975 square feet
Second Floor: 1,024 square feet
Total: 1,999 square feet

WALK IN
CLOSET

DN.

LINEN

BED RM.
12⁰ x 11⁰

BATH

BED RM.
11⁰ x 17⁶

● Sleek, modern lines
define this contemporary
two-story home. The open
combination of the dining
room, the U-shaped kitchen
and the gathering room with
its warming fireplace make
this a favorite place for
informal gatherings. The
large master suite features a
huge walk-in closet and a
private balcony, offering a
welcome retreat. Completing
the second floor are two
secondary bedrooms and a
full bath. For information on
customizing this design, call
1-800-521-6797, ext. 800.

40'-4"

TERRACE

52'-0"

GATHERING RM.
18⁰ x 13⁶

DINING RM.
13⁴ x 13⁶

SNACK BAR

STORAGE

RANGE

OVEN

KITCHEN
13⁰ x 10⁰

PANTRY

REF'G.

CL

WASH
RM.

STUDY
11⁰ x 9⁰

ENTRY

CL

PORCH

CURB

GARAGE
21⁴ x 21⁸

Design by
Home Planners,
Inc.

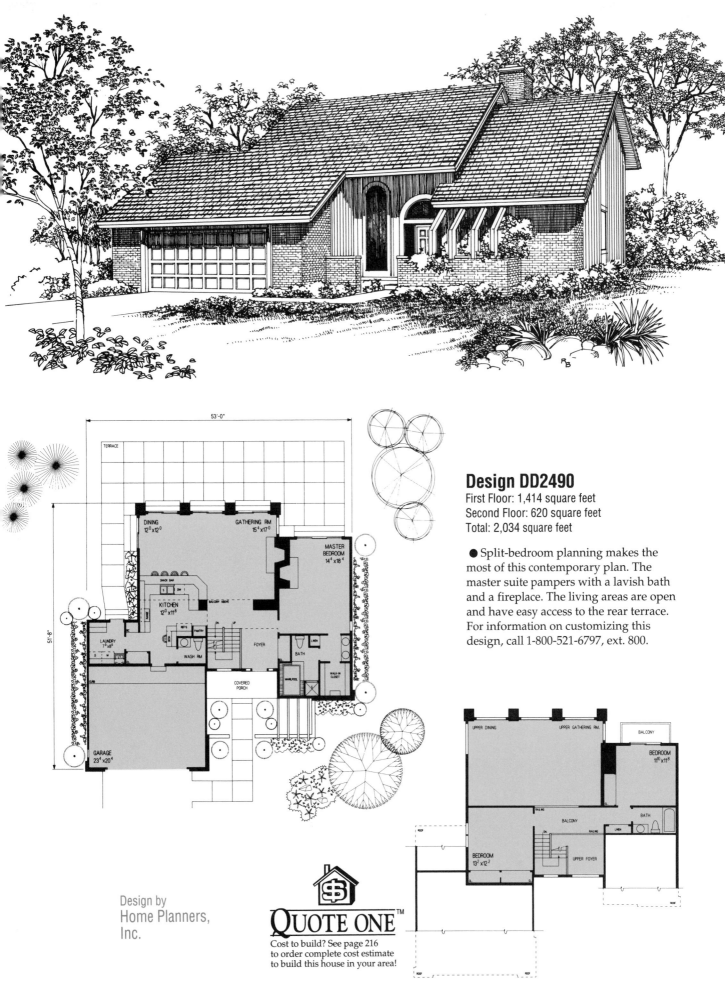

Design DD2490

First Floor: 1,414 square feet
Second Floor: 620 square feet
Total: 2,034 square feet

● Split-bedroom planning makes the most of this contemporary plan. The master suite pampers with a lavish bath and a fireplace. The living areas are open and have easy access to the rear terrace. For information on customizing this design, call 1-800-521-6797, ext. 800.

Design by
Home Planners,
Inc.

QUOTE ONE™

Cost to build? See page 216
to order complete cost estimate
to build this house in your area!

193

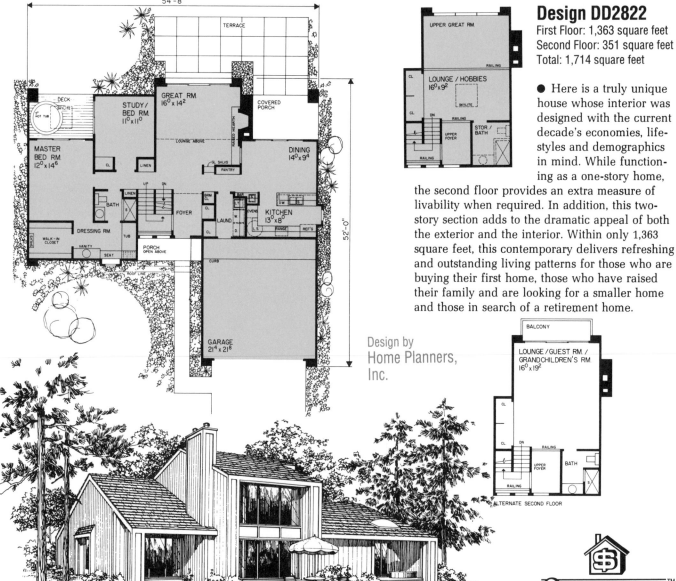

54'-8"

TERRACE

DECK

HOT TUB
SKYLITE

STUDY / BED RM.
11⁰ x 11⁰

GREAT RM.
16⁰ x 14²

COVERED PORCH

LOUNGE ABOVE

RAISED HEARTH

MASTER BED RM.
12⁰ x 14⁶

CL

LINEN

GL. SHLVS
PANTRY

DINING
14⁰ x 9⁴

BATH

LINEN CL

UP DN

BRM CL

DW

WALK-IN CLOSET

DRESSING RM.

TUB

FOYER

LAUND.

OVENS

KITCHEN
13⁰ x 8⁰

RANGE

REF'G

VANITY

SEAT

PORCH OPEN ABOVE

CURB

52'-0"

ROOF LINE

GARAGE
21⁴ x 21⁸

Design by
Home Planners, Inc.

Design DD2822

First Floor: 1,363 square feet
Second Floor: 351 square feet
Total: 1,714 square feet

● Here is a truly unique house whose interior was designed with the current decade's economies, life-styles and demographics in mind. While function-ing as a one-story home, the second floor provides an extra measure of livability when required. In addition, this two-story section adds to the dramatic appeal of both the exterior and the interior. Within only 1,363 square feet, this contemporary delivers refreshing and outstanding living patterns for those who are buying their first home, those who have raised their family and are looking for a smaller home and those in search of a retirement home.

UPPER GREAT RM.

CL

LOUNGE / HOBBIES
16⁰ x 9²

SKYLITE

DN

RAILING

UPPER FOYER

STOR. / BATH

RAILING

BALCONY

LOUNGE / GUEST RM. / GRANDCHILDREN'S RM.
16⁰ x 19²

CL

CL

DN

RAILING

UPPER FOYER

BATH

RAILING

ALTERNATE SECOND FLOOR

QUOTE ONE™

Cost to build? See page 216
to order complete cost estimate
to build this house in your area!

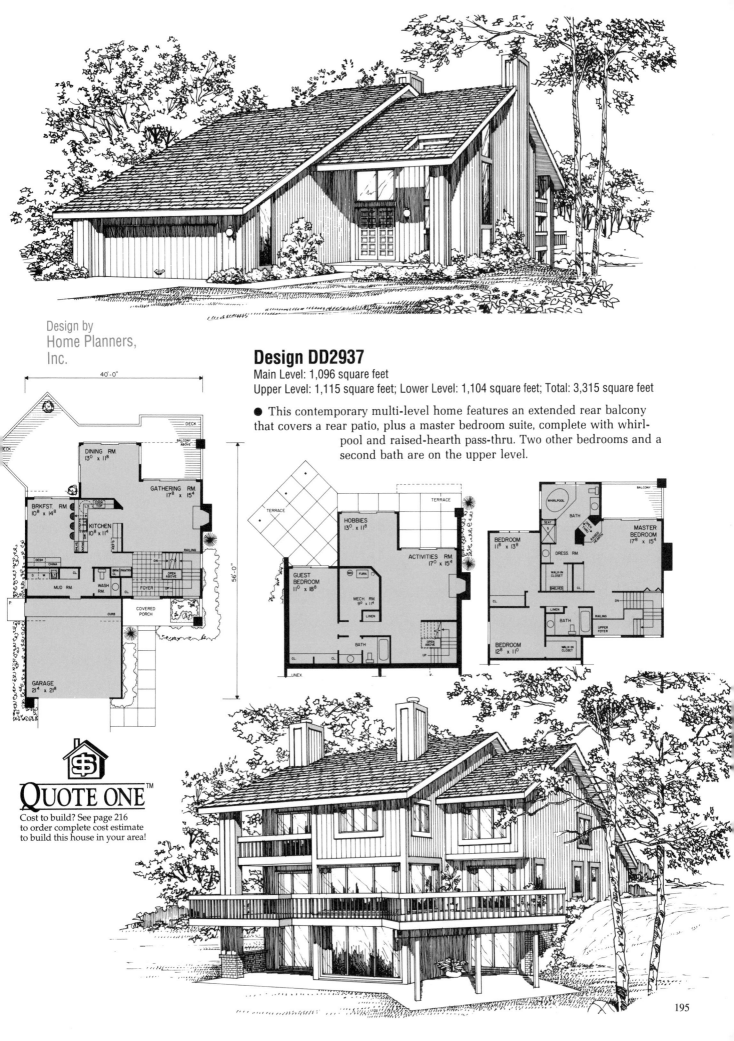

Design by
Home Planners,
Inc.

Design DD2937

Main Level: 1,096 square feet
Upper Level: 1,115 square feet; Lower Level: 1,104 square feet; Total: 3,315 square feet

● This contemporary multi-level home features an extended rear balcony that covers a rear patio, plus a master bedroom suite, complete with whirlpool and raised-hearth pass-thru. Two other bedrooms and a second bath are on the upper level.

QUOTE ONE™

Cost to build? See page 216
to order complete cost estimate
to build this house in your area!

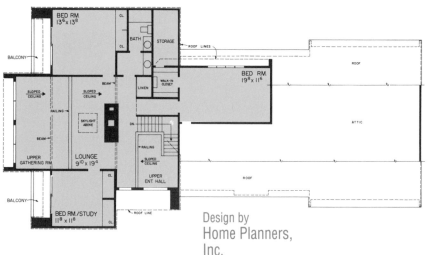

Design by
Home Planners,
Inc.

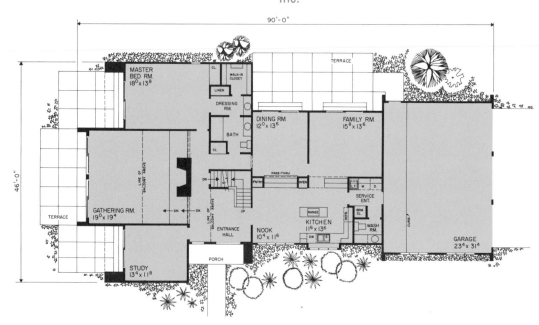

Design DD2781

First Floor: 2,132 square feet
Second Floor: 1,156 square feet
Total: 3,288 square feet

● This beautifully designed two-story could be considered a dream house of a lifetime. The exterior is sure to catch the eye of anyone who takes sight of its unique construction. The front kitchen features an island range, adjacent breakfast nook and pass-thru to formal dining room. The master bedroom suite, with its privacy and convenience on the first floor, has a spacious walk-in closet and dressing room. The side terrace is accessible through sliding glass doors from the master bedroom, gathering room and study. The second floor has three bedrooms and storage space galore. Also notice the lunge which has a sloped ceiling and a skylight above. This delightful area looks down into the gathering room. The outdoor balconies overlook the wrap around terrace. Surely an outstanding trend house for decades to come.

Design DD2826 First Floor: 1,112 square feet
Second Floor: 881 square feet; Total: 1,993 square feet

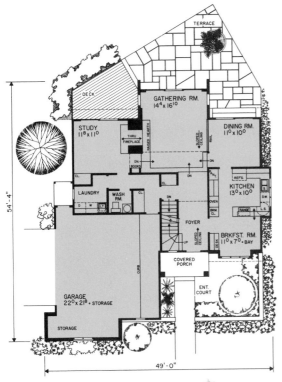

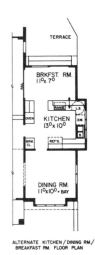

ALTERNATE KITCHEN / DINING RM./
BREAKFAST RM. FLOOR PLAN

● This home offers the type of transitional architecture that captures the imagination. The interior plan houses the most sought-after amenities: a spacious gathering room, both formal and informal dining areas, an efficient kitchen, master suite and two secondary bedrooms. Outdoor living is easy with the rear terrace and deck. For information on customizing this design, call 1-800-521-6797, ext. 800.

Design by
Home Planners,
Inc.

197

COPYRIGHT 1993 LARRY E BELK

Design DD8041

First Floor: 1,937 square feet
Second Floor: 1,215 square feet
Total: 3,152 square feet
Bonus Room: 451 square feet

● A massive, stacked-stone gable highlights the entrance to this magnificent European plan. The two-story foyer and the living room—coupled with ten-foot ceilings throughout the remainder of the first floor—provide an open and spacious feeling. The dining room is located to the right of the foyer and is open on two sides. An efficient kitchen with a work island is conveniently grouped with the breakfast room and the family room, sharing a warming fireplace and providing the ideal area for informal gatherings. An adjacent living room provides space for more formal entertaining. The first-floor master suite shares a luxurious master bath with dual vanities, His and Hers walk-in closets and a corner whirlpool tub. Upstairs are three bedrooms, a bath and an oversized game room. In addition, a large area over the garage is available for future expansion, making this a perfect plan for the growing family. This plan is available with either a crawlspace or slab foundation. Please specify when ordering.

Design by
Larry E. Belk
Designs

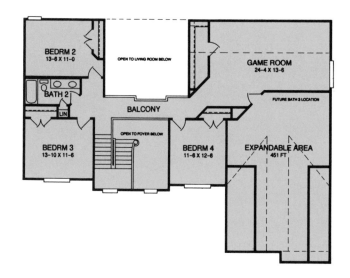

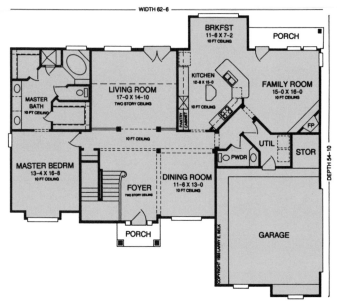

Design by
Larry E. Belk
Designs

Design DD8066

Square Footage: 2,237

● Brick, siding and an accent of wood shingles give this one-story home its distinctive appearance. The foyer leads through a series of columns with graceful, connecting arches to the formal dining room and great room that share a see-through fireplace. An L-shaped kitchen sports an eating bar, a large pantry and a cooktop work island for added convenience. Outdoor dining is easy thanks to an adjacent covered porch. Thoughtful planning makes the master suite a relaxing retreat. Indulge yourself in the soothing whirlpool tub. Other amenities include His and Hers vanities, a separate shower with a seat and an extra-large walk-in closet. Bedrooms 2 and 3 have walk-in closets and share a full bath. Bedroom 4 serves as a study, opening from the foyer through double French doors. However, by interchanging the position of the closet and doors, the study becomes a fourth bedroom with access from the hall. This plan is available with either a crawlspace or slab foundation. Please specify when ordering.

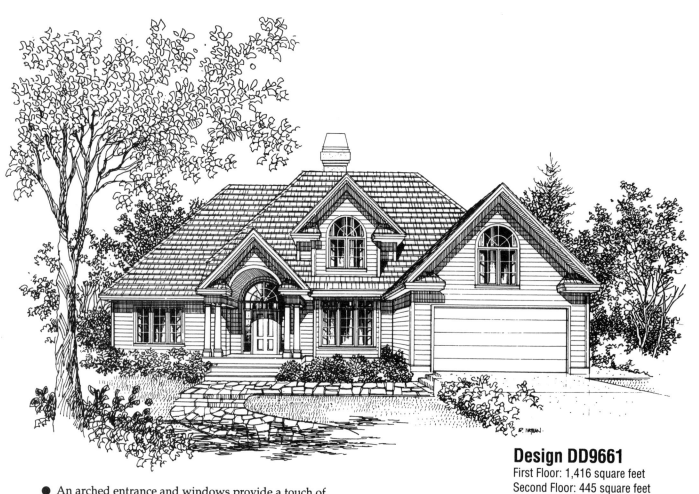

● An arched entrance and windows provide a touch of class to the exterior of this plan. The foyer leads to all areas of the house minimizing corridor space. The dining room displays round columns at the entrance while the great room boasts a cathedral ceiling, fireplace and arched window over exterior doors to the deck. In the master suite is a walk-in closet and lavish bath. On the second level are two bedrooms and a full bath. Bonus space over the garage can be developed later. The plan is available with a crawl-space foundation.

Design DD9661
First Floor: 1,416 square feet
Second Floor: 445 square feet
Total: 1,861 square feet

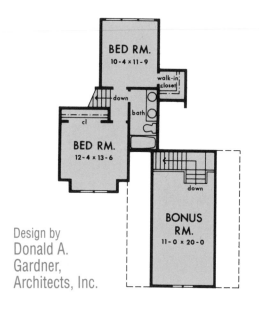

Design by
Donald A.
Gardner,
Architects, Inc.

200

Design by
Donald A.
Gardner,
Architects, Inc.

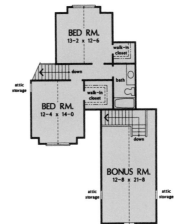

Design DD9736

First Floor: 1,839 square feet
Second Floor: 527 square feet
Total: 2,366 square feet
Bonus Room: 344 square feet

● An arched entrance and windows combine with round columns to develop a touch of class on the exterior of this four-bedroom plan. The plan layout allows no wasted space. The foyer leads to all areas of the house, minimizing corridor space. The large, open kitchen with an island cooktop is convenient to the breakfast and dining rooms. The master bedroom suite has plenty of walk-in closet space and a well-planned master bath. A nearby bedroom would make an excellent guest room or study, with an adjacent full bath. An expansive rear deck boasts a location for a spa tub and generous space for outdoor living. The second level offers two bedrooms, with sloped ceilings and walk-in closets, and a full bath. A bonus room is available over the garage. This plan includes a crawlspace foundation.

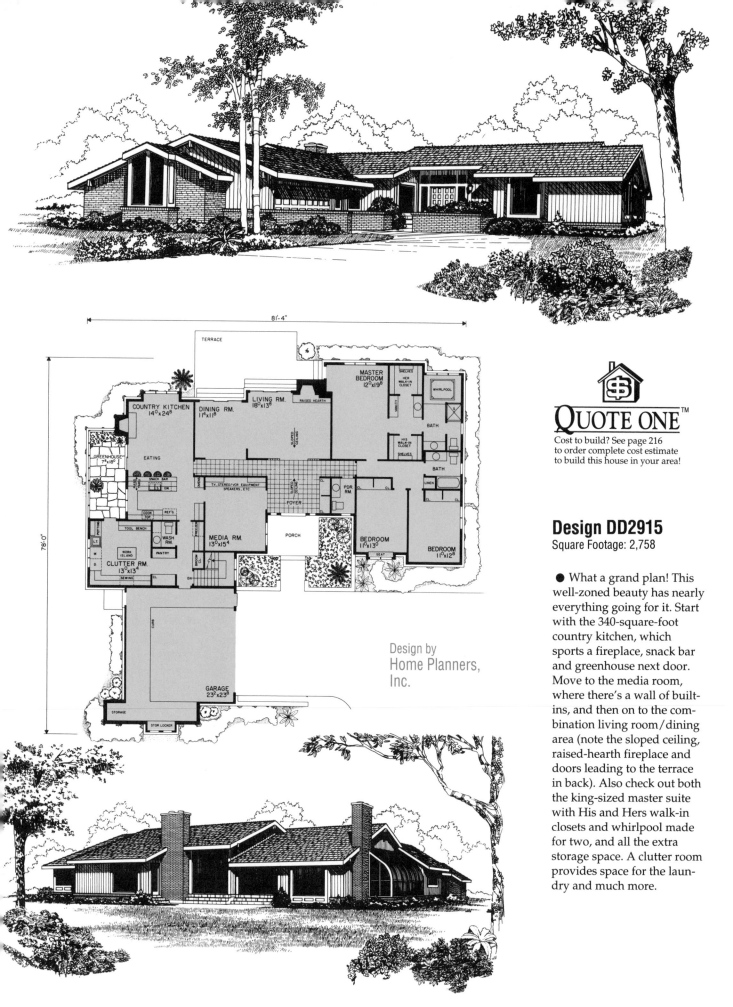

QUOTE **ONE**™

Cost to build? See page 216
to order complete cost estimate
to build this house in your area!

Design DD2915

Square Footage: 2,758

● What a grand plan! This
well-zoned beauty has nearly
everything going for it. Start
with the 340-square-foot
country kitchen, which
sports a fireplace, snack bar
and greenhouse next door.
Move to the media room,
where there's a wall of built-
ins, and then on to the combination living room/dining
area (note the sloped ceiling,
raised-hearth fireplace and
doors leading to the terrace
in back). Also check out both
the king-sized master suite
with His and Hers walk-in
closets and whirlpool made
for two, and all the extra
storage space. A clutter room
provides space for the laundry and much more.

Design by
Home Planners,
Inc.

Design by
Home Planners,
Inc.

QUOTE ONE™

Cost to build? See page 216
to order complete cost estimate
to build this house in your area!

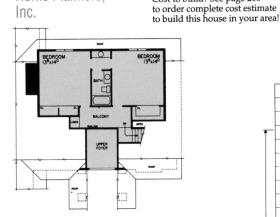

Design DD2920

First Floor: 3,067 square feet
Second Floor: 648 square feet; Total: 3,715 square feet

● This sleek contemporary design has a great
deal to offer. A fireplace opens up to both the
living room and the country kitchen. Privacy is
the key word when describing the sleeping
areas. The secluded first-floor master bedroom
is split from the two secondary bedrooms and
features a dressing/exercise room, a relaxing
whirlpool tub, a separate shower, a huge
walk-in closet, and skylights for plenty of natural light. The cheerful sunroom adds 296
square feet to the total. For information on
customizing this design, call 1-800-521-6797,
ext. 800.

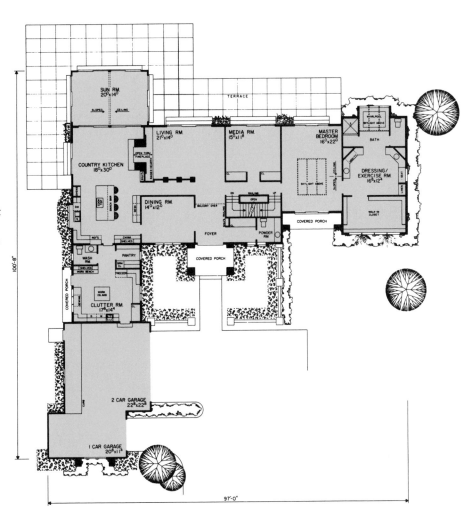

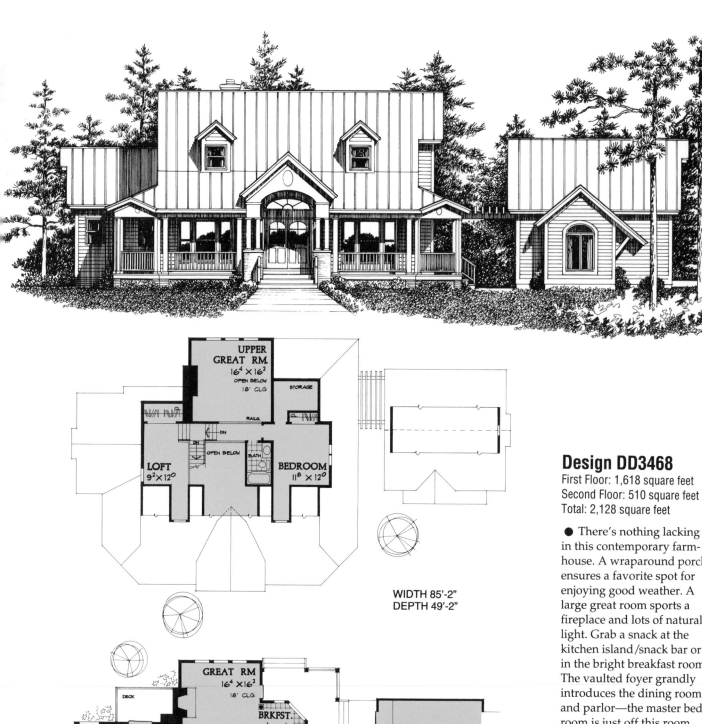

UPPER
GREAT RM.
16⁴ × 16²
OPEN BELOW
18' CLG
STORAGE

RAILG.

DN

LOFT
9² × 12⁰
OPEN BELOW
BATH
BEDROOM
11⁸ × 12⁰

WIDTH 85'-2"
DEPTH 49'-2"

GREAT RM
16⁴ × 16²
18' CLG

BRKFST.
9⁴ × 21⁶

DECK

TRAY CLG
TUB
MASTER BATH
SHWR
W.I.C.

MASTER
BEDRM
13⁰ × 16⁰
12' CLG

PANTRY

KITCHEN

PDR RM
REF.

GARAGE
21⁴ × 20⁴

PARLOR
12⁰ × 11²
9' CLG

FOYER

DINING
RM
12⁰ × 11²
9' CLG

COVERED PORCH

Design DD3468

First Floor: 1,618 square feet
Second Floor: 510 square feet
Total: 2,128 square feet

● There's nothing lacking in this contemporary farmhouse. A wraparound porch ensures a favorite spot for enjoying good weather. A large great room sports a fireplace and lots of natural light. Grab a snack at the kitchen island/snack bar or in the bright breakfast room. The vaulted foyer grandly introduces the dining room and parlor—the master bedroom is just off this room. Inside it: tray ceiling, fireplace, luxury bath and walk-in closet. Stairs lead up to a quaint loft/bedroom—perfect for study or snoozing—a full bath and an additional bedroom. Designated storage space also makes this one a winner.

Design by
Home Planners,
Inc.

Design DD3466

Square Footage: 1,800

● Small but inviting, this one-story contemporary ranch-style farmhouse is the perfect choice for a small family or empty-nesters. It's loaded with amenities even the most particular homeowner can appreciate. For example, the living room and dining room each have plant shelves, sloped ceilings and built-ins to enhance livability. The living room also sports a warming hearth. The master bedroom contains a well-appointed bath with a dual vanity and a walk-in closet. The additional bedroom has its own bath with linen storage. The kitchen is separated from the breakfast nook by a clever bar area. Access to the two-car garage is through a laundry area with washer/dryer hookup space. For information on customizing this design, call 1-800-521-6797, ext. 800.

Design by
Home Planners,
Inc.

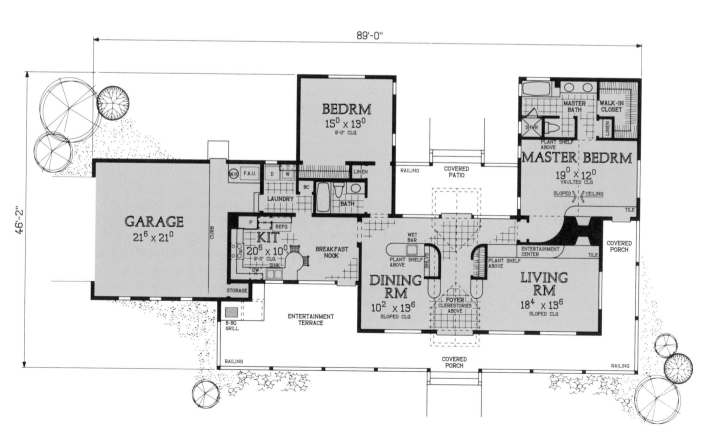

Design DD3469

First Floor: 1,066 square feet
Second Floor: 1,006 square feet
Total: 2,072 square feet

● Our neo-classic farm-
house offers plenty of room
for delightful diversions; a
sheet-metal roof adds old-
fashioned flair; front and
rear porches accommodate
out-of-doors lounging.
Inside, a large living area
with a fireplace affords
grand lounging; a dining
room, cozy interludes. A
fully functional kitchen,
powder room and utility
room round out the first
floor. The second floor provides well-arranged sleeping quarters—with large
master bedroom—and two
full baths. Don't forget the
interesting mud yard separating the garage from the
house.

Design by
Home Planners,
Inc.

COVERED PORCH

DINING RM. 11⁰ × 13² 9' CLG

KITCHEN 13⁰ × 13² 9' CLG

PANTRY

STOR.

STOR.

GARAGE 21⁴ × 20⁸

LIVING ROOM 19⁶ × 17¹⁰ 9' CLG

PWDR. RM.

DN

FOYER

DN

CL.

DN

COVERED PORCH

WIDTH 70'-4"
DEPTH 50'-4"

BEDROOM 13⁰ × 11² 8' CLG

BATH

BEDROOM 13⁰ × 11² 8' CLG

LINEN

W.I.C.

MASTER BATH

OPEN BELOW

DN

MASTER BEDROOM 15⁶ × 15⁶ 8' CLG

COVERED BALCONY

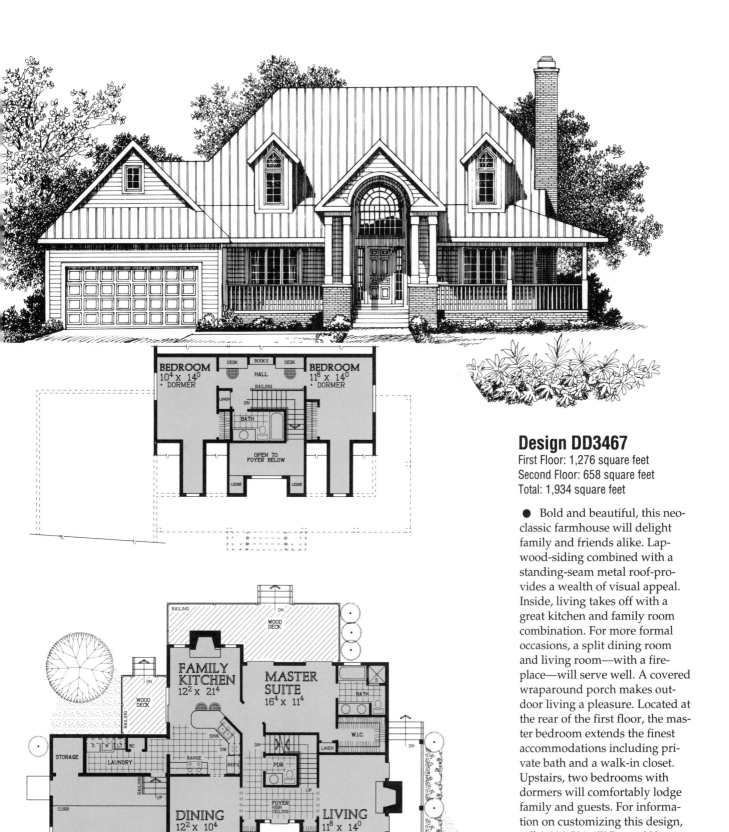

BEDROOM
10⁴ x 14⁰
+ DORMER

DESK BOOKS DESK

HALL

RAILING

BEDROOM
11⁸ x 14⁰
+ DORMER

LINEN

DN

BATH

OPEN TO
FOYER BELOW

LEDGE   LEDGE

Design DD3467

First Floor: 1,276 square feet
Second Floor: 658 square feet
Total: 1,934 square feet

● Bold and beautiful, this neo-classic farmhouse will delight family and friends alike. Lap-wood-siding combined with a standing-seam metal roof provides a wealth of visual appeal. Inside, living takes off with a great kitchen and family room combination. For more formal occasions, a split dining room and living room—with a fireplace—will serve well. A covered wraparound porch makes outdoor living a pleasure. Located at the rear of the first floor, the master bedroom extends the finest accommodations including private bath and a walk-in closet. Upstairs, two bedrooms with dormers will comfortably lodge family and guests. For information on customizing this design, call 1-800-521-6797, ext. 800.

RAILING

DN

WOOD
DECK

FAMILY KITCHEN
12² x 21⁴

MASTER SUITE
16⁴ x 11⁴

BATH

WOOD
DECK

DN

RAILING

STORAGE

LAUNDRY

D W LT BC

RANGE

SINK

DW

REF

PDR

DN

LINEN

W.I.C.

RAILING

UP

UP

DINING
12² x 10⁴

FOYER
HIGH
CEILING

LIVING
11⁸ x 14⁰

GARAGE
20⁰ x 22⁰

CURB

COVERED PORCH

RAILING

UP

RAILING

Width 65'
Depth 51'-8"

Design by
Home Planners,
Inc.

Design DD9498

First Floor: 2,270 square feet
Second Floor: 788 square feet
Total: 3,058 square feet

● Dramatic on the highest level, this spectacular plan offers a recessed entry, double rows of multi-paned windows and two dormers over the garage. On the inside, formal living and dining areas reside to the right of the foyer and are separated from it by columns. A private den is also accessed from the foyer through double doors. The family room with fireplace is to the rear. It adjoins the breakfast nook and attached island kitchen. The master suite is on the first floor to separate it from family bedrooms. They are found on the second floor—there are two with the option of another. There are also two full baths on this floor. Bonus space over the garage can be developed at a later time.

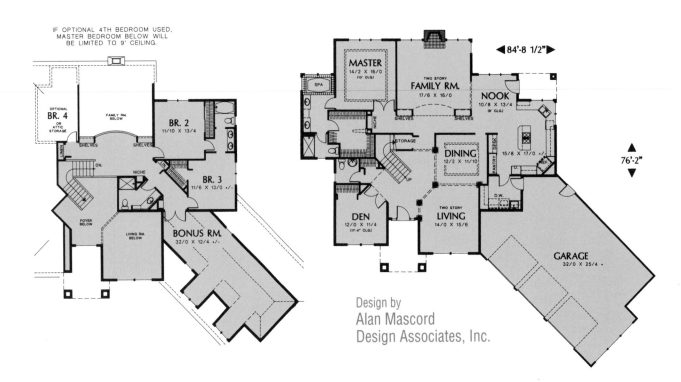

Design by
Alan Mascord
Design Associates, Inc.

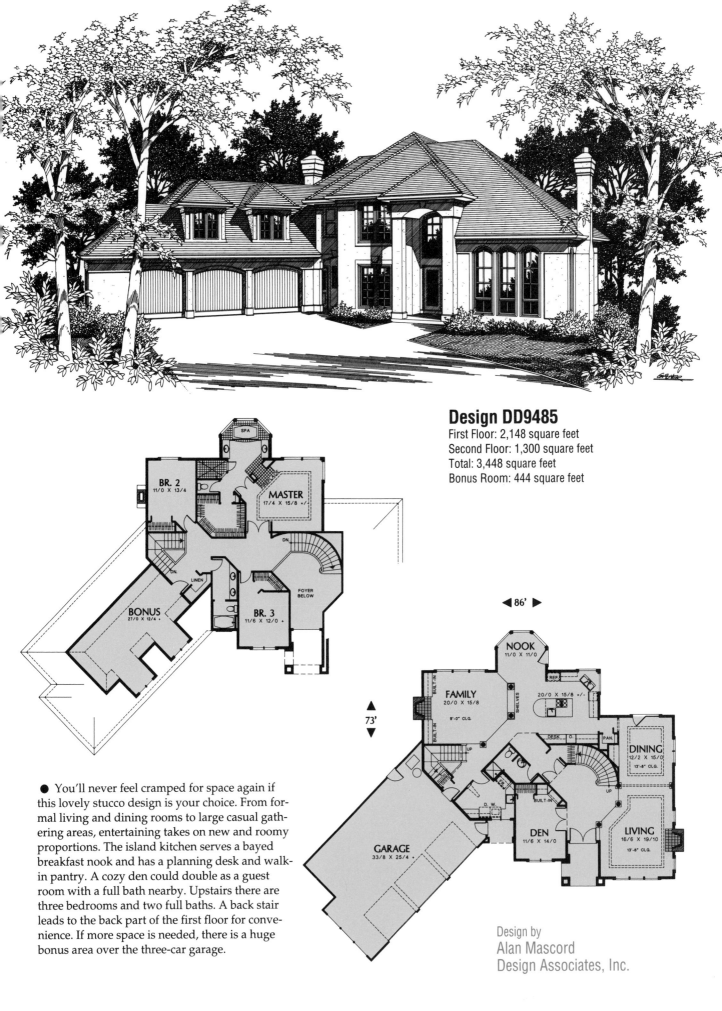

Design DD9485

First Floor: 2,148 square feet
Second Floor: 1,300 square feet
Total: 3,448 square feet
Bonus Room: 444 square feet

BR. 2
11/0 X 13/4

SPA

MASTER
17/4 X 15/8 +/-

DN.

BONUS
27/0 X 12/4 +

DN.

LINEN

BR. 3
11/6 X 12/0 +

FOYER BELOW

◀ 86' ▶

NOOK
11/0 X 11/0

REF.

FAMILY
20/0 X 15/8
9'-0" CLG.

20/0 X 15/8 +/-

SHELVES

BUILT-IN

BUILT-IN

DESK

PAN.

DINING
12/2 X 15/0
13'-8" CLG.

UP

73'

UP

BUILT-IN

D. W.

GARAGE
33/8 X 25/4

DEN
11/6 X 14/0

LIVING
16/6 X 19/10
13'-8" CLG.

● You'll never feel cramped for space again if this lovely stucco design is your choice. From formal living and dining rooms to large casual gathering areas, entertaining takes on new and roomy proportions. The island kitchen serves a bayed breakfast nook and has a planning desk and walk-in pantry. A cozy den could double as a guest room with a full bath nearby. Upstairs there are three bedrooms and two full baths. A back stair leads to the back part of the first floor for convenience. If more space is needed, there is a huge bonus area over the three-car garage.

Design by
Alan Mascord
Design Associates, Inc.

Design DD9521

First Floor: 2,145 square feet
Second Floor: 1,342 square feet
Total: 3,487 square feet

● Here is the best of contemporary design to suit the best of contemporary times. A dynamic floor plan is housed in this elegant exterior. Enter the foyer and find a glass-walled living room to the left, and a glass-walled dining room to the right. Straight ahead, the gracious family room sports a fireplace with high windows flanking each side. Columned arches lead into the bumped-out nook with double doors opening to the rear grounds. An L-shaped kitchen features a double-windowed corner sink, a large walk-in pantry and a convenient cooktop prep island. A den with built-ins and shelves, and a sizable laundry room complete the first floor. Upstairs, double doors open to a master suite fit for a king and queen. The master bedroom delights with a cozy fireplace and a pampering bath with a relaxing spa tub and a giant walk-in closet. Two family bedrooms and a full bath complete the second floor.

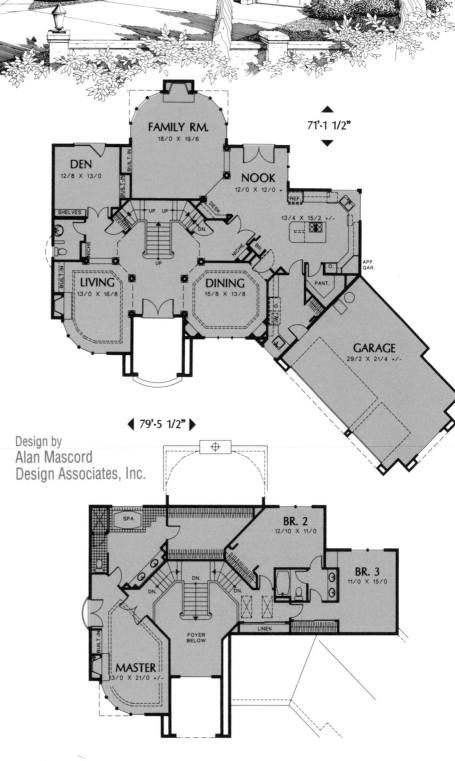

Design by
Alan Mascord
Design Associates, Inc.

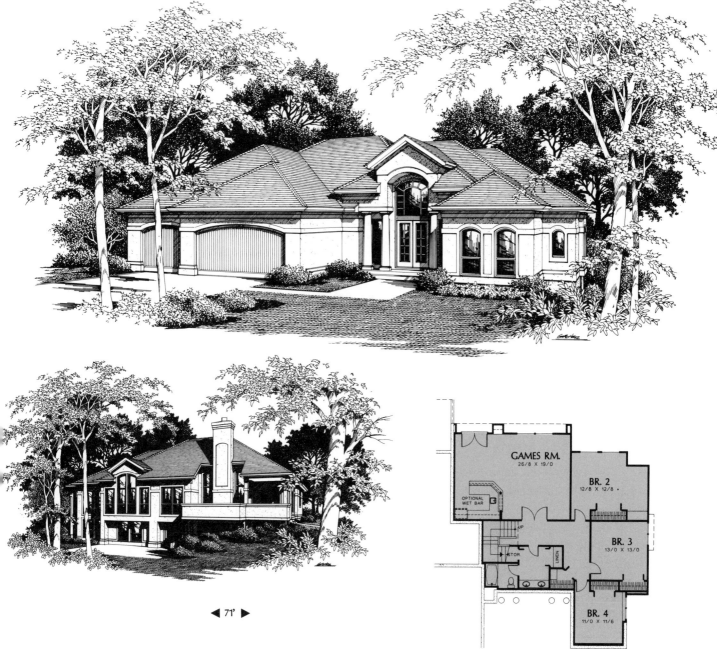

◄ 71' ►

GAMES RM.
26/8 X 19/0

OPTIONAL WET BAR

BR. 2
12/8 X 12/8 +

BR. 3
13/0 X 13/0

UP
STOR.
LINEN

BR. 4
11/0 X 11/6

COVERED DECK

DECK

DINING
10/8 X 14/0

LIVING
16/8 X 15/0

BUILT-INS

NOOK
10/0 x 10/4

FAMILY
14/8 X 16/0

BOOKSHELF

MASTER
17/8 X 15/0

SPA

GALLERY

DN.

D. W.
PAN.

BUILT-IN

▲
56'
▼

GARAGE
32/4 X 23/2 +/-

DEN
12/4 X 14/4 +/-

Design by
Alan Mascord
Design Associates, Inc.

Design DD9417

First Floor: 2,196 square feet
Lower Level: 1,542 square feet
Total: 3,738 square feet

● This refined transitional home is designed to work especially well with lots that slope toward the rear and offers dramatic views out the back. The kitchen and eating nook wrap around the vaulted family room with its arched transom windows flanking the fireplace. Directly off the nook is a covered deck. Don't miss the huge game room on the lower level.

Design DD3409

First Floor: 1,481 square feet
Second Floor: 1,287 square feet
Total: 2,768 square feet

● Glass block walls and a foyer with barrel vaulted ceiling create an interesting exterior. Covered porches to the front and rear provide for excellent indoor/outdoor living relationships. Inside, a large planter and through-fireplace enhance the living room and family room. The dining room has a stepped ceiling. A desk, eating area and snack bar are special features in the kitchen. The master suite features a large walk-in closet, bath with double bowl vanity and separate tub and shower, and a private deck. Three additional bedrooms share a full bath.

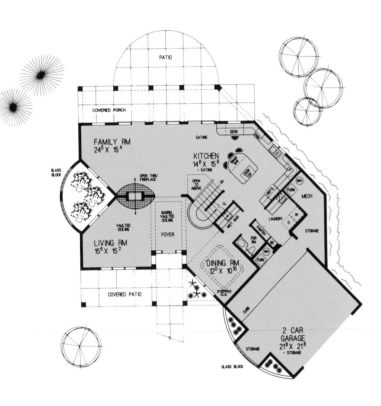

Width 64'
Depth 67'-4"

Design by
Home Planners,
Inc.

QUOTE ONE™

Cost to build? See page 216
to order complete cost estimate
to build this house in your area!

Design DD3403

First Floor: 2,240 square feet
Second Floor: 660 square feet
Total: 2,900 square feet

Design by
Home Planners,
Inc.

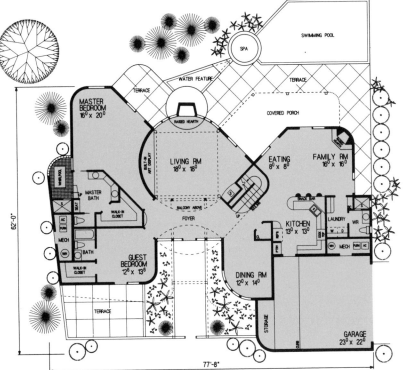

● There is no end to the distinctive features in
this Southwestern contemporary. Formal living areas are concentrated in the center of the
plan, perfect for entertaining. To the right of the
plan, the kitchen and family room function
well together as a working and living area. Also
note the separate laundry room. The optional
guest bedroom or den and the master bedroom
are located to the left of the plan. Upstairs, the
remaining two bedrooms are reached by a balcony overlooking the living room and share a
bath with twin vanities.

When You're Ready To Order . . .

Let Us Show You Our Home Blueprint Package.

Building a home? Planning a home? Our Blueprint Package has nearly everything you need to get the job done right, whether you're working on your own or with help from an architect, designer, builder or subcontractors. Each Blueprint Package is the result of many hours of work by licensed architects or professional designers.

QUALITY

Hundreds of hours of painstaking effort have gone into the development of your blueprint set. Each home has been quality-checked by professionals to insure accuracy and buildability.

VALUE

Because we sell in volume, you can buy professional-quality blueprints at a fraction of their development cost. With our plans, your dream home design costs only a few hundred dollars, not the thousands of dollars that custom architects charge.

SERVICE

Once you've chosen your favorite home plan, you'll receive fast, efficient service whether you choose to mail or fax your order to us or call us toll free at 1-800-521-6797.

SATISFACTION

Our years of service to satisfied home plan buyers provide us the experience and knowledge that guarantee your satisfaction with our product and performance.

ORDER TOLL FREE 1-800-521-6797

After you've looked over our Blueprint Package and Important Extras on the following pages, simply mail the order form on page 221 or call toll free on our Blueprint Hotline: 1-800-521-6797. We're ready and eager to serve you.

Each set of blueprints is an interrelated collection of detail sheets which includes components such as floor plans, interior and exterior elevations, dimensions, cross-sections, diagrams and notations. These sheets show exactly how your house is to be built.

Among the sheets included may be:

Frontal Sheet
This artist's sketch of the exterior of the house gives you an idea of how the house will look when built and landscaped. Large ink-line floor plans show all levels of the house and provide an overview of your new home's livability, as well as a handy reference for deciding on furniture placement.

Foundation Plan
This sheet shows the foundation layout includ-

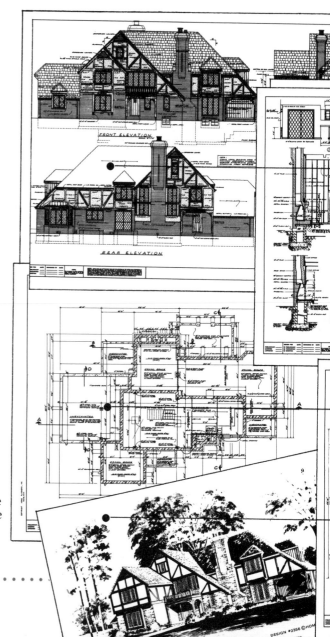

ing support walls, excavated and unexcavated areas, if any, and foundation notes. If slab construction rather the basement, the plan shows footings and details for a monolithic slab. This page, or another in the set, may include a sample plot plan for locating your house on a building site.

Detailed Floor Plans

These plans show the layout of each floor of the house. Rooms and interior spaces are carefully dimensioned and keys are given for cross-section details provided later in the plans. The positions of electrical outlets and switches are shown.

House Cross-Sections

Large-scale views show sections or cut-aways of the foundation, interior walls, exterior walls, floors, stairways and roof details. Additional cross-sections may show important changes in

floor, ceiling or roof heights or the relationship of one level to another. Extremely valuable for construction, these sections show exactly how the various parts of the house fit together.

Interior Elevations

These large-scale drawings show the design and placement of kitchen and bathroom cabinets, laundry areas, fireplaces, bookcases and other built-ins. Little "extras," such as mantelpiece and wainscoting drawings, plus moulding sections, provide details that give your home that custom touch.

Exterior Elevations

These drawings show the front, rear and sides of your house and give necessary notes on exterior materials and finishes. Particular attention is given to cornice detail, brick and stone accents or other finish items that make your home unique.

Sample Package

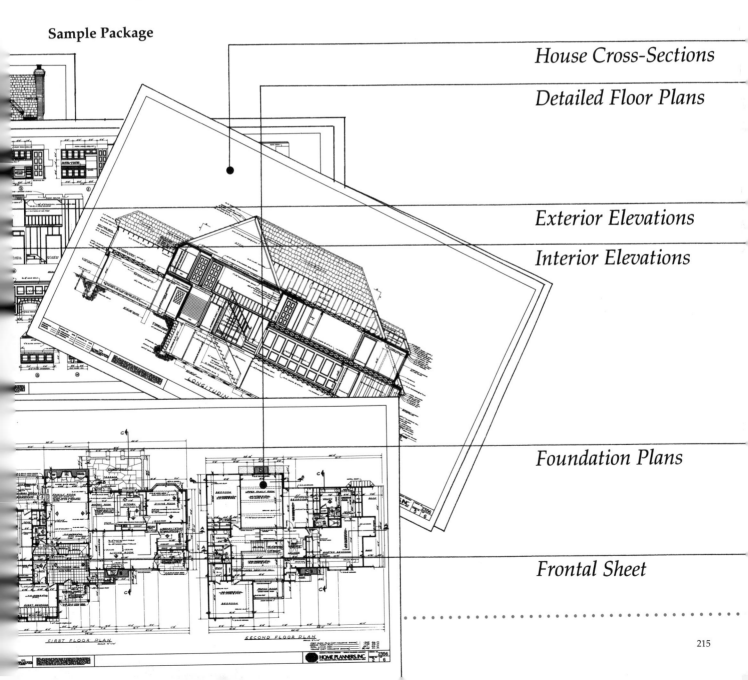

House Cross-Sections

Detailed Floor Plans

Exterior Elevations

Interior Elevations

Foundation Plans

Frontal Sheet

215

*I*mportant Extras To Do The Job Right!

Introducing eight important planning and construction aids developed by our professionals to help you succeed in your home-building project.

MATERIALS LIST

For many of the designs in our portfolio, we offer a customized materials take-off that is invaluable in planning and estimating the cost of your new home. This comprehensive list outlines the quantity, type and size of materials needed to build your house (with the exception of mechanical system items). Included are:

- framing lumber
- roofing and sheet metal
- windows and doors
- exterior sheathing material and trim
- masonry, veneer and fireplace materials
- tile and flooring materials
- kitchen and bath cabinetry
- interior drywall and trim
- rough and finish hardware
- many more items

This handy list helps you or your builder cost out materials and serves as a ready reference sheet when you're compiling bids. It also provides a cross-check against the materials specified by your builder and helps coordinate the substitution of items you may need to meet local codes.

(Note: Because of differing local codes, building methods, and availability of materials, our Materials Lists do not include mechanical materials. To obtain necessary take-offs and recommendations, consult heating, plumbing and electrical contractors. Materials Lists are not sold separately from the Blueprint Package.)

SPECIFICATION OUTLINE

This valuable 16-page document is critical to building your house correctly. Designed to be filled in by you or your builder, this book lists 166 stages or items crucial to the building process. It provides a comprehensive review of the construction process and helps in making choices of materials. When combined with the blueprints, a signed contract, and a schedule, it becomes a legal document and record for the building of your home.

QUOTE ONE™

A new service for estimating the cost of building select Home Planners designs, the Quote One™ system is available in two separate stages: The Summary Cost Report and the Detailed Cost Estimate. The Summary Cost Report shows the total cost per square foot for your chosen home in your zip-code area and then breaks that cost down into ten categories showing the costs for building materials, labor and installation. The total cost for the report (including three grades: Budget, Standard and Custom) is just $15 for one home; $25 for two and additionals are only $5. These reports allow you to evaluate your building budget and compare the costs of building a variety of homes in your area.

The Detailed Cost Estimate furnishes an even more detailed report. The material and installation (labor + equipment) cost is shown for each of over 1,000 line items provided in the Standard grade. Space is allowed for additional estimates from contractors and subcontractors. This invaluable tool is available for a price of $100 ($110 for a Schedule E plan) which includes the price of a materials list which must be purchased at the same time.

To order these invaluable reports, use the order form on page 221 or call **1-800-521-6797**.

CONSTRUCTION INFORMATION

If you want to know more about techniques—and deal more confidently with subcontractors—we offer these useful sheets. Each set is an excellent tool that will add to your understanding of these technical subjects.

Plan-A-Home®

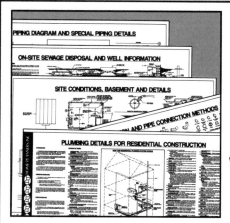

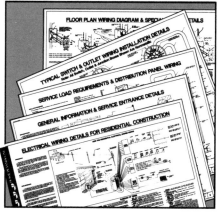

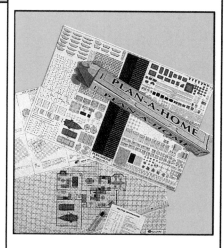

PLUMBING

The Blueprint Package includes locations for all the plumbing fixtures in your new house, including sinks, lavatories, tubs, showers, toilets, laundry trays and water heaters. However, if you want to know more about the complete plumbing system, these 24x36-inch detail sheets will prove very useful. Prepared to meet requirements of the National Plumbing Code, these six fact-filled sheets give general information on pipe schedules, fittings, sump-pump details, water-softener hookups, septic system details and much more. Color-coded sheets include a glossary of terms.

ELECTRICAL

The locations for every electrical switch, plug and outlet are shown in your Blueprint Package. However, these Electrical Details go further to take the mystery out of household electrical systems. Prepared to meet requirements of the National Electrical Code, these comprehensive 24x36-inch drawings come packed with helpful information, including wire sizing, switch-installation schematics, cable-routing details, appliance wattage, door-bell hookups, typical service panel circuitry and much more. Six sheets are bound together and color-coded for easy reference. A glossary of terms is also included.

Plan-A-Home® is an easy-to-use tool that helps you design a new home, arrange furniture in a new or existing home, or plan a remodeling project. Each package contains:

- **More than 700 reusable peel-off planning symbols** on a self-stick vinyl sheet, including walls, windows, doors, all types of furniture, kitchen components, bath fixtures and many more.

- **A reusable, transparent, 1/4-inch scale planning grid** that matches the scale of actual working drawings (1/4-inch equals 1 foot). This grid provides the basis for house layouts of up to 140x92 feet.

- **Tracing paper** and a protective sheet for copying or transferring your completed plan.

- **A felt-tip pen**, with water-soluble ink that wipes away quickly.

Plan-A-Home® lets you lay out areas as large as a 7,500 square foot, six-bedroom, seven-bath house.

CONSTRUCTION

The Blueprint Package contains everything an experienced builder needs to construct a particular house. However, it doesn't show all the ways that houses can be built, nor does it explain alternate construction methods. To help you understand how your house will be built—and offer additional techniques—this set of drawings depicts the materials and methods used to build foundations, fireplaces, walls, floors and roofs. Where appropriate, the drawings show acceptable alternatives. These six sheets will answer questions for the advanced do-it-yourselfer or home planner.

MECHANICAL

This package contains fundamental principles and useful data that will help you make informed decisions and communicate with subcontractors about heating and cooling systems. The 24x36-inch drawings contain instructions and samples that allow you to make simple load calculations and preliminary sizing and costing analysis. Covered are today's most commonly used systems from heat pumps to solar fuel systems. The package is packed full of illustrations and diagrams to help you visualize components and how they relate to one another.

To Order, Call Toll Free 1-800-521-6797

To add these important extras to your Blueprint Package, simply indicate your choices on the order form on page 221 or call us Toll Free 1-800-521-6797 and we'll tell you more about these exciting products.

House Blueprint Price Schedule and Plans Index

These pages contain all the information you need to price your blueprints. In general the larger and more complicated the house, the more it costs to design and thus the higher the price we must charge for the blueprints. Remember, however, that these prices are far less than you would normally pay for the services of a licensed architect or professional designer. Custom home designs and related architectural services often cost thousands of dollars, ranging from 5% to 15% of the cost of construction. By ordering our blueprints you are potentially saving enough money to afford a larger house, or to add those "extra" amenities such as a patio, deck, swimming pool or even an upgraded kitchen or luxurious master suite.

To use the Index below, refer to the design number listed in numerical order (a helpful page reference is also given). Note the price index letter and refer to the House Blueprint Price Schedule at right for the cost of one, four or eight sets of blueprints or the cost of a reproducible sepia. Additional prices are shown for identical and reverse blueprint sets, as well as a very useful Materials List for some of the plans.

House Blueprint Price Schedule
(Prices guaranteed through December 31, 1995)

	1-set Study Package	4-set Building Package	8-set Building Package	1-set Reproducible Sepias
Schedule A	$240	$300	$360	$460
Schedule B	$280	$340	$400	$520
Schedule C	$320	$380	$440	$580
Schedule D	$360	$420	$480	$640
Schedule E	$480	$540	$600	$700

Additional Identical Blueprints in same order ....$50 per set
Reverse Blueprints (mirror image) ....$50 per set
Specification Outlines...$10 each
Materials Lists (for Home Planners', Larry Belk's, Design Basics', Alan Mascord's, and Donald Gardner's Plans only):
  ▲ Home Planners' Designs
      Schedule A-D $40
      Schedule E $50
  ≠ Larry Belk's Designs $50
  † Design Basics' Designs...$75
  ◆ Donald Gardner's Designs $40
  ✳ Alan Mascord's Designs $40
Exchanges.........................$50 exchange fee for the first set; $10 for each additional set
                        $70 total exchange fee for 4 sets
                        $100 total exchange fee for 8 sets

To Order: Fill in and send the Order Form on page 221—or call us Toll Free 1-800-521-6797.

DESIGN	PRICE	PAGE	CUSTOMIZABLE	QUOTE ONE™	CALIFORNIA PLANS
DD9046	C	23			
DD9056	D	126			
DD9067	D	123			
DD9082	D	170			
DD9083	D	171			
DD9085	D	120			
DD9087	D	54			
DD9088	C	102			
DD9089	C	103			
DD9095	E	33			
DD9097	C	98			
DD9098	C	101			
DD9108	D	55			
DD9126	D	32			
DD9131	C	147			
DD9156	D	104			
DD9161	C	99			
DD9182	C	100			
DD9183	D	116			
DD9185	C	146			
† DD9211	E	118			
† DD9214	D	73			
† DD9235	C	75			
† DD9242	E	86			
† DD9251	D	138			
† DD9268	D	140			
† DD9270	C	137			
† DD9274	D	87			
† DD9277	D	139			
† DD9288	C	136			
† DD9297	E	89			
† DD9298	D	88			
† DD9299	D	34			
† DD9300	C	72			
† DD9312	D	74			
† DD9343	C	7			
† DD9344	D	8			
† DD9346	E	119			
† DD9367	E	37			
† DD9390	E	35			
✳ DD9400	D	188			
✳ DD9403	E	149			
✳ DD9417	E	211			
✳ DD9420	D	134			
✳ DD9439	B	148			
✳ DD9468	B	77			
✳ DD9475	C	135			
✳ DD9477	C	189			
✳ DD9485	E	209			
✳ DD9497	C	76			
✳ DD9498	E	208			
✳ DD9513	E	186			
✳ DD9517	C	60			
✳ DD9518	B	150			
✳ DD9519	B	151			
✳ DD9520	E	187			
✳ DD9521	E	210			
◆ DD9606	C	47			
◆ DD9611	C	156			
◆ DD9621	C	46			
◆ DD9632	D	48			
◆ DD9645	C	49			
◆ DD9661	C	200			
◆ DD9662	C	95			
◆ DD9664	B	96			
◆ DD9666	C	154			
◆ DD9669	D	51			
◆ DD9709	D	43			
◆ DD9711	C	94			
◆ DD9714	C	42			
◆ DD9726	B	157			
◆ DD9728	C	112			
◆ DD9734	C	113			
◆ DD9735	D	115			
◆ DD9736	D	201			
◆ DD9737	C	163			
◆ DD9740	C	162			
◆ DD9741	D	114			
◆ DD9742	C	50			
DD9804	D	63			
DD9821	C	14			
DD9822	C	15			
DD9837	D	38			
DD9844	B	40			
DD9851	D	78			
DD9853	B	79			
DD9861	D	81			
DD9862	C	159			
DD9884	C	41			
DD9898	D	158			
DD9899	D	39			
DD9908	D	80			
DD9918	D	62			
DD9919	D	64			
DD9920	E	65			
DD9921	E	66			
DD9922	D	67			

Before You Order . . .

Before filling out the coupon at right or calling us on our Toll-Free Blueprint Hotline, you may want to learn more about our services and products. Here's some information you will find helpful.

Quick Turnaround
We process and ship every blueprint order from our office within 48 hours. Because of this quick turnaround, we won't send a formal notice acknowledging receipt of your order.

Our Exchange Policy
Since blueprints are printed in response to your order, we cannot honor requests for refunds. However, we will exchange your entire first order for an equal number of blueprints at a price of $50 for the first set and $10 for each additional set; $70 total exchange fee for 4 sets: $100 total exchange fee for 8 sets. . . *plus* the difference in cost if exchanging for a design in a higher price bracket or *less* the difference in cost if exchanging for a design in a lower price bracket. One exchange is allowed within a year of purchase date. **(Sepias are not exchangeable. No exchanges can be made for the California Engineered Plans since they are tailored to your specific building site.)** All sets from the first order must be returned before the exchange can take place. Please add $10 for postage and handling via ground service; $20 via 2nd Day Air.

About Reverse Blueprints
If you want to build in reverse of the plan as shown, we will include an extra set of reverse blueprints (mirror image) for an additional fee of $50. Lettering and dimensions will appear backward. Right-reading reverses of Home Customizer® plans are available. Call 1-800-521-6797, ext. 800 for more details.

Modifying or Customizing Our Plans
With such a great selection of homes, you are bound to find the one that suits you. However, if you need to make alterations to a design that is customizable, you need only order our Customizer® kit or call our Customization representative at 1-800-521-6797, ext. 800 to get you started. We strongly suggest you order sepias if you decide to revise non-Customizable plans significantly.

Architectural and Engineering Seals
Some cities and states are now requiring that a licensed architect or engineer review and "seal" your blueprints prior to building due to local or regional concerns over energy consumption, safety codes, seismic ratings or other factors. For this reason, it may be necessary to talk to a local professional to have your plans reviewed. In some cases, Home Planners can seal your plans through our Customization Service. Call 1-800-521-6797, ext. 800 for more details.

Compliance with Local Codes and Regulations
At the time of creation, our plans are drawn to specifications published by the Building Officials and Code Administrators (BOCA) International, Inc.; the Southern Building Code Congress (SBCCI) International, Inc.; the International Conference of Building Officials; or the Council of American Building Officials (CABO). Our plans are designed to meet or exceed national building standards. Some states, counties and municipalities have their own codes, zoning requirements and building regulations. Before building, contact your local building authorities to make sure you comply with local ordinances and codes, including obtaining any necessary permits or inspections as building progresses. In some cases, minor modifications to your plans by your builder, architect or designer may be required to meet local conditions and requirements. Home Planners may be able to make these changes to Home Customizer® plans providing you supply all pertinent information from your local building authorities.

Foundation and Exterior Wall Changes
Most of our plans are drawn with either a full or partial basement foundation. Depending on your specific climate or regional building practices, you may wish to change this basement to a slab or crawlspace. Most professional contractors and builders can easily adapt your plans to alternate foundation types. Likewise, most can easily change 2x4 wall construction to 2x6, or vice versa. For Home Customizer® plans, Home Planners can easily make the changes for you.

How Many Blueprints Do You Need?
A single set of blueprints is sufficient to study a home in greater detail. However, if you are planning to obtain cost estimates from a contractor or subcontractors—or if you are planning to build immediately—you will need more sets. Because additional sets are cheaper when ordered in quantity with the original order, make sure you order enough blueprints to satisfy all requirements. The following checklist will help you determine how many you need:

_____Owner

_____Builder (generally requires at least three sets; one as a legal document, one to use during inspections, and at least one to give to subcontractors)

_____Local Building Department (often requires two sets)

_____Mortgage Lender (usually one set for a conventional loan; three sets for FHA or VA loans)

_____TOTAL NUMBER OF SETS

Have You Seen Our Newest Designs?

Home Planners is one of the country's most active home design firms, creating nearly 100 new plans each year. At least 50 of our latest creations are featured in each edition of our New Design Portfolio. You may have received a copy with your latest purchase by mail. If not, or if you purchased this book from a local retailer, just return the coupon below for your FREE copy. Make sure you consider the very latest of what Home Planners has to offer.

Yes! Please send my FREE copy of your latest New Design Portfolio.

Name _____

Address _____

City _____ State _____ Zip _____

HOME PLANNERS, INC.
3275 West Ina Road, Suite 110,
Tucson, Arizona 85741

Order Form Key

TB35NDP

The Home Customizer®

Many of the plans in this book are customizable through our Home Customizer® service. Look for this symbol on the pages of home designs. It indicates that the plan on that page is part of The Home Customizer® service.

Some changes to customizable plans that can be made include:

- exterior elevation changes
- kitchen and bath modifications
- roof, wall and foundation changes
- room additions
- and much more!

If the plan you have chosen to build is one of our customizable homes, you can easily order the Home Customizer® kit to start on the path to making your alterations. The kit, priced at only $29.95, may be ordered at the same time you order your blueprint package by calling our toll-free number or using the order blank at right. Or you can wait until you receive your blueprints, spend some time studying them and then order the kit by phone, FAX or mail. If you then decide to proceed with the customizing service, the $29.95 price of the kit will be refunded to you after your customization order is received. The Home Customizer® kit includes:

- instruction book with examples
- architectural scale
- clear acetate work film
- erasable red marker
- removable correction tape
- ¼" scale furniture cutouts
- 1 set of Customizable Drawings with floor plans and elevations

The service is easy, fast and *affordable*. Because we know and work with our plans and have them available on state-of-the-art computer systems, we can make the changes efficiently at prices much lower than those charged by normal architectural or drafting services. In addition, you'll be getting custom changes directly from Home Planners—the company whose dedication to excellence and long-standing professional experience are well recognized in the industry.

Call now to learn more about how simple it can be to have the *custom home* you've always wanted.

California Customers!!

For our customers in California, we now offer California Engineered Plans (CEP) and California Stock Plans (CSP) to help in meeting the strict California building codes. Check Plan index for homes that are available through this new service or call 1-800-521-6797 for more information about the availability of the service and prices.

☎ **Toll Free 1-800-521-6797, Ext. 800**

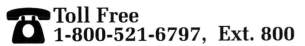

BLUEPRINTS ARE NOT RETURNABLE

ORDER FORM

 HOME PLANNERS, INC., 3275 WEST INA ROAD
SUITE 110, TUCSON, ARIZONA 85741

THE BASIC BLUEPRINT PACKAGE

Rush me the following (please refer to the Plans Index and Price Schedule in this section):

_____ Set(s) of blueprints for plan number(s) _____.	$_____
_____ Set(s) of sepias for plan number(s) _____.	$_____
_____ Additional identical blueprints in same order @ $50 per set.	$_____
_____ Reverse blueprints @ $50 per set.	$_____
_____ Home Customizer® Kit(s) for Plan(s)_____ @ $29.95 per kit.	$_____

IMPORTANT EXTRAS

Rush me the following:

_____ Materials List: Home Planners' Designs (Not available for CEP service) @ $40 Schedule A-D; $50 Schedule E; $50 Larry Belk's Designs; $75 Design Basics' Designs; $40 Alan Mascord's Designs; $40 Donald Gardner's Designs. $_____

Quote One™ Custom Quoting System

_____ Quote One™ Summary Cost Report @ $15 for 1, $25 for 2, $5 for each additional, for plans _____. $_____

_____ Quote One™ Detailed Cost Estimate @ $100 Schedule A-D; $110 Schedule E for plan_____. $_____

(must be purchased with Materials List and Blueprints set)

_____ Specification Outlines @ $10 each. $_____

_____ Detail Sets @ $14.95 each; any two for $22.95; any three for $29.95; all four for $39.95 (save $19.85). $_____

❑ Plumbing ❑ Electrical ❑ Construction ❑ Mechanical
(These helpful details provide general construction advice and are not specific to any single plan.)

_____ Plan-A-Home® @ $29.95 each. $_____

SUB-TOTAL $_____

POSTAGE AND HANDLING	1-3 sets	4+ sets
DELIVERY (Requires street address - No P.O. Boxes)		
•Regular Service (Allow 4-6 days delivery)	❑ $8.00	❑ $10.00
•2nd Day Air (Allow 2-3 days delivery)	❑ $12.00	❑ $20.00
•Next Day Air (Allow 1 day delivery)	❑ $22.00	❑ $30.00
POST OFFICE DELIVERY If no street address available. (Allow 4-6 days delivery)	❑ $10.00	❑ $14.00
OVERSEAS DELIVERY Note: All delivery times are from date Blueprint Package is shipped.	fax, phone or mail for quote	

POSTAGE (From shaded box above) $_____

SALES TAX (Arizona residents add 5% sales tax; Michigan residents add 6% sales tax.) $_____

TOTAL (Sub-total, postage, and tax) $_____

YOUR ADDRESS (please print)

Name _____

Street _____

City _____ State_____ Zip _____

Daytime telephone number (_____) _____

FOR CREDIT CARD ORDERS ONLY

Please fill in the information below:

Credit card number _____

Exp. Date: Month/Year _____

Check one ❑ Visa ❑ MasterCard ❑ Discover Card

Signature _____

Please check appropriate box: ❑ Licensed Builder-Contractor
❑ Home Owner

 ORDER TOLL FREE
1-800-521-6797 or
602-297-8200

Order Form Key
TB35BP

Additional Plans Books

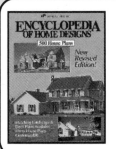

1. ENCYCLOPEDIA OF HOME DESIGNS (EN) Our best collection of plans is now bigger and better than ever! Over 500 plans organized by architectural category. Includes all types and styles. The most comprehensive plan book ever. 352 pages. $9.95 ($12.95 Can.)

2. THE ESSENTIAL GUIDE TO TRADITIONAL HOMES (ET) Over 400 traditional homes in one special volume. American and European styles from Farmhouses to Norman French. Best sellers shown in color photographs and renderings. 304 pages. $9.95 ($12.95 Can.)

3. THE ESSENTIAL GUIDE TO CONTEMPORARY HOMES (EC) More than 340 contemporary designs from Northwest Contemporary to Post-Modern Victorian. Color section of best sellers; two-color illustrations throughout. 304 pages. $9.95 ($12.95 Can.)

4. AFFORDABLE HOME PLANS (AH) For the prospective home builder with a modest or medium budget. Features 430 one-, 1½-, two-story and multi-level homes in a wealth of styles. Cost-saving ideas for the budget-conscious included. 320 pages. $8.95 ($11.95 Can.)

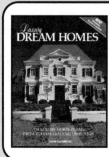

5. LUXURY DREAM HOMES (LD2) New Edition! Completely updated with 50% new designs, this exciting collection of 154 designs now contains the home you've been waiting for! 192 pages. $14.95 ($18.95 Can.)

6. ONE-STORY HOMES (V1) A collection of 470 homes to suit a range of budgets in one-story living. All popular styles, including Cape Cod, Southwestern, Tudor and French. 384 pages. $9.95 ($12.95 Can.)

7. TWO-STORY HOMES (V2) 478 plans for all budgets in a wealth of styles: Tudors, Salt-boxes, Farmhouses, Victorians, Georgians, Contemporaries and more. 416 pages. $9.95 ($12.95 Can.)

8. MULTI-LEVEL AND HILLSIDE HOMES (V3) 312 distinctive styles for both flat and sloping sites. Includes exposed lower levels, open staircases, balconies, decks and terraces. 320 pages. $6.95 ($9.95 Can.)

9. VACATION AND SECOND HOMES (V4) 258 ideal plans for a favorite vacation spot or perfect retirement or starter home. Includes cottages, chalets and one-, 1½-, two-story, and multi-level homes. 256 pages. $5.95 ($7.95 Can.)

10. STARTER HOMES (ST) 200 easy-to-build plans—from simple do-it-yourself houses to more stylish contemporary designs. Features the all-new Economy Building Series. 224 pages. $6.95 ($9.95 Can.)

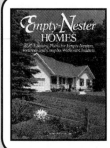

11. EMPTY-NESTER HOMES (EP) Perfect for empty-nesters, retirees and couples without children. These 206 plans feature sophisticated designs and upgraded amenities. 224 pages. $6.95 ($9.95 Can.)

12. 200 FAMILY-FAVORED HOME PLANS (FF) Expanded designs for expanding families! Seven top designers present move-up homes combining beautiful styling with more living space. 224 pages. $7.95 ($10.95 Can.)

13. 200 NARROW-LOT HOME PLANS (NL) The largest collection ever of homes that meet the unique challenges of today's narrow lots. Up to 3,000 square feet at less than 60-ft. widths! 224 pages. $7.95 ($10.95 Can.)

14. 200 FARMHOUSE AND COUNTRY HOME PLANS (FH) Styles and sizes to match every taste and budget, from Classic Farmhouses to Country Capes and Cottages. Expertly drawn floor plans and renderings enhance the sections. 224 pages. $7.95 ($10.95 Can.)

15. 200 BUDGET-SMART HOME PLANS (BS) The definitive source for the home builder with a limited budget—have your home and enjoy it too! Amenity-laden homes, in many sizes and styles, can all be built from our plans. 224 pages. $7.95 ($10.95 Can.)

16. MOST POPULAR HOME DESIGNS (MP) 400 of our customers' favorites! One-story, 1½-story, two-story and multi-level homes in a variety of styles. Designs feature-laden with lounges, clutter rooms, media rooms and more. 304 pages. $9.95 ($12.95 Can.)

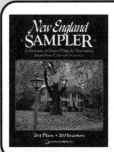

17. NEW ENGLAND SAMPLER (NES) New England architecture—inside and out! 264 Cape Cods, Saltboxes, Garrisons, Georgians and other Colonial classics—many developed for *Colonial Homes* magazine. 200 interior illustrations included. 384 pages. $14.95 ($18.95 Can.)

18. VICTORIAN DREAM HOMES (VDH) 160 Victorian and Farmhouse designs by three master designers. Victorian style from Second Empire homes through the Queen Anne and Folk Victorian era. Beautiful renderings with modern floor plans. 192 pages. $12.95 ($16.95 Can.)

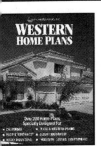

19. WESTERN HOME PLANS (WH) Over 215 home plans from Spanish Mission and Monterey to Northwest Chateau and San Francisco Victorian. Historical notes trace the background and geographical incidence of each style. 208 pages. $8.95 ($11.95 Can.)

20. THE HOME REMODELER (HR) A revolutionary book of 31 remodeling plans backed by complete construction-ready blueprints and materials lists. Kitchens, baths, master bedrooms and much more. Ideas, advice, suggestions. 112 pages. $7.95 ($10.95 Can.)

21. DECK PLANNER (DP) 25 practical plans and details for decks the do-it-yourselfer can actually build. How-to data and project starters for a variety of decks. Construction details available separately. 112 pages. $7.95 ($10.95 Can.)

22. THE HOME LANDSCAPER (HL) 55 fabulous front and backyard plans that even the do-it-yourselfer can master. Complete construction blueprints and regionalized plant lists available for each design. 208 pages. $12.95 ($16.95 Can.)

TO ORDER BOOKS BY PHONE
1-800-322-6797

CANADIAN CUSTOMERS: Order books toll-free: 1-800-561-4169. Or, complete this form, using Canadian prices and adding postage, and mail with Canadian funds to: The Plan Centre, 20 Cedar Street North, Kitchener Ont. N2H 2W8. FAX: 1-519-743-1282.

23. THE BACKYARD LANDSCAPER (BYL) Sequel to *The Home Landscaper*, contains 40 professionally designed plans for backyards. Do yourself or contract out. Complete construction blueprints and regionalized plant lists available. 160 pages. $12.95 ($16.95 Can.)

Additional Books Order Form

To order your Home Planners books, just check the box of the book numbered below and complete the coupon. We will process your order and ship it from our office within 48 hours. Send coupon and check (in U.S. funds) to: Home Planners, Inc, 3275 W. Ina Rd., Ste.110, Dept. BK, Tucson, AZ 85741

YES! Please send me the design books I've indicated:

1: **Encyclopedia of Home Designs (EN)** ....$9.95 ($12.95 Can.)
2: **403 Traditional Home Plans (ET)** ....$9.95 ($12.95 Can.)
3: **340 Contemporary Home Plans (EC)** ....$9.95 ($12.95 Can.)
4: **Affordable Home Plans (AH)** ....$8.95 ($11.95 Can.)
5: **Luxury Dream Homes (LD2)** ....$14.95 ($18.95 Can.)
6: **One-Story Homes (V1)** ....$9.95 ($12.95 Can.)
7: **Two-Story Homes (V2)** ....$9.95 ($12.95 Can.)
8: **Multi-Level & Hillside Homes (V3)** ....$6.95 ($9.95 Can.)
9: **Vacation & Second Homes (V4)** ....$5.95 ($7.95 Can.)
10: **Starter Homes (ST)** ....$6.95 ($9.95 Can.)
11: **Empty-Nester Homes (EP)** ....$6.95 ($9.95 Can.)
12: **200 Family-Favored Home Plans (FF)** ....$7.95 ($10.95 Can.)
13: **200 Narrow-Lot Home Plans (NL)** ....$7.95 ($10.95 Can.)
14: **200 Farmhouse & Country Home Plans (FH)** ....$7.95 ($10.95 Can.)
15: **200 Budget-Smart Home Plans (BS)** ....$7.95 ($10.95 Can.)
16: **400 Most Popular Home Designs (MP)** ....$9.95 ($12.95 Can.)
17: **New England Sampler (NES)** ....$14.95 ($18.95 Can.)
18: **Victorian Dream Homes (VDH)** ....$12.95 ($16.95 Can.)
19: **Western Home Plans (WH)** ....$8.95 ($11.95 Can.)
20: **The Home Remodeler (HR)** ....$7.95 ($10.95 Can.)
21: **Deck Planner (DP)** ....$7.95 ($10.95 Can.)
22: **The Home Landscaper (HL)** ....$12.95 ($16.95 Can.)
23: **The Backyard Landscaper (BYL)** ....$12.95 ($16.95 Can.)

Home Planners, Inc.
3275 W Ina Road, Suite 110, Dept. BK, Tucson, AZ 85741

Additional Books Sub-Total $_____
Ariz. residents add 5% Sales Tax; Mich. residents add 6% Sales Tax $_____
ADD Postage and Handling $ __3.00__
YOUR TOTAL (Sub-Total, Tax, Postage/Handling) $_____

YOUR ADDRESS (Please print)

Name _____

Street _____

City _____ State _____ Zip _____

Phone (_____) _____ — _____

YOUR PAYMENT

Check one: ☐ Check ☐ Visa ☐ MasterCard ☐ Discover Card
Required credit card information:

Credit Card Number _____

Expiration Date (Month/Year) _____ / _____

Signature Required _____

TB35BK

223

Design DD9621

OVER 3 MILLION BLUEPRINTS SOLD

"We instructed our builder to follow the plans including all of the many details which make this house so elegant... Our home is a fine example of the results one can achieve by purchasing and following the plans which you offer... Everyone who has seen it has assured us that it belongs in 'a picture book.' I truly mean it when I say that my home 'is a DREAM HOUSE.'"

S.P.
Anderson, SC

"We have had a steady stream of visitors, many of whom tell us this is the most beautiful home they've seen. Everyone is amazed at the layout and remarks on how unique it is. Our real estate attorney, who is a Chicago dweller and who deals with highly valued properties, told me this is the only suburban home he has seen that he would want to live in."

W. & P.S.
Flossmoor, IL

"Your blueprints saved us a great deal of money. I acted as the general contractor and we did a lot of the work ourselves. We probably built it for half the cost! We are thinking about more plans for another home. I purchased a competitor's book but my husband wants only your plans!"

K.M.
Grovetown, GA

"We are very happy with the product of our efforts. The neighbors and passersby appreciate what we have created. We have had many people stop by to discuss our house and kindly praise it as being the nicest house in our area of new construction. We have even had one person stop and make us an unsolicited offer to buy the house for much more than we have invested in it."

K. & L.S.
Bolingbrook, IL

"The traffic going past our house is unbelievable. On several occasions, we have heard that it is the 'prettiest house in Batvia.' Also, when meeting someone new and mentioning what street we live on, quite often we're told, 'Oh, you're the one in the yellow house with the wrap-around porch! I love it!'"

A.W.
Batvia, NY

"I have been involved in the building trades my entire life... Since building our home we have built two other homes for other families. Their plans from local professional architects were not nearly as good as yours. For that reason we are ordering additional plan books from you."

T.F.
Kingston, WA

"The blueprints we received from you were of excellent quality and provided us with exactly what we needed to get our successful home-building project underway. We appreciate your invaluable role in our home-building effort."

T.A.
Concord, TN